INTENDED

A Marriage in
Black & White

SHARON NESBIT-DAVIS

Ten|16
PRESS

www.ten16press.com - Waukesha, WI

For family . . . past, present, and future

• One •

I know how to get to Dewey School. I go down to the corner, cross the street, and walk three blocks. But Mother makes me wait for my brothers. John and Roger take too long to eat lunch, but if I ask them to hurry, they eat slower. When they come outside, I run to get there before someone else takes my doll.

My brothers go to the baseball diamond, and I go across the playground to the little schoolhouse for the retarded kids. During the summer, it's open in the afternoons to play, read, and do arts and crafts. There is one big room that smells like my attic, and it's dark like my attic too. School desks are stacked a corner. Shelves are filled with books, games, and puzzles. Some kids paint or play with trucks, but the only place I ever go is where the baby dolls are.

My doll is in a crib with the others. They are naked and hard rubber with curls carved in their heads. They are identical except for color. Three are white and one is dark brown, and the dark brown one is mine. I give her my favorite name. Nancy.

My doll at home is named Alice and has clothes handmade by my grandmother. Each outfit has a matching knit sweater and cap. Alice has brown hair like mine, and I comb it every night before we go to bed. Her eyes have lashes and shut when we lie down. While Alice sleeps, I stare at shadows on the ceiling and think of Nancy; she lies watching moon shadows, wondering where I am.

A new girl comes to the playhouse and wants my doll. I point to the crib. "There are more dolls in there."

She says, "I want that one."

"No."

"I'm telling."

I shrug. "Go ahead."

She stomps off to talk to the woman who wears glasses, sits at a desk in the corner, and never laughs. The woman walks over with the girl and says, "Sharon, this is Regina. Be nice and let her play with the doll."

I hug Nancy against my chest. "It's not fair. I had her first."

The woman stands over me and frowns. I hold Nancy behind my back and get one of the other dolls. "You can have this one."

Regina won't take her. She points at Nancy and says, "I want that one."

The woman leans in close to my face. She smells like my grandmother but doesn't smile. "How about you play with this other doll and let her play with the one she wants?"

A sick feeling comes over me like when my mother is mad at me for something, but I don't know why.

My next-door neighbor, Lucille, comes over. She is a year older, and I never argue with her. She protects me in the neighborhood from the older boys, and we pretend to be sisters.

Lucille says, "Give her the doll."

Tears start. I hold Nancy tighter, knowing something bad is about to happen.

Lucille whispers, "That girl is Colored, and that doll is Colored, so she should get it." She gives me a hard look. "Why do you want it anyway?"

I loosen my grip, and the woman takes Nancy and gives her to Regina. She points to the White doll I had gotten out for Regina. "You two could play together."

Lucille goes back to the paint table, the woman goes back to her desk, and I put the White doll back in the crib, sit down, and wait to get Nancy back.

Regina doesn't talk to, hold, or feed her. She lays Nancy on the dirty wood floor while she plays with blocks and watches me watch her. An older boy with brown skin comes to the door. "Regina! Time to go!" She buries Nancy beneath the White dolls and runs after him.

I dig Nancy out, hug her, and whisper, "I'm sorry."

I still run to the playhouse every day, but if Regina shows up, I give her my doll.

For Christmas, I get a rubber baby doll with carved curls on her head. She has bright blue eyes that open and close. She and Alice sleep with me every night, and I tell them about their faraway sister.

• Two •

Karen lives two houses away from us. She is a teenager and pretty enough to be in movies. I want her to be my babysitter instead of Shirley, who wears her hair like an old lady and acts like one, which is why my mother likes her. When I ask for Karen, Mother says, "We'll see," which is practically a "No." But it could happen if my parents need a babysitter and Shirley, who is never busy on Saturday nights, finally finds a boyfriend.

One rainy Saturday night, Karen and her girlfriend come to our house and ask to change clothes. She says her parents aren't home and she is locked out. My mother hesitates, but I don't. "They can use my room!"

Karen grins and follows me upstairs. I ask if I can stay, and Karen flashes a smile. "Sure."

I sit on the bed and watch them giggle and whisper. Karen's hose snags, and she sends me on an errand for clear nail polish.

Mom wants to know what they're doing. I do not tell her that they are getting ready for dates and their boyfriends are waiting in a car parked down the block.

When I get back to my room, they are putting makeup on each other. I ask if they'll put some on me. Karen shakes her head. "Your mother would kill me." I pout, and she says, "Come here." We stand in front of the mirror. "I'll show you a trick. This is what you do when you don't have makeup." She pinches my cheeks to make them red. "See? You're so cute." She dabs perfume on my wrist, gives me a hug, and leaves.

After they are gone, my mother goes into the bathroom and screams. They used her guest towels to clean their muddy shoes. For a week, my mother fusses about Karen and her friend. "There's something fishy going on. Where did that mud come from? And Karen lied about her parents being gone. The lights were on in the house."

Karen will never be my babysitter.

A few months later, Lucille makes me pinky-swear not to tell a secret. "Karen has to get married." I don't know what that means. Lucille says it means she is pregnant, but I think she's lying. That doesn't happen until after you get married.

That summer, Lucille and I are playing outside and we see Karen walking with a baby buggy. Lucille nudges me. "See?"

Karen's face is fatter than it was, but she is still pretty. She lifts her daughter out of the buggy and holds her so we can see. This baby has black, curly hair and golden-brown skin. I look closely and touch it. "How did she get a tan?"

Karen laughs and says, "She was born that way. See you later, girls." She goes inside, and Lucille hits me. "You are so dumb. Don't you know that baby is Colored? *Karen married a Negro.*"

I do feel dumb. I didn't know that was possible.

That night, through the heat vent, I listen to my parents talk. My father knows the Colored boy's family and says it's a shame. This boy was going to college, and now he's working in a factory. "He ruined his life for a girl who is nothing but trash."

My mother agrees. "Remember what she did to my towels?"

I see the baby one more time before Karen and her husband move far away. Karen's mother takes the baby for a walk in a stroller.

I ask, "Can I see her?"

Karen's mother lifts her out and helps me hold her.

The baby smells like Karen. Her eyes are open, and she smiles. I look up at Karen's mother. "She is the most beautiful baby in the world."

Karen's mother takes the baby and puts her back in the stroller. She searches pockets, finds a handkerchief, and wipes her eyes. "I think she is beautiful too."

• Three •

I am wearing the chicken costume my mother made. It survived two brothers, and a cousin, and now it's my turn. The beak is bent. The crepe paper feathers are wrinkled and brown around the edges. Mother replaced missing ones, and Dad says it looks like it's molting.

Lucille is a ballerina princess. She says her crown has real diamonds in it and it cost a million dollars. I don't believe her, but I don't want to make her mad because this year I get to go trick-or-treating with her instead of my brothers.

Mother's orders are to be back in an hour and only go to houses with porch lights on. Almost everyone says the same thing: "Why, it's a beautiful princess . . . and a chicken?"

Lucille stops at a gate and whispers, "I dare you to go to this house." The chicken head makes me almost blind, so I take it off to see where I am.

This is the Colored lady's house. Nobody knows her name or talks to her. My mother told me not to bother her, but I want to see if her house is as nasty as Lucille says it is, because if she lied about the house, she probably lied about the Colored lady growing a tail at midnight and hunting cats to eat.

I put my hand on the gate, but Lucille pulls me back and says, "Don't be stupid. You can't eat Negro candy. It'll make you Colored."

This might be true. The other Colored lady I've seen is dark brown and fat and looks like she eats a lot of candy. This lady is skinny and light brown. Maybe that's why she lives here, around White people. She had been White, but someone slipped her the candy.

The door opens, and the Colored lady yells at us. "You best be going! I'm not putting up with your tricks tonight!" She is holding something in her hand and shaking it at us. Lucille and I take off running and don't stop until we reach my front porch.

Lucille catches her breath. "Did you see that axe she shook at us?"

"It was a fly swatter."

Lucille swears it was an axe and swears the woman started running after us but we were too fast.

I'm sure it was a fly swatter. But I'm not going back to see.

That winter, I have Girl Scout cookies to sell. It's easy if I pretend to be Pollyanna. I saw the movie three times and practice her squint, head tilt, and English accent in my mirror. "A lovely day, isn't it? I was passing by and thought you might like some cookies."

I have sold to everyone on our block except the Colored lady. Pollyanna would go, even if she might get in trouble. And they'd become friends.

I open the gate, step up to the porch, and take a deep breath, because that is what Pollyanna does when she's scared. I knock. I hear a television. I knock louder and make myself smile.

A tall, brown woman opens the door, and the Colored lady is behind her. "Mama, it's just a little girl selling cookies."

I open my mouth to talk, but feel Pollyanna slip away. Now it's just me. The Colored lady's eyes are the same color as mine, and I am almost as tall. She is old, but not wrinkled like my grandma.

She shakes her head and says, "I don't want any cookies."

Her daughter smiles. "Yes, she does, but she can't have sugar."

I nod. I know about this and add, "My grandfather can't have sugar, and he gives himself a shot. I watched him do it once, but it made me throw up."

The Colored lady busts out laughing. "Girl, you are a mess." Then her daughter laughs.

I laugh too, but I am not a mess. I took a bath last night and combed my hair this morning, but it is rude to correct an adult. I bow and curtsy like Pollyanna would do if she were here. The Colored lady laughs harder and says, "I'll buy a box for company."

The daughter opens the door wider, and I step inside a Negro house. I look around quick because it is not polite to stare. There is a bookshelf with thick books, a picture of Jesus, a braided rug, and a couch with lace doilies. The kitchen has daisy wallpaper and a big pot of something cooking on the stove.

Her daughter watches me. I have to say something, but what I'm thinking, I shouldn't say, so I don't tell her that Lucille was wrong about her mother's house being nasty. Instead I say, "I like this house. It smells better than mine."

The Colored lady starts up laughing again. "You really are a mess, girl."

She serves tea in a real china cup and Thin Mint cookies on a matching plate. She says God made her the color she is, not candy. Her name is Fanny, and she doesn't mind that it makes me giggle.

I don't even have to ask about the tail.

• Four •

Valerie is Colored, and Belinda is Italian, and I am White, and that's all I know because my parents won't tell me anything else. They say it doesn't matter.

Valerie, Belinda, and I play together every recess and sit in class as close as the teacher lets us. We know how to pass notes and not get caught. We are in the highest reading group and play flute in the school band until Belinda drops out because her mother is divorced and can't make the payment on the flute rental.

One recess, we play tag and I'm "It." Instead of going after the slow girls, I go after Valerie, who dodges, runs, and thinks I'll give up and go after someone easy. But I don't. She glances back to see where I am, and I chase her into a crowd of older girls playing jump rope. Valerie bumps into a girl, and the girl yells, "Get out of here, nigger!!!" They all circle around Valerie and laugh. And it's a mean laugh. Valerie pushes through them and runs.

I follow Valerie to the alley and find her behind the dumpster. I wait for her to talk, but she doesn't. I don't know what that word means, but it has to be bad because this is the first time I've seen Valerie cry.

After dinner, I tell my father, and he explains about the word, and about slavery and prejudice and how wrong this all is. He tells me this is the reason he and Mom moved into this neighborhood. "Dewey School is the only grade school in town with both White and Colored children. We wanted you to know for yourself that people are people, so when you hear racist ideas, you will know what is true."

I nod and go to bed because this lecture took all night.

Valerie is the nicest girl I know. Nicer than Belinda and nicer than me. I am mad that God made Valerie a Negro. This isn't fair.

Now that I know the word nigger, I hear it everywhere. Kids say it when they're deciding teams: "Eeny, meeny, miney, mo, catch a . . ." Belinda's grandmother says it the day Belinda invites me to come play at her house. She and her mother live with the grandmother in the smallest house I've ever seen. You walk in and see everything: the living room, the kitchen, and the bedroom without a door. When we get there, the screen door is locked, and Belinda yells to get in. "I have Sharon with me."

We hear an old woman's voice. "If that's the nigger, you ain't bringing her in my house!"

Belinda rolls her eyes and yells back, "No, Grandma, Sharon's White."

Uncle Mack says it. Sometimes he says it in a joke at the dinner table, and everyone laughs except me, Mom, Dad, and my brothers. My mother says he doesn't have any Negro friends, so he doesn't know any better.

Sometimes my uncle says it when he isn't joking. I look at my father, but he looks down at his hands, or up at the ceiling. He doesn't tell Uncle Mack to stop. Mom says it's because Uncle Mack is eleven years older, and Daddy respects him too much.

Uncle Mack is handsome like a movie star, and he's funny. When we pull up to his house, I hear his laughter before the door opens. He smiles when he sees me, and I grin back. He winks at me with his one good eye then pops out his glass eye to scare and tease.

I love my uncle. I wish he didn't say nigger.

Valerie's skin is dark and smooth. It feels soft and slippery, and she says it's the oil she uses so her skin won't get cracked and white. "If I didn't use it, I'd be White too."

Valerie swears it's true. Her mama told her.

"Then stop, so you can be White."

Valerie shakes her head and says, "I don't want to be White. White people are mean."

"I'm not mean."

Valerie laughs. "You aren't all White." She points to my cheeks. "You have brown freckles."

That night, I dream my freckles connect and spread.

In the morning, I look in the mirror. I'm still White. It was just a nightmare.

• Five •

I am turning eight, and Mother says I can have a birthday party. She finally says yes after I am invited to Joyce's, Sally's, and Debby's parties. Mother doesn't like birthday parties because she thinks they make people greedy. "You don't need more presents," she says.

I like presents, but that's not why I want a party. I want the girls to come to my house. On television, people have friends come into their houses. Mothers invite friends into the kitchen for coffee, and bosses come over for dinner. That doesn't happen in our house. My mother only talks to friends on the phone and neighbors outside. No one comes to dinner except relatives who invite themselves. When I ask if Lucille can come inside to play, Mother says we should be out in the fresh air.

I want a birthday party so my friends will see my silver and pink flowered wallpaper room, play with my toys, and bounce on my bed. I'll show them how I take off my window screen, climb out the window, and sit on the slanted porch roof. I want my room to be loud with laughter. I want to remember them here.

Mother looks over my class list. There are twelve girls, and one of them is Valerie. She asks, "Do you think we should invite Regina?" Regina is in the other third grade class. "Maybe Valerie will be more comfortable if she isn't the only Colored girl."

I think it's an odd question. "Valerie won't care." Valerie is my best friend, and we only play with Regina when the teachers make us. "If I invite Regina, the other girls in her class will want to come too."

That would be thirteen more girls, and Mother says it's too many.

On the day of the party, my mother watches out the window and yells for me to come open the door for my guests.

Valerie is the last to arrive, and her father walks with her up to the house. My mother yells for me but opens the door herself. "Mr. Mason, I'm so glad Valerie could come. Sharon talks about Valerie all the time. She was driving me crazy asking if she was here yet."

My mother is almost lying. I only asked twice.

Valerie stands close to her father. She holds his hand and looks like she's ready to cry. He smiles at my mother, then down at Valerie, and says, "Okay, honey."

Valerie grins up at him. "Thank you, Daddy." She hugs him, and he gives her the present, leans down, and whispers, "Behave yourself."

She nods. "I promise."

On the way upstairs, Valerie says, "My daddy wasn't going to let me stay. We came to bring you the present."

"But why?"

"We don't go into White peoples' houses."

I remember Valerie wasn't at the other birthday parties. I never asked her why.

Valerie and the other girls like my room. We make faces in the mirror that was once my great-grandmother's. It has waves in it, and when you stare at it, you feel dizzy. Girls are staring, falling down, and giggling.

My mother calls us down for party games. She makes us wear the crepe paper hats she made. I open the presents and get books, a jump rope, and fancy barrettes. My favorite present is from Valerie: a gold, sparkly baton.

Valerie's father is the first parent to come back.

Valerie thanks my mother, and my mother thanks Valerie for

coming. Mother looks up at Valerie's father. "Mr. Mason, Valerie is welcome here anytime."

The next Saturday, Valerie and I play in my room with our dolls and batons. She has one now too.

And the week after that, I go to Valerie's house.

Her room is painted pink. It's bigger and taller than mine. It makes our laughter echo.

• Six •

There is a Voice inside me that tells me things. Like I should be nicer to my brothers. When I wake up scared in the dark, it's there. *Go back to sleep.* The Voice is not God because it is a whisper. I think God's voice would be louder. But I think the Voice works for God.

My mother talks to God. I've heard her when she didn't know I was there. She would never tell my father. He gets mad when the preachers on television say they talk to God and He answers. My father would say, "They are lying and taking money from poor people." I think my grandma sends money. She has the Jesus books they sell on TV.

We are Presbyterians because the minister gives sermons that are short, smart, and funny. No one prays out loud in my house unless one of the grandmothers comes for dinner: *"Bless this food to our use, and us to His service."*

Belinda is Catholic, but her parents are divorced so they can't go to church. On Sunday mornings, her grandmother makes her scrub the kitchen floor with a toothbrush so she won't become a sinner like her mother.

Valerie is Baptist and goes to church all day. There isn't just one minister. There's a bunch of them, and they all preach. The church ladies make a big dinner with chicken and ham and dressing and cakes. And then everyone has Bible study classes. After that, there's soup and sandwiches for evening supper. And after that, they pray and sing again.

I feel bad for Valerie having to be at church all day, but she says Sunday is her favorite day. She brings the old people their plates, and they put pennies in her socks.

Sunday is my favorite day because we eat supper in the living room and watch *The Wonderful World of Disney*. We have popcorn and a bottle of pop. Sometimes we have root beer floats. That's better than getting pennies in your socks.

Valerie says, "If White folks spent more time with God, maybe they wouldn't be so mean."

My minister tells stories about how a long time ago, God got mad at people and made them get sick. I say, "God could make the mean ones die. Why doesn't He do that?"

Valerie worries I am going to hell for asking questions like that. She's going to pray for me next Sunday and hopes I don't die before then.

That night in bed, under the covers, I ask God, "Why do you let people be bad?"

There is a long silence. I hear crickets and smell my toothpaste breath.

The next morning, my mother yells me awake. If God answered, I didn't hear what He said.

• Seven •

My mother stays in the kitchen while I eat breakfast, and I can tell she is going to tell me something I don't want to hear. "Sharon, I know Valerie is your friend, but you can't let her borrow your hairbrush." There is no point in asking why. She has that because-I-said-so face. "You have to promise, or you can't take your brush to school."

I give her the nastiest look I can without getting into trouble. "Fine." I slam the door and wait until she can't see me to stick out my tongue.

When we line up for recess, I am behind Valerie, and I study her hair. It is pulled tight into braids and held by blue, plastic barrettes. Our hair is different. Hers is thick and stays still when she runs. Mine blows in my face.

Valerie has never asked to use my hairbrush, but Belinda does, and I let her.

The next day, Belinda has new lipstick she stole from her mother. During recess, while Belinda puts on Fire Engine Red and dabs it off so the teacher won't notice, Valerie and I brush our hair. She watches me in the mirror and then holds out her brush. "Let's trade."

In the space of a second, I think about what my mother said. Valerie didn't ask to borrow my brush. It's a trade.

I take it and give her mine.

We brush our bangs and trade back. Valerie inspects hers and removes a brown hair. "You can't tell anyone we did this. My mother told me never to let you White girls use my brush."

I tell her what my mother said.

We laugh so hard we have to run to the stalls to pee.

• Eight •

I have a bride doll. I don't give her a name because she is me. She has short, brown hair the same color as mine, and fake pearl earrings. I jam pins in her head to hold the veil. My brothers tease that I'll never be a bride, and that could be true. I don't like any of the boys in my class, especially Donny. We have the same wavy, brown hair and freckles, and substitute teachers think we are twins. I think that means I have to marry him, but he makes me sick. He eats his own boogers.

Donny makes me want to run away and grow up somewhere else, but I don't know how to get anywhere. I've read about people jumping on trains, but the only train station is across the Mississippi bridge, and unless I went at night, someone would see me crossing it and tell.

If I did make it, I wouldn't be old enough to get a job. I'd have to hide in somebody's barn and steal the farmer's wife's pie from her kitchen window. Maybe the farmer's wife would catch me and ask why I was there, and when I explained about Donny, she'd let me live with them because they always wanted a daughter. I'd send a letter to my family, so they wouldn't worry. My mom would be happier without me there, since she is always mad because my room is a mess, and I don't want to learn how to sew, and I'm not polite like my cousin Carol.

But that only happens on television. Real grown-ups would make me go home, and I'd be in the biggest trouble I've ever been in.

One night family goes to the movies to see *The Music Man* because my mother loves musicals. My father doesn't, but he loves her. My brothers and I go because they won't let us stay home alone.

The librarian in the movie believes her future husband is out in the world somewhere, and she sings to him. She doesn't know she's already met him.

I sit in the dark and dream about getting married to someone besides Donny. Maybe my husband doesn't live in my town.

My father was born in Colorado, where his father had a ranch. A mean son-of-a-gun won land in a poker game and was going to make all the ranchers pay to use his land to get their cattle to the only watering hole. My grandpa got his gun to kill this man, but my grandmother stopped him. She said, "We're moving back to Illinois." They moved where they had family, and my dad became the new kid in my mother's class. I think that's when she fell in love with him because she always smiles when she tells the story. But when I ask, she says I'm being silly. They were thirteen when they met, and I'm ten, so maybe my husband isn't here yet.

When I should be in bed, I climb out my window and onto the roof of the porch. I look up to the stars and sing, "Goodnight, my someone, Goodnight, my love . . ."

A thought floats up: *He lives in Chicago.*

That summer, we go on vacation to Wisconsin and make a stop in Chicago. My father wants to see the Cubs, my brothers want to see dinosaur bones, and I want to look for my husband.

But I didn't know Chicago was so big. Everywhere we go, there are huge crowds and hundreds of boys.

I don't know how I will ever find him.

• Nine •

My fifth-grade teacher, Mrs. Heinz, is young and pretty and fun. She laughs and smiles every day and tells us how happy she is to be our teacher. By the second quarter, my grades are the best they have ever been. The one time she is disappointed in me, I want to crawl away and cry. Later that day, she squeezes my shoulder and whispers, "It's okay, don't be so sad," and then I do cry.

One afternoon after we have cleaned up to go home, she says to our class, "I have something to tell you." Her eyes are teary, but her face is smiling. "My husband and I are going to have a baby." We cheer, and she blushes. "In a couple weeks after Easter break, I won't be coming back to school." She looks around the room at each one of us. "I will miss you all very much." The bell rings, but we don't leave. We crowd around her desk and beg her to stay.

On the last day before Easter break, we have a party. Mrs. Heinz tells each of us why she likes us. She says I am smart, and kind, and funny. I give her a card I made with hearts and sad faces. She makes us promise to be good for our new teacher.

Our new teacher is not young, pretty, or fun. Mrs. Baker has bluish-silver hair pulled tight in a French twist, black rimmed glasses, and a mouth that is frozen across a wrinkled face. She does not put stickers on our papers or turn our rope at recess. But worst of all is what she says: "I never wanted to teach at your school because there are Negro children here. But your principal says they are well-behaved. I hope he is right."

In our class, there are three: my friend Valerie and two boys, Ralph and Richard. Ralph is quiet, and Richard is funny, but after Mrs. Baker says this, Richard becomes quiet like Ralph.

One day after recess, Mrs. Baker stands at the front of the class and smiles. She says, "Just a little while ago, I passed Richard on the stairs, and his arm brushed against mine. I went to the bathroom to wash it off... but there was nothing there!"

Mrs. Baker holds out her arm to show us. "I always thought if I touched a Negro, the color would rub off on me. It doesn't!" She laughs and looks around the room. A few White girls laugh with her. I look at Valerie, who stares down at her hands. They are drawn up into two small fists.

I tell my parents what Mrs. Baker says and how awful she is. "She is too dumb to be our teacher."

My mother says she is old and set in her ways. My father says, "You have to respect her" and reminds me of his rule: "If you get in trouble at school, you will be in more trouble at home."

One day when the dismissal bell rings, Mrs. Baker asks me to stay for a few minutes.

Valerie walks past and whispers, "What did you do?"

I shrug. I can't think of anything I did wrong. I thought bad things about Mrs. Baker, but I didn't say any of them. Maybe she's a witch and can read my mind.

After everyone leaves, she tells me to sit in the chair next to her desk, the chair kids sit in when they're in trouble. "Sharon, you come from a good family." She leans in so close I see a hair growing under her chin. "But I've noticed you are friends with the Colored girl. If you stay friends with her, people are going to say unkind things about you and your family. You don't want that, now, do you?"

I sit still and stare at her chin hair until her neck muscles twitch. She sighs and says, "Go on home, but remember what I said."

The next day, Valerie, Belinda, and I plan a protest like ones we've seen on the news. We'll do a sit-in during gym class, and when the principal comes, we'll tell him all the things Mrs. Baker has said. If he won't listen, we'll refuse to go home, and then our parents will come to the school and we'll tell them. And then the television people will find out and we'll get on the news.

We tell most of the girls, but not everyone. We don't trust the girls who laugh with Mrs. Baker.

At dinner, I eat lima beans without complaining and do my homework and go to bed before bedtime. My mother asks what's wrong, and I say my stomach hurts, which is true. It hurts like when I'm sitting in the doctor's office waiting to get a shot.

In my bed, in the dark, I imagine the look on Mrs. Baker's face when she blows the whistle for us to run relays and, one by one, we sit down.

The next morning, we say the pledge and take our seats. Belinda is absent. She must have chickened out, so it will be up to Valerie and me to do this. I look back to smile at Valerie, but she is staring at the door. Mr. Terrill, the principal, is there and motions for Mrs. Baker to come out into the hall. My heart is beating so loud I can't hear anything else.

Mrs. Baker returns with Mr. Terrill, followed by Belinda. Belinda goes to her desk to get her books. Her face is red and sweaty. That happens when she's mad. Her desk is behind mine, and she whispers, "Someone tattled on me."

Someone told on Belinda, but not Valerie and me.

I look up and see Mr. Terrill frowning at me. Maybe Mr. Terrill knows about Valerie and me but is afraid of our fathers. My father went to school once and yelled at him about something. I asked why, but he said it didn't concern me. I don't know if Mr. Mason has ever yelled at him, but he and my dad are both tall with loud voices. Belinda doesn't have a father.

I think about standing up and saying, "We planned a protest because Mrs. Baker is prejudiced and should not be our teacher." If he tells me to sit down, I will stand on my desk and refuse to get down until Mrs. Baker leaves. Maybe everyone will get on their desks.

I look back at Valerie. She shakes her head and looks away.

I hear my father's voice in my head: *"If you get in trouble at school, I'll double the punishment. Doesn't matter if it was fair or not. You will respect your elders."*

At recess, Valerie and I make a pact. We will do our schoolwork, but we won't volunteer to answer questions in class. If Mrs. Baker asks us a question, we will nod yes, or shake our head no, or shrug. If she asks us to read aloud, we won't.

We are silent for a day. A week. A month. Until the school year ends.

Mrs. Baker never asks why.

• Ten •

Valerie and I play flutes in the Quincy Area Elementary Band. Every Thursday after school, we take a bus downtown to rehearse at Quincy Junior High School. Our mothers give us money to ride the bus there and back, but we can get home as quick as the bus if we run. We save the bus ride money, and after a month, there is enough to buy ice cream sundaes at the soda shop.

The day we plan to go to the shop, Valerie doesn't want to go. "I'm going to be in trouble for getting home so late."

I tell her, "Just say we missed the bus." Valerie pouts, but considers. "Come on. It's not a lie. We have missed the bus." Valerie laughs, and we race each other to the soda shop.

The tables all have customers, but no one is at the counter. We jump up onto the tall stools and spin so fast we almost fall off. The store owner's back is to us, but he sees us in the big mirror. We both stop and straighten. He doesn't turn around, so I clear my throat like my father does when he wants a clerk to wait on him.

He stands there, looking at us but not moving, not doing anything.

Valerie nudges me and whispers, "Let's go."

I shake my head and say in a loud (but not yelling) voice, "Excuse me, Mister. We'd like some ice cream, please."

He turns around, crosses his arms, and glares hard at us.

Valerie jumps off her stool and pulls me off mine. "Come on . . . NOW." She runs out the door, and I chase after her.

"Why did you do that?"

She says, "He won't wait on ME!"

I look back at the soda shop and see the owner scrubbing Valerie's stool.

This is the North. That isn't supposed to happen here.

On the way home, we plan a boycott. Valerie will ask people from her church to help. That's how Dr. King does it. Maybe some people from my church will. Maybe my parents. They like Valerie.

But when I get home, I don't tell my parents. I don't know how to tell them this without confessing how we got the money for ice cream.

The next day, Valerie says we can't do the boycott. Her parents say we don't understand the kind of trouble it will cause for them and other Negroes in town. Valerie got a whipping for thinking she could go anywhere a White girl can.

The week after that, we walk by the soda shop. We stand in front of the door and wait until the owner sees us. We smile, wave, and blow kisses.

Then spit on the door and run.

• Eleven •

My mother is mad because all her soap operas are canceled. "Why does every TV station cover this?" The crowd is enormous. Most are Colored, but there are White people too. A bus took people from here, and Regina's father and Valerie's uncle went.

Mother washes clothes, irons, pays bills, and yells to me from the kitchen, "If you're going to watch that, dust the living room."

I dust the mantel, the television cabinet, three sets of venetian blinds, two lamps, my father's chemistry books, my mother's murder mysteries, and my grandmother's Bible. I am done when Dr. King steps up to the microphone.

I like his voice. He talks and my heart hurts. If he were my minister, I'd go to church every Sunday.

My father watches the news that night, and I tell him I saw the whole thing. He says he understands the Negro position, but you can't force people to change. "Dr. King wants too much too soon. He's going to get more people killed."

My father is smart. He is the smartest man I know, but he is wrong about this, and I tell him what I heard today. "It's been a hundred years, Daddy. One hundred years!"

"In terms of history, that's a short time."

"But what if we were Negroes? How long would you want us to wait?"

My father doesn't answer. He goes back to reading his newspaper.

School starts the day after Labor Day. Valerie is in my class, and during recess, we make plans to join the Freedom Riders next summer. We have a year to convince our parents. We'll ask for that instead of birthday and Christmas presents.

We practice what we'll say when we meet Dr. King: *"We saw your speech and want you to know we go to school together and we are best friends."*

Maybe our picture will be in *Life Magazine*.

Before Valerie or I talk to our parents, four little girls die in Birmingham, bombed in church on a Sunday morning. I watch the news that night with my father. "This is exactly what I was telling you. Because of Dr. King, children are getting killed."

The next day at school, Valerie is quiet, quieter than she ever is. At recess, we play hopscotch and take turns on the swings.

We never talk about going on the Freedom Rides again.

• Twelve •

"Are there any Colored girls on your relay?" My father was a track man in college. He watches it on TV and builds a high jump for us to practice. My brothers disappoint him with their lack of skills. I want to become his track star, and my first meet is coming up. He coaches me on the weekend, and he's worried.

Daddy says, "You're going to be running against Jackson schoolgirls." Every Colored child in town goes to Jackson School, except the ones who go to my school.

Dad has a theory: Negroes are better in sports than Whites because only the strongest survived slavery.

But in my class, there are two Colored girls and only Valerie runs good, and she's on our relay. The other Colored girl is Regina, and she runs funny. Nobody wants her on their team, so she gets picked last.

In gym class, Valerie wins most races, but not always. The boys have their own races, and the two Colored boys in my class hardly ever win.

I tell Dad this so he will stop worrying. He says, "Every rule has its exceptions."

Valerie's cousin is on the Jackson School track team. I ask Valerie, "Is she fast? Can you beat her?"

"Sometimes, but when I win, she says she let me."

I laugh. "She's just saying that."

"She says she is the slowest one on their team."

"I bet she's lying. She's afraid of us."

Valerie shrugs. "Maybe."

The morning of the meet, Daddy goes to the stadium to check out the early races. He comes home and has me run around the yard three times. I pass by him and see his frown, but when I stop, he switches it to a smile. "Good job, Punky. No matter what happens today, just do your best."

Mom finds me in my room getting ready and says, "Daddy saw the Colored girls you'll race against, and they are fast. He doesn't think you can beat them. I thought you should know."

I wish I had another mother. A mother with long legs who likes me. I have my mother's short, fat legs, and she never thinks I can do anything.

Now I have to win, to prove them both wrong. I stare into the funny wavy mirror that was my great-grandmother's. It makes me feel light and dreamy.

I see myself running. I run so fast that people stand and cheer. I see Dad yelling for me, and Mom is shocked and silent. I get a trophy, and my mother hugs me and apologizes. "I didn't know you were that good."

I hear the girls from Jackson before I see them. Their laughter floats up and explodes, forcing us to look. They are stretching their long legs, practicing baton hand-offs, and acting like they don't know we are watching.

My team calls to me. Their voices are louder than they need to be, and we laugh at nothing. We do our warm-ups. The ones who can, do splits. My flashiest move is touching my toes.

I ask Valerie which one is her cousin. She shakes her head. "She didn't make the team. They have a coach who makes them practice every night and race every week to see who's the fastest." Their coach must be the tall man who is now walking the track with them.

Our teacher let us choose our own teams, and we practice during recess. Except for my dad who has me run around our yard on Saturdays, no one coaches us.

There are two other teams we will be racing, and they are all White. One of the teams is looking at the rest of us and laughing, and the other is sitting in a circle holding hands and praying.

The announcer calls for the sixth grade girls' relay. I'm running the third leg and will pass the baton to Valerie, our last runner. I'm in a lane next to the Jackson girl. She is jumping and stretching and makes quick practice takeoffs. She says, "What are you looking at?"

"Nothing." I stretch and practice my takeoff. She laughs, points to her butt, and says, "You'll be looking at this."

I make the unimpressed look I give my brothers when they tease, but I can't think of a good comeback. She smirks and takes her position, fixing her eyes ahead. Her body quivers, waiting for release.

Up the track, I see the girls in place and hear a faint "On your mark, get set, GO!"

The starting runners are off, and within seconds, the Jackson girl is ahead. By the time it's my turn, this girl's prediction is right. I chase her behind. The race is between the rest of us, so I pull even with the others and pass the baton to Valerie, who tries to catch the Jackson girl. She doesn't, but she wins second place for us.

We get our ribbons, and I find my parents in the stands. Mom puts the ribbon in her purse. "Those Colored kids are beating everyone."

I say, "That's because they have a coach and they practice every day."

Dad clears his throat. "Like I explained, they were built for this."

I start to argue, but make myself stop. He isn't going to listen to me. There are things I know that he won't understand.

• Thirteen •

The girls in my class won't talk to me. They whisper, point, and laugh . . . draw me ugly and drop the picture on my desk. They hold their noses and hurry past. At recess, I ask my teacher if I can study for the quiz on tornadoes. She tells me to go play, and I tell her my stomach hurts. She writes a pass for the bathroom, but they will find me there. I walk along the edge of the baseball diamond where no girl ever goes. I crouch low behind a small hill, close my eyes, and wish myself gone.

This happened to other girls, and I didn't do anything to stop it. No one does. There isn't anything to do except wait until Donna decides it's enough. Donna is new, and everyone wants to be her friend. She has green cat eyes and looks like a model. She teaches us a secret code and picks a girl to be the enemy. When she gets bored, she picks someone new. Now, it's me.

I've seen Dr. King tell his people what to do when people hate them: Don't get angry. Don't fight back. They know in their hearts they are wrong, and one day, they will be ashamed.

During class, I stare at the teacher, or the blackboard, or my math problems. Donna makes nasty gestures at me. The others do too, except Valerie. She won't talk to me now, but she doesn't treat me bad. She is scared to stand up for me. Her parents made her swear on the Bible not to argue with White girls. They say that's all the excuse some of these crazy White folks need to burn their house.

My banishment has been ten days now, longer than anyone's. Maybe Donna hates me more. Or maybe I didn't notice when it wasn't me.

When I get to school today, it's just Valerie and me at the bike stand. "I'm sorry," she says. "I don't know why Donna picked you."

I try to smile, but I can't.

Valerie runs off and yells back, "I still like you!"

I go to the swings and pump my legs so hard it hurts.

When I get home from school, I have a fever and it hurts to swallow. It's the mumps, and I stay home for two weeks. My teacher drops off homework and Get Well cards from the class. Valerie's card is covered with hearts. Donna drew a picture of the two of us holding hands. She drew our matching ponytails.

Mom didn't let me wash my hair while I was sick. It's dirty and oily, and she suggests for the hundredth time to get it cut. I surprise her and agree.

The beautician asks, "Are you sure you want to do this?" She winks at me in the mirror. "I told your mother that girls want to look like their friends." She combs through my hair and winks again. "How about I just cut the split ends? We'll say you changed your mind."

I say, "Cut it off."

* * *

"Well, class, we have a new student!" Miss Gordon is a lousy actress. "Wait!" She comes close and squints. "It's our Sharon!"

The class laughs, and Miss Gordon says everyone missed me. "Your new haircut shows off your big, brown eyes!" I keep those eyes on her and blur everyone else. I've been practicing this trick.

At recess, I go to the end of the line. Donna, Belinda, and Valerie wait outside. Donna waves, grins, and says, "Come on, slowpoke."

I walk measured and unhurried because my legs are weak. And because they hurt me, and I want them to know it.

We play together at recess again, and they let me take longer turns on the swing. Only Valerie says she is sorry.

In a month, school is out, and I won't be coming back to this school.

There will be a summer, and then junior high with hundreds of new kids.

• Fourteen •

Lucille was in junior high last year, and this summer, she doesn't want to ride bikes, climb the trees in her backyard, or put on shows for the neighborhood kids and mothers.

She says I need to get ready for junior high and will help me get into the popular crowd. Lucille didn't make it because she made friends with the wrong people. But if I make it, maybe she will have another chance. "Figure out who the popular people are and make friends with them."

Most afternoons, we lay out on towels in our swimsuits to get tans. Her suit is a baby-blue-and-white, checkered two-piece with spaghetti straps. Mine is a nylon, black one-piece with a junior lifeguard patch. We read Lucille's teen magazines, the ones my mother won't let me buy even with my own allowance. The articles are about movie stars, fashion, hair, pimples, and advice on boys: Be a good listener. Don't talk about yourself. Ask the boy about his interests.

Lucille adds her own: "Don't let them know how smart you are. They want to be the smart one."

I think about my brilliant father and my mother. Whatever he says about the news, she listens. Later, she repeats it to my brothers, or somebody on the phone, or me. I can't remember Daddy ever asking her what she thinks. Maybe Mother is hiding how smart she is.

Lucille puts on gobs of tanning lotion hoping her pink skin will turn tan. I have my mother's brown hair and my red-headed father's freckled skin. She tans, and he burns, and I do both. "Isn't it weird how White people want tans but are so prejudiced against Blacks?"

Lucille sighs. "If you want to be popular, you can't say stuff like that." She pauses and says, "In junior high, Whites and Blacks aren't friends."

I shake my head. "Valerie and I will always be friends."

"You'll see." She turns to look at me. "And none of them ever get into the popular crowd."

I won't pray to God to make me popular. That's silly, but I want Him to know what I want.

Every night, I go to sleep with a wish dream: *I see myself walk down the halls, and everyone I pass smiles and calls my name. I stop at my locker, and boys surround me and ask for my number. I walk to class with other girls. I say funny things, and they laugh. Valerie walks next to me and laughs too.*

Mother drives me to school on the first day. Her hair is in curlers, she is wearing my father's red flannel shirt, and the car is an old pink Pontiac. We are stopped at a red light several blocks away. "I'll get out here." I open the door and jump out before she can say anything. I turn back to wave, but she won't look at me. She's got that ready-to-cry face.

I don't want to hurt her feelings, but if I have any chance of getting into the popular crowd, I can't be seen with her. Lucille says the popular kids' moms look like Jackie Kennedy.

There are hundreds of seventh graders, and not one kid from my grade school is in any of my classes except for Band. Valerie and I sit together in the flute section, and she asks, "Do we have lunch together?" We compare our schedules. Valerie frowns.

I say, "Maybe you can find someone from your church—or a cousin to sit with." Valerie has dozens of cousins.

"They all hate me. They say I'm stuck-up because I went to a White school."

Valerie has lunch after Band. I watch her walk slowly down the hall and wish we were back on the playground, trading sandwiches under the trees and claiming first dibs on the swings.

I have PE before lunch and share a locker with a girl who is in my English and Social Studies classes. Susan looks like she could be in a teen magazine. No pimples, eyes highlighted by a delicate black line, and under a baby blue wool skirt and mohair sweater is a pink lace bra with matching panties. She smiles, and I smile back but don't know what to say. I pretend to look for something in my bag and wait until she leaves to undress. I'm wearing thick cotton underwear and a training bra.

The lunchroom is in the basement. It's the only time seventh, eighth, and ninth graders are together. It's easy to spot the popular crowd. They all have tans and hair bows that match their outfits. Some wear cheerleader uniforms because there is a pep assembly today. The middle tables are theirs. Nervous seventh graders go through the line and search for a place to sit. If the popular crowd has chosen them, they get a wave.

Susan gets her food and waits. A cheerleader stands up and yells, "Susan! Over here!"

I don't wait. I go to a table at the back of the room. Now that I've seen them, there's no point in hoping anymore.

• Fifteen •

My first English assignment is to write my life story. Two pages and due tomorrow.

My life will take half a page: Born and raised in Quincy, Illinois. Two older brothers who get all A's and are Eagle Scouts. One dog found in an alley and a parakeet that whistles. My mother is a housewife. My father is a scientist, but he isn't looking for a cure for cancer. He makes feed for cows and pigs and chickens so they'll taste good. I want to be a writer.

I can write a better life story than the boring one I have.

I was born on the island of Hawaii, the youngest of four children and the only girl. My father was a scientist for the government, and my mother took care of orphans during the day.

Our school was a hut in the jungle. We took a canoe to get there. Once, the canoe tipped over, and I was caught underneath. My oldest brother, Michael, saved me. He was the best swimmer of the island and a champion surfer.

When I was five, Michael took me for rides, and when I got older, he taught me how to surf. He taught me which waves to go after and which ones to leave alone. We had dreams of being the first brother-sister world champions.

For my tenth birthday, Michael gave me my own surfboard. He had

*painted my surfer name on it: Shar-o-line. That day, there was a tropical
storm coming, and everyone warned I shouldn't go. But I snuck out and
caught the biggest wave of my life. I crashed and lost my board. Before
anyone could stop him, Michael went after it. He never came back, and
we never found his body.*

*My parents were grief-stricken having lost their most favorite child.
My father quit his job, and my mother left the orphans. We moved to the
mainland, and my father got a research job with a company in Quincy,
Illinois.*

*I miss Hawaii, but I have an uncle who flies a cargo plane and drops
off supplies to the natives. Sometimes I go with him to see my friends, and
see if Michael has come back.*

I expect the teacher will know that I made this up, so when she
asks, I'll tell her I misunderstood the assignment. I think she'll give me
an A anyway.

A few days later, Mrs. Talcott says to the class, "I enjoyed reading
your stories and getting to know you, but there is one story I want to
read to all of you." She glances at me.

I put my head down. This woman is cruel. Everyone will laugh at
me and tell the whole school. And Valerie will be mad at me for lying
and say the devil is in me and her mother won't let us be friends now.

Maybe I can convince my parents to move . . . perhaps to the
islands.

Mrs. Talcott comes to the part about Michael's body, and her voice
trembles. I look up and see a tear slide down her cheek.

She finishes and says, "This was written by Sharon Nesbit."
Students clap, and when the bell rings, they circle around my desk.
They want to know what their names are in Hawaiian.

Susan waits for me, and we walk to our next class. She says, "Wow,
Hawaii." I almost tell her the truth, but she says, "I'm sorry. It must be
hard to talk about, with your brother and all." I nod and say nothing.

In PE, Susan and I are partners for square dancing. I take the man's part, lower my voice, and say hilarious things. We giggle in the locker room and in the lunch line.

When we get to the end of the line, I start to head to my back table, then hear my name. "Sharon!" Susan smiles and says, "Come sit with us."

That night at dinner, my mother wants to know what happened at school. So do my brothers and father. "You look happy."

I can't share this with them. These people have no appreciation for social achievements. I say, "Nothing happened," and readjust my face to neutral.

In my room, I tell my mirror, "I'm in," and practice my smile and wave.

Susan's friends are now mine. I listen to their conversations to know what to say and how to say it. After a week, I know who they like and who they don't. I make up funny names for the people they hate. I buy Beatles trading cards and tape them inside my locker. I use their slang words . . .

"Way out." "Cool." "Tough."

In the morning before the first bell rings, we walk the halls and say hi to the other popular kids. They say hi back, and some call out my name. I see kids from grade school but pretend I don't. If they yell out to me, I nod but keep going. My stomach jumps, but I ignore that too.

One morning, I see Valerie. She is walking with some Black girls I don't know. They wear matching sweaters. Valerie sees me too. We walk past each other, faces turned away to laugh with our new friends.

* * *

My new friends come to my house, and I ask them to not mention Hawaii. "My mother will cry, and my brothers will get mad. They all blame me for Michael's death, and so do I."

I need to end this story. I'm afraid someone will find out, and I think Carla, Susan's best friend, is suspicious. She asks when I will go to Hawaii with my uncle again, and I tell her what I've been practicing in my mirror for a week:

"I was going to go with him last weekend, but I had too much homework." I pause, and my lip quivers. "His plane crashed, and they haven't found his body." A tear slides down my cheek. "I will never talk about Hawaii again. Never."

Carla tells everyone.

Maybe I'm not supposed to be a writer. I think I'm an actress.

• Sixteen •

My new girlfriends are not rich, but their mothers work and buy them clothes. It's been three months, and they wear a different dress every day.

I ask my mother if I can get more clothes, and she says what she always says: She had one school dress and washed it every night. I have five outfits—one for each day of the week. I should be grateful. She says, "Real friends don't care about your clothes."

But my mother doesn't have any girlfriends, and maybe that's why.

Carla brings up my lack of clothes. She says, "We were wondering why."

I tell her my mother hates me and is crazy. "When I asked if I could have more clothes, she gave me my dead grandmother's dresses. They are hanging in my closet now."

Part of this is true. I have some of my grandmother's dresses in my closet. But that's because I asked for them after she died.

Carla and Susan bring extra clothes for me to wear at school.

There are five of us in our group: Susan, Carla, Marcia, Diane, and me. We have sleepovers and go to school games and dances. We talk about boys, and movie stars, and boys, and clothes, and boys. When they like a boy, I deliver the notes. When they fight, I help them make up. When it's over, I say he's a jerk.

I am the joker, the messenger, the healer of breakups. This is my role. My membership dues.

I have a boyfriend for two days. Stephen is new to town. He's blond, blue-eyed, and handsome. He says someday he'll be taller than me. He wants to hold my hand at the football game, and I put on a big fuzzy mitten. Everyone laughs but him, and later he tells Carla to tell me that he has broken up with me.

Carla says I don't know how to act with boys.

That is correct. I tease and argue with them—like I do with my brothers.

The advice from teen magazines is "Be yourself."

I can't do that.

I'll lose everything.

• Seventeen •

I talk with Susan or Carla on the phone almost every night. We help each other through braces, acne, and cramps. We save seats at pep rallies, and when the rich, popular girls have birthday parties at the Country Club, we are on the guest list. We spend most of every summer at each other's houses, the mall, and the pools of the popular kids.

My family doesn't like the way I act around my friends. They say I act silly and stupid. My brother thinks they are frivolous. He asks, "What do they think about Vietnam, or nuclear proliferation, or civil rights?"

I don't answer because I don't know. We only talk about boys, movies, and other girls.

In tenth grade, our history teacher assigns current events.

Carla complains. "I don't want to read about niggers."

Susan agrees, and neither of them notices my silence.

I knew they might be prejudiced. They went to an all-White grade school, and once Carla saw me talking with Valerie and gave me a funny look. But until now, no one said it.

They don't know better because they've never had a Negro friend, just like Uncle Mack. I've learned how to deal with my uncle. When he says something racist, I scream at him in my head so loud that I can't hear what he is saying. If I can still love Uncle Mack, I can find a way to keep these friends.

• Eighteen •

Carla tells a racist joke, and I go off to the bathroom. When I come back, she says Dr. King and all his followers need to go back to Africa if they don't like it here. Others agree, and I sit silent. Susan asks what's wrong. "Are you sick?"

I tell her the truth. "Yes, I feel sick."

Carla asks if we saw the news last night. I did. White police used hoses and dogs on Black protesters. Carla says they deserve it. "They need to remember their place." Heads nod. No one disagrees. Carla's eyes settle on me. I pull out a book and pretend to read. My stomach hurts, and I can't eat. I want to go home, crawl in bed, and sleep until this goes away.

But it won't go away.

I have a new friend, and the friendship makes me feel worse.

I met Brother Daniel because my father asked me to please go back to the Sunday School class I had quit weeks ago. "A Franciscan brother is coming, and your teacher wants you there since you are the only one who asks questions." My father grins. I know it's because he is glad I question the church and the Bible. He does too, but he keeps quiet about it, and now he's a Presbyterian Elder.

Brother Daniel wears long, brown robes tied by a rope. He answers my first question before I ask it: "Yes, I am wearing pants." His whole face smiles. Comparison to Sidney Poitier is unavoidable. They look different, but their brown skin color matches. They both tilt their heads to listen and throw them back to laugh. I've had a crush on Sidney since I saw *Lilies of the Field*.

Brother Daniel is young, smart, and takes us seriously. He wants to know what we think and welcomes questions. I ask mine and discover he has the same ones. If there is a God, how could He let people become this evil? It makes no sense that only Christians would get into heaven, especially with all the horrid things they have done like steal land and people and make them slaves. The creation story makes no sense.

Brother Daniel doesn't give me answers because he doesn't know them. But he's sure there is a God, and he wants to spend his life doing His Will. And no, he doesn't know what His Will is.

By the third class, we share stories. Brother Daniel talks about growing up in the South and the separate White and Colored bathrooms. I tell about my friendship with Valerie and the protests we wanted to do but never did. He tells about the little White boy who became his friend. They played together every day in a park until the boy's mother came looking for him. She said, "Get away from that nigger." And the boy said he wasn't a nigger, he was his friend. The mother grabbed him away, and that night, the boy was beaten by his father. Neighbors called the police, and they put the father in a motel room until relatives could come and get the boy. Brother Daniel tells the story, and I can't look at him. His voice is so sad when he says, "After that, I stayed away from White children."

After class, Brother Daniel says he watched my reaction to his story. He says, "There are only a few White people I trust. I've added you to my list."

He shouldn't have. But I want to become the person he thinks I am.

• Nineteen •

Sunday night, I am doing the homework I've put off all weekend. My father yells for us from the living room. Walter Cronkite is on television with a face more serious than his usual. "Dr. Martin Luther King, Jr. was shot and killed tonight."

President Johnson says the nation is "shocked and saddened." They show clips from King's speech last night. "I've seen the Promised Land . . . I might not get there with you . . ." The National Guard is on alert. There are already eruptions of violence in Washington, D.C. and Nashville.

I watch until my parents make me go to bed. I drift in and out of sleep and wake myself up crying. I cry for his wife, his children, and myself. I am one of those Whites he admonished—the White folks who know better, but don't speak up.

The next morning, the school halls are quiet. All I see are White people. Maybe the Black students are taking the day off.

I'm at my locker, waiting for the bell to ring. I don't want to talk to anyone. I know they will say something stupid.

A girl runs down the hall, and more follow. They get books out of lockers and head to the exit doors. I see parents in cars waiting for them.

One of my friends stops to tell me the Black students are marching in the streets carrying spears and doing African war chants. She swears it's true. A woman called the radio station, and it's on the news. That is why parents are picking up their kids.

During morning announcements, the principal echoes President Johnson. "We are shocked and saddened by the assassination of Dr. Martin Luther King." He coughs and whispers to someone in the office. "We do not expect any disturbances, but to ensure everyone's safety, police officers are stationed at all entrance doors."

My first hour French teacher gives the daily vocabulary quiz. She doesn't mention Dr. King or the five absent Black students. She looks out the window and gives us more time than usual for the quiz. It won't matter because I didn't study last night.

Between classes, I go into the bathroom and find two girls hiding in a stall. They peek out and ask, "Have they come yet?"

I almost laugh, but another girl runs in and yells, "They're here!"

We wait and listen and hear nothing. The door opens, and two Black girls walk in. They look at us looking at them and shake their heads. "Stupid-ass crackers . . ."

In the halls, Black students head to lockers. No one has spears.

My U.S. History teacher says there is no point in discussing what none of us read. "We can talk about Dr. King and what is happening now in our country." There is silence until a Black boy says the school bus didn't come this morning. "So we walked, and then we get here and police are waiting for us."

A White boy says, "What do you expect? You were marching down the street with spears shouting African war chants."

Black students bust out laughing. "We were on the sidewalk singing 'We Shall Overcome' . . . And just where are we supposed to get spears? Do they sell them at Sears?"

The White boy's face turns red. Everyone laughs. Whites have looks of relief and embarrassment. Blacks look amused and annoyed. Nobody wants to talk, so the teacher lectures on what we should have read last night.

At lunch, rumors spread that there will be a riot after school. White students call parents to pick them up or make plans to leave early with others who have cars. My brother drives our pink Pontiac. Carla finds me at my locker. "Can you ask your brother to leave now and give us all a ride?"

Carla is ready to cry, and I almost feel sorry for her. "Nothing is going to happen."

Her eyes are wide and wild. "You don't know that. You think you're safe because you had some Black friends. But you are White, and they hate you too."

She leaves in search of another ride, and I walk to my next class.

• Twenty •

The nation burns, and I wait to see if anything changes. It seems
it has. My friends aren't talking racist crap, but it's not gone. They are
silent now because they are scared.

Maybe this is my opportunity.

My talent is writing stories. I get A's on all my creative writing
assignments, and my friends ask for help in writing theirs. Maybe this
is how I can give them Black friends.

I write about a White girl who is funny, smart, and sad.

*Emily's mother died when Emily was born. Grown folks say she looks
like her mother, but she knows that's a lie. Emily looks in the mirror and
sees freckles and frizzled hair. Her mother was beautiful. She's seen the
pictures her father hides under the bed. Her daddy doesn't say she looks
like her. He doesn't say anything much. Most days he forgets she is there.*

*Church ladies bring her clothes, and Emily cuts her own hair with
a pocketknife. None of the kids ever play with her, but she has books, and
trees in the woods. Her favorite is a big oak tree by the creek. She likes to sit
quietly and watch animals come up and drink. She's seen raccoons, deer,
and a fox; they see her but don't run.*

*One day, Emily sits by the creek with her legs in the water and hears
singing from the sky. The singing is good, but some of it is off-key, so she
knows it is not an angel. She looks up and sees a crude shelter high up in*

her oak tree, almost hidden. She is afraid of heights, so she won't climb it, but yells up to ask who is there.

The singing stops. She waits until she can't stand it. "I know that was no bird. Who are you? Why are you hiding up there? Are you an escaped prisoner?"

A boy sticks his head out. "It's me. Henry."

Emily had seen Henry at school. They were not in the same class, but they had the same lunch and recess. He didn't have friends either.

Most days after that, Emily and Henry meet at the tree. Henry sings songs from his hideout. Emily yells up stories from the books she's reading, and then tells the stories she has been thinking up in her head. He likes them better.

Henry tells her not to come to the tree for a week. He is making a surprise for her. It feels like Christmas Eve all week long.

When Emily comes back to the tree, Henry is standing next to it, and hanging down is a ladder made from ropes.

"I want you to see what I see."

He promises he won't let anything happen to her, and talks her up the ladder, one step behind.

In the treetops, the wind is stronger, the sky bigger, the world smaller. She laughs, and so does Henry.

"Look at what else we can do."

Henry pulls the ladder up, holds on, and lets go. It bounces him up and down. He screams and laughs louder than anybody she's ever heard. She forgets she's afraid and tries it too.

At school the next day, they eat lunch together.

That day, they go to their Oak tree and skip stones in the creek. They climb to the tree house, and Emily talks about her newest story. It's about a lost princess who finds a magic house in the jungle. No one can feel sad in the house. It sucks your tears into the walls.

She doesn't know how to end the story, and Henry tells her to ask for a dream.

"That's how I find songs. I ask for them."

They stay in the tree house, talking, laughing, singing . . . until they can't see each other's eyes.

Emily comes home, and her father is standing on the porch with his belt, waiting.

The next day, it hurts to move. Emily finds her Aunt Millie in the kitchen.

"About time you got up. We need to be gone before your daddy gets home."

Millie had packed Emily's clothes in a grocery sack and made an egg salad sandwich for her to eat in the car. Millie touches Emily's swollen lip. "I didn't put any salt or pepper in the sandwich so I don't think it'll sting you."

Millie frowns and shakes her head.

"What were you thinking? Taking up with a Colored boy?"

Emily stays in her aunt's house until the bruises are gone. Millie takes her shopping for new clothes and to the beauty parlor. The woman cuts her hair like the teenagers in the magazine. Millie turns Emily to face the mirror. "See? You do look like your mama." She whispers, "Act right, and someday your daddy will forgive you."

Millie takes Emily to the new school and says, "Never, ever tell anyone why you came to live with me."

The girls are nice. They invite her to eat lunch and ask where she's from. When she names the town, they remember it was in the news a few weeks ago.

It's where a Colored boy's body was found in a creek. He didn't drown. He was tied up with ropes.

My friends read this story and cry. Even Carla tears up.

I'll write more stories during the summer, and by next school year, they'll regret every ignorant racist joke and comment they've made.

The last day of school before summer break, Derrick, one of Valerie's cousins, asks for a ride to the college by my house.

I just got my driver's license, and Roger and I now share the pink Pontiac. "Okay, let's go. I'll get to drive if we get there before my brother does." Derrick and I run to the parking lot and are in the front seat waiting when my brother arrives. He sighs and climbs in the back.

On the way out of the parking lot, a carload of my friends spots me. They smile and wave until they are close enough to see who sits next to me. Mouths drop open, and every hand snaps back. Derrick sees but says nothing.

To break the silence, I turn on the radio and we sing with Marvin Gaye:

I heard it through the grapevine
Not much longer would you be mine . . .

After supper, Carla calls. "Why didn't you put the nigger in the back?"

I am too angry to think.

Carla says, "We've all talked, and you have to choose. Give up your Black friends or give up us."

I slam down the phone so hard it hurts my hand.

These girls were never my friends. It's not all their fault. I've been pretending who I was from the beginning.

Mother suggests I call my old friends from grade school, but that won't work. Valerie finally has Black friends. She doesn't need me to ruin that. Belinda has new friends too. They wear heavy eye makeup, smoke in the parking lot, and have boyfriends with motorcycles. When Belinda passes me in the hall, she doesn't look at me.

For three months, no one calls me or invites me to the birthday parties at the Quincy Country Club.

I spend the summer reading books, sitting under trees, and wishing I could disappear.

• Twenty-One •

School starts again. My old crowd sees me walk in the halls, but act as if they don't. Sometimes they bump me and laugh. A note written on flower-bordered stationery is taped to my locker:

Nigger Lover

At lunch, I stand against the wall and read. At night, I do extra credit homework and daydream about being a famous actress. When I win the Oscar, they'll regret this.

I walk to classes alone and make my face look like it doesn't care. There is a boy I walk behind every day. Freddy is skinny and dark. He holds his head high, appearing taller than he is. We are in first-hour English, second-hour Biology, third-hour World History, and fourth-hour French together. The first time he talks to me is because we both choose Langston Hughes poems to recite.

Freddy says, "Not trying to tell you what to do, but I'll be doing it better than you ever could." If I hadn't looked up at the right moment, I might have changed poems. But there was a half-second smile he covered up as soon as I caught it.

We walk together to the next class and talk about the poems. And then the next class, because he isn't sure he heard the assignment. And, after our third class, he walks slow so I can catch up to him. After a week of us walking together, a White girl who has a Black boyfriend stops at my locker and says, "I've been sent to talk to you."

I know who this girl is. She and other White girls who date Black boys hang out together.

She leans against the locker. "We've seen you walking with Freddy. He belongs to Christina."

Freddy told me about Christina the first day we purposely walked together. Last year, a teacher called her parents to tell them she had a Black boyfriend, and her father almost killed her. She was taken to the emergency room and committed to the state mental institution. She isn't allowed to write letters to Freddy or her friends, but her sister delivers messages.

This girl is standing so close, I can smell the tobacco on her breath. I fight with my brothers, so I know how to act tough. I stand solid, but relaxed, on both feet—and stare at this girl without smiling.

I say, "Freddy told me about Christina. He's a friend, that's all." I turn back to my locker but watch her. She doesn't leave.

"If you don't want Freddy, which one do you want?"

I could point out the racism in asking who I wanted, as if they were up for bid, but I shake my head and hope my voice doesn't crack when I say, "I don't want anyone. I'm not after any of your boyfriends."

She leans closer. "If you ever do, we'll beat your ass."

I shrug and ignore her until she walks away. And then I breathe.

I tell Freddy about the girl at the locker and that rumors are spreading about us. He grins and says, "You're lucky it was the White girls. If the Black girls came at you, your ass would have been whooped. They did that to Christina." I think he is lying, but he swears he isn't. "They don't care about me anymore after I jumped over to White. But if you get yourself a brother they want, they'll be coming after you."

Freddy's face becomes serious. "If this bothers you, I won't walk with you anymore."

I don't want it to bother me. I say, "I don't care, I thought you might."

* * *

White boys on the bus tease a girl about her mother. Her mother is Mrs. McNeely, my World History teacher. She wears bright-colored clothes with loud patterns, and her voice matches. Her daughter, Cathy, and I are the same age. Cathy is nice, but all she ever says to me is "Hi," then she sits with other girls and laughs with them.

Her mother adores Gandhi and Dr. King. Their pictures are in her classroom, and she teaches about the civil rights movement even though it isn't in our history book. She divides the class into what she calls "encounter groups." It's something she did at a conference in California. We share the way we feel about racism and the civil rights movement. "Be truthful. Make it personal." Others in the group can challenge us. She hopes it will lead to greater understanding. Within minutes, we are screaming and yelling at each other. Mrs. McNeely abandons the encounter groups and gives a reading assignment: *The Autobiography of Malcolm X*. Students complain because it's a big book, so she gives the option of writing a paper on the history of slavery in America.

I do both.

The boys on the bus tease Cathy about her mother having the hots for Black men. "I bet she wants you to marry one."

This is what always comes up. Always. In every debate about civil rights, someone says, "Well, if you think everyone is equal, would you ever marry one?" I usually give them a mean look and stop talking. Or say, "Of course not. Don't be stupid."

"Hey Cathy! Are you going to marry a Negro?"

Cathy says, "Maybe. If the man I love is Black." She turns away and stares out the window.

The boys say she's a nigger lover like her mother. She ignores them, and they lose interest. Or can't think of anything else to say.

Damn. Why have I not thought to say that? Why have I not considered that possibility?

That night after dinner, I tell my mother since I believe everyone is equal, I might marry someone from another race. "What will happen if I bring home someone who isn't White?"

My mother is washing the dishes and keeps working without turning around. "Your father and I love you, so we'd have to accept it."

I can't see her face, but my mother is the most honest person I know. I believe her and go to sleep happy. My chance of finding a husband has increased by the millions.

And my mother said she loves me.

• Twenty-Two •

I work on my term paper about U.S. slavery, and Freddy tells me more things I haven't found yet. He is in training to be a preacher, and he preaches it. He takes his fist and pounds it into his hand, emphasizing the atrocities. "They raped wives in front of their husbands, and whipped sons in front of their mamas. Whites are the devil."

I listen and agree. Whites are the devil, and I hate them too.

Freddy laughs when I get upset. "What's the matter? Was it your people? Did your great-great-grandpa own slaves? Did he fuck little girls?"

I don't think so, but I don't know. My family won't talk about where we come from. I ask and get no answers. Dad says people care too much about that and it makes no difference what ancestors did or didn't do. "You have no right to be proud or ashamed of anything except your own life." He could be hiding a family secret.

In my bedroom mirror, I imitate Freddy's rage and deliver speeches about evil White people. "I, a White woman, am sorry." I imagine a crowd of Black people weeping with me.

Every day, Freddy lectures and I listen. He says things that hurt, and when he sees that it does, he strikes harder and harder until I feel like I can't breathe. He looks pleased.

I wake up one morning thinking, "It isn't fair." None of this is fair, and what Freddy is doing to me isn't fair either.

That day, he starts it up with me, and I say, "Shut up. I didn't do any of this. Stop accusing me of shit I did not do."

Freddy doubles over laughing. "I knew I could break you. Someday you are going to get so mad, you'll call me nigger. You are thinking that right now, aren't you?"

I am, and it's his fault. I wasn't thinking it until he said that. The thought came two seconds after he said it, or maybe while he was saying it. Or did it come one second before? "Freddy, you are so full of shit."

I walk away and hear his taunts: "You're going to say it. I know you are."

I'm terrified he's right.

I stop walking to classes with Freddy. There are 435 days until I graduate from high school. Maybe I'll get some disease and can have a teacher come and teach me at home. Then I will never have to walk around school alone again with their eyes watching. I won't see the hate stares. I don't care what they think, but I don't want to be here to see it anymore.

Josephine is a big Black girl. People make fun of her behind her back, but never to her face. She stops me in the hall and says, "Mrs. McNeely showed me your report on slavery. It was good."

I mumble, "Thank you . . ." before she walks away.

Later, I stand against the wall, eating my lunch, and Josephine yells to me, "You think you too good to sit down?" She makes a space next to her and grins.

Every day at lunch, Josephine saves me a seat, and nobody messes with me. Not even Freddy.

• Twenty-Three •

Josephine is my friend, and her friends are my friends because she says they are.

I am the lone White girl in an all-Black crowd, and I am the only one with a car and money for gas. I don't have a job but get an allowance. My friends think I'm joking when I tell them that. They say, "White folks spoil their kids." I can't argue the point.

After a school basketball game, I give rides home. My passengers are all girls because my mother makes me promise. She says, "No boys, or you can't have the car."

When I get to Josephine's house, the cops pull up behind me.

"Oh, crap! What did I do?" It's a serious question, but the girls laugh.

The policeman asks for my license, but I can't find it. "I brought the wrong purse. It's at home."

The cop shakes his head. "Get out of the car."

That's when I cry.

Josephine's mother is already there, yelling at the cop. "This is a nice girl." She gets close to his face. "She isn't what you think she is."

He eases away from her, opens the door of the squad car, and orders me to get in. Josephine's mom runs to the other side of the car and jumps in next to me. "You ain't taking this girl down there alone."

People surround the car, so the cop rolls the window a crack and says, "Go on home," then inches his way through the crowd.

Josephine's mom has watched me play cards and dance with her daughters, but she has never spoken to me. Now she pats my hand and says, "Stop your crying, girl. I won't let them do nothing to you."

My mother doesn't know who called, but says it was a girl who yelled, "Sharon got arrested, and the cops took her to jail!"

My father is at a meeting, and Mother doesn't have a car, so Josephine's cousin comes to get her. His car doesn't have a muffler, and it stalls at every red light.

An officer brings my mother to the interrogation room. She looks more scared than I do. Josephine's mom was going to leave when my mother came, but she stays.

The policeman asks Mother if I had permission to drive her car. She looks up at the ceiling and nods.

"Mrs. Nesbit, do you know where your daughter was tonight?"

Mother looks at me. "You were supposed to be at the game."

"I was, and then I gave Josephine and the girls a ride home."

Mother turns to the officer. "Yes, I knew she was doing that."

Josephine's mom laughs, and the officer grunts and leaves. My mother looks around the room but won't look at me. Josephine's mother introduces herself and tells what happened, but doesn't mention that I cried. She lies and says, "You've got a brave daughter here."

The cop comes back with the car keys and papers for the court date. "She is released into your custody." He stares hard at me, and I make my face look like it doesn't care.

In the lobby, Josephine and kids from school and people I have never seen before are waiting, jeering the police officers for arresting a White girl for once.

Josephine's uncle and cousin give us a ride back to our car. They tell their stories of first-time arrests and tease me about getting off easy. "They let you sit in a room with your momma. They threw our asses in jail and forgot we had mommas." I laugh, but my mother doesn't.

Once we're alone in our car, I say, "I can't believe this. I wasn't doing anything wrong."

Mother screams, "Nothing wrong? Nothing? Police don't arrest people for nothing." Her hands grip the steering wheel. "Do you have any idea how humiliating this is? What will the neighbors think?"

I let her scream and yell the rest of the way home. You can't reason with a crazy woman.

My father comes home and listens to my mother's rants and my defense. He reads the paperwork. The charge is driving without a license. He's angry, but not at me. "All they had to do was look up the records."

The next day at school, Black kids are talking about it. Kids I don't know tell me their arrest stories. A Black student activist says this is an opportunity to expose racist attitudes of the cops. Witnesses for me could cite their own experiences. He is excited this happened.

At dinner that night, my father says he called a judge who is a friend of a friend. "You had twenty-four hours to produce your license. The police overreacted."

I say, "Good. In court, we're going to show how racist they are. They've done worse things to my friends."

My father shakes his head. "You're not going to court. The judge called the chief of police, and they dropped the charges. The policeman who arrested you will wish he hadn't."

I act mad but feel relieved. I am only courageous in my fantasies. Real life has not demanded it from me.

My Black friends tease, "Ask your daddy to adopt us."

I apologize to the student activist, but he shrugs me off and says, "Not your problem."

"I really am sorry. Maybe there is something else I could do to help." He doesn't answer. He walks away and catches up with other Black students. They do the soul-brother greeting, fake punch each other, and laugh.

Their laughter rolls down the hall, and I walk alone to class.

• Twenty-Four •

Mrs. McNeely is the advisor for the Human Relations Club. She asks permission to share my report on slavery with the group and invites me to come to the meeting. She smiles. "You could join the club."

Everyone is Black except one other White girl. I know who she is, but we are not friends. Jan doesn't have any friends. She is the daughter of a minister, dresses like a grown woman, and has no sense of humor.

The club doesn't do much. We talk about racism and agree that our country is racist. Leon, the president of the club, says, "The people who need to hear this aren't here."

I feel eyes on me. "They aren't going to listen to me. They think I'm a traitor."

Jan nods. "They do. And nobody likes me."

And then Mrs. McNeely brings an opportunity. This is the year after Dr. King's assassination, and racial tensions are high across the country. While there are no strong protests in our city, there is tension. The school district hires a team of professors from Western Illinois University to do "encounter group" training with the entire school staff, elementary through high school, to confront racism. The leaders want students here to share their perspectives, and Mrs. McNeely offers our club.

Out of the entire school district staff, there is one Black teacher who teaches PE. The encounter group trainers are two men: one Black and one White. They arrive five minutes late after everyone is seated and waiting. The principal who is hosting the meeting approaches the White man on the team and asks him if the room is arranged correctly. He asks him what they need. The White man won't answer. The principal asks again, and the White man remains silent. The principal looks confused and turns to the teachers, who also look confused. The Black man steps forward and says, "The room is arranged just fine, thank you."

That is the first lesson. "Who did you assume was in charge?"

After the first session, people are afraid and angry. One man says, "I wasn't prejudiced when I came, but I am now." Others agree. There is a sadness that permeates.

The leaders are not concerned. The White one says, "It will be worse before it gets better. We have to recognize the problem before we can solve it."

The second session starts badly. The leaders announce the Human Relations Club will do their presentation and then will be assigned to join the breakout discussion groups. Teachers object. They can't speak freely with us there. The leaders say we need to be there to make them face the truth.

The Black students speak first about their experiences and the injustices: Not being called on in class, a curriculum that negates contributions made by Blacks, White kids getting reprieves for minor infractions when Black students receive suspensions.

It's my turn. I say I have Black friends who are smarter than me and didn't get into the college track. "I didn't earn my place. I have it because I am White and my father went to college. That isn't right, and it isn't fair." I look at the faces in the crowd and spot former teachers. A few smile, but most look angry.

"I know how to stay out of trouble. If I'm quiet, and pretend to listen, and pretend to be nice, you'll leave me alone. But you watch the Black students and wait for them to do something wrong. Anything. If they talk or laugh, they get in trouble for being too loud. If they are quiet, you think they are up to something. You look for excuses to punish them.

"You demand students treat you with respect. But respect is something, even you, need to earn. I've seen how you treat students when no other adult is watching. You can't treat us like that and expect us to be respectful."

A teacher stands. He says he's known me since I was a little girl, and this wasn't the way I had been raised. He says I am saying things I don't mean.

I turn to the Black facilitator and whisper, "I don't know who that man is, but everything I said is true."

He says, "Tell them again."

I repeat it, but the way I say it changes.

The Black leader asks if the teachers saw what just happened. Most shrug, or look at the ceiling. A few teachers nod. "What she said offended you. This man's comment made it clear she had forgotten her place. So when I asked her to tell you again, she was quieter, and she smiled. She hid the anger to be more acceptable. And it worked. I saw heads nodding. Be honest with yourselves. Would you have given her a second chance if she had been Black?"

As he says this, I feel my face redden. I did this without knowing I had. It feels like a betrayal.

At the end of the session, the teachers get up and leave without the lingering talk and laughter. A few thank the leaders for coming, but most make a quick exit.

I offer to help carry a box to the car and ask the Black leader, "Will you be coming back?"

He frowns. "I doubt it."

It is the first time I see him sad, rather than serious. I take it as an invitation to rant against the teachers for being bigoted, hypocritical, and unwilling to confront their prejudices. "They teach that America believes in equality but don't practice it themselves."

He sighs. "You don't need me to tell them that. You can tell them."

"But they won't listen to me."

"Find a way to make them."

This isn't what I want him to say. I want him to be amazed at finding an unprejudiced White girl who gives him hope the world will one day be united, just like Dr. King's dream.

He takes the box I am carrying and puts it in the trunk. He hesitates before stepping into the car and then says, "If you want to help, talk to your people. Or forget about it. Slip back into the White world and live a nice little life. You have that choice."

He smiles before driving away.

• Twenty-Five •

In classes at school, I start speaking up about racism. Most kids argue, but some listen, and a few become friends. They are Black and White, male and female. We all feel like outsiders—like we don't belong anywhere. And now we do.

On the weekends, we go to a coffeehouse managed and owned by a married couple who are my parents' age, but are fun. They convert an apartment above Bowman's Shoe Store into a space for young people to gather and make world-changing plans. Their son serves in the Peace Corps, and they envy him and us. We are young, and it's a new world. More things are possible now. We just need to wake up our minds and question everything.

We make up The Coffee House rules because the city will shut us down if we don't. No drugs, alcohol, or sex on the premises. It closes thirty minutes before curfew.

Every weekend, we have guitar performances, poetry readings, and discussions. No subject is off-limits. We talk about race, religion, politics, our families, hurts, disappointments, hopes, fears, discouragements, beliefs, and doubts. Some believe in prayer, and others mock it. When feelings are hurt, there are apologies. That becomes another rule.

The spring of my senior year, The Coffee House shuts down. The cool old couple are done with it. Too many problems, and the tea and coffee purchases don't pay the rent. They leave town to travel the world, and our crowd has nowhere to go.

We try a park, but mosquitoes, flies, and no food are a problem. We go to Shakey's Pizza, but after two nights are banned. We try other restaurants, but the same thing happens: they want us to leave after we eat. A church offers to host, but we have to pray first. The atheists won't, and the Jewish kids won't pray in the name of Jesus.

We consider our homes, and everyone's is eliminated except mine. My parents are the only ones who will tolerate Blacks and Whites, boys with long hair, and barefooted, braless girls.

I ask my parents, and they say, "Why us?" I want to give a smart-aleck answer, but I want them to say yes, so I tell them the truth. No other parent will allow us all to be there. White families don't want the Black kids, and Black families don't want the White kids.

My parents give each other the look. The one they gave when we brought home stray animals, even the baby bats I once found in our yard after a storm.

They don't say yes immediately. They will talk it over and let me know.

The next morning, Mother says my friends can come over on the weekends but will have to leave to get home by curfew. No smoking or drinking. They are the same rules as The Coffee House. Mother is going to the grocery store and asks for their snack and soda preferences.

My friends hang out in our kitchen, and Mother makes sandwiches and serves homemade chocolate chip cookies. The sideshow is a pair of doves my oldest brother brought home from college. In the university lab, they wouldn't look at each other. In my mother's kitchen, they won't stay off each other. When the male starts his courting dance, Mom turns off the lights and makes us be quiet.

My father talks about rock formations, constellations, sports, and the fall of the Roman Empire. I warn my friends to not talk to him about politics. "And don't tell him you're going to go to Canada to

avoid the draft." Dad doesn't like the Vietnam War, but he's a veteran
and a Republican.

My mother says, "With all your friends and their problems, you
don't need to watch soaps." I am irritated that she sees my friends as
entertainment, but I know what she means. There is always someone in
crisis, someone who needs help. She offers her observations and advice
if they ever ask. What is most irritating is that she is right.

Family dinner conversations are now about my friends. "Did Mike
get his term paper done? Will he graduate? Did Laura's mother let her
move back into the house? Did Leon hear about the scholarship yet?
And if he gets it, how will he move away to college if nobody in his
family has a car?" They aren't making the offer yet, but if nothing else
works out . . .

"Your parents are cool." I roll my eyes, and my friends state the
evidence.

Their parents despise Black people, or distrust White people, or
walk around in their underwear, and would never stock the pantry
with their friends' favorite snacks or send them home with chocolate
chip cookies.

I will never think of them as cool, but I'm glad they're my parents.

• Twenty-Six •

Freddy and I are friends again, and he invites me to hear him preach for the first time. In his church, you don't have to go to seminary to be a preacher. If God touches you, you are a preacher. Freddy says God talks to him and told him to bring me to Jesus.

I tell Freddy I'm an atheist, but that's not true. I want to be, but can't because of what happened at church camp: I was arguing with the girls in my bunk room about whether God exists, and we decided to ask God for proof. We held hands in a circle and counted slowly to one hundred. While we counted, one of the girls begged God to show us a miracle by the time we got to one hundred. We reached eighty and heard wind swirl outside. At eighty-five, it thundered. We said, "One hundred!" and lightning struck the tree by our window and knocked out the camp's electricity.

The weatherman said it was an odd storm. It erupted without warning and left as suddenly as it came. The only place that got hit was the camp.

It's a childish thought that God would play this game, but it makes me doubt my doubts.

I doubt because what I've learned about religion makes no sense. Presbyterians believe people are predestined to go to heaven, and no one knows who. I found that out in my catechism class and questioned the minister, who told the story of Martin Luther, which did nothing to answer my question. I asked my father if he knew Presbyterians believed this, and he said yes, but you don't have to believe everything to be one. That makes no sense either.

But what bothers me most is Jesus. I like Jesus, but it isn't fair that if other people like Muhammad, or Krishna, or Buddha, or never heard of Jesus, they won't go to heaven. I don't believe God would be that cruel, but every Christian I know does. Freddy preaches it to me every day.

Freddy asks again if I'll come to hear his sermon and promises he won't try to make me come to Jesus. "I want friends in the pews for my first sermon."

My mother asks if I'll be the only White person. "Probably, but I'll be fine. Don't worry about it."

She shakes her head. "I'm not worried. But I want to come with you."

That Sunday morning, Mom puts food in the Crock-Pot and tells Dad he's on his own for dinner. "This church goes on all day."

On the way there, I tell her what Freddy told me. "There will be a minister preach before him, and another one after. There's a choir, and you can sing and clap along. People will shout and get smacked by the Holy Ghost or the devil. Don't offer to help someone if they fall down. You won't know if it's the Holy Ghost or the devil. They have trained nurses for that."

Mother says, "I've wanted to go to a Black church ever since I heard Mahalia Jackson sing."

Freddy's church is brick, and the foundation is slightly tilted. I hear laughter before we open the door. We step in and are surrounded by people who take our hands, smile into our eyes, and say, "So happy to see your lovely faces here with us today." No one acts surprised.

My church is elegant and somber. It makes you whisper. The Presbyterians assign greeters. My parents take a shift once a year, so we arrive fifteen minutes early that day. They hand out programs, and if someone new comes, they point to a seat not claimed by one of the regulars.

At Freddy's church, everyone greets and talks to us until the choir lines up.

A grey-haired woman with a pink hat says, "It's time for us to sit down." She leads us to a seat next to her. The choir dance-walks down the aisle. They sing, "Well the Lord woke me up this morning, and I'm glad . . ." Some people jump up, some bodies sway in the seats, others wave hands. Pink Hat Lady puts her hand on her chest and cries.

The choir reaches its seats and sings more songs until the minister stands. Then they hum. He starts quiet, asking for help to get himself going. People yell at him, "Go on now!" The preacher closes his eyes and raises his hands, and people shout, "Help him, Lord!" You see the moment the Lord does. It starts with the hands and shimmies down to his feet. He opens his eyes and sings out his sermon. His body moves to the rhythm. When he's done, he collapses into a chair and a nurse fans him.

The choir takes off again with more songs. They turn quiet when Freddy rises. He begins too loud, too hard, and the congregation tells him, "Easy now." He stops, shakes his head, like he's ready to fight someone. "No. I'm not going to take it easy. I'm in a fight with the devil." Someone hollers, "All right now!" And Freddy punches out his words and people clap to the beat.

The four-hour service ends with a hug line. Pink Hat Lady grabs our hands and pulls us in line. We circle around the church, and the main preacher starts by hugging the person next to him, and then everyone follows. Everyone hugs and blesses everyone. My mother, who doesn't hug her own children, hugs and holds on to people as if they were lost friends. I hug everyone and receive blessings and invitations to come again anytime. The last person to hug is my mother. Pink Hat Lady looks at my face, laughs, and says, "Girl, what's wrong with you? Hug your mama!" Before I do, my mother's arms are around me like I can't ever remember.

The next day, Freddy is pleased with himself. Kids at lunch call him "Preacher." He walks me to my locker and asks if I'm ready to come to Jesus. "Let me baptize you. That little sprinkle on the head you had is not enough." He takes a strand of my hair and tugs it. "You got to go all the way with me." His face has that horny boy look, and I push him away. He laughs and walks off. "I'm just playing."

He is. Freddy is a good actor. He'll never get me to come to Jesus because I know that. But there are people in his church who believe, like Pink Hat Lady. There are believers in my church too.

But I'm not one of them.

• Twenty-Seven •

I want to be an atheist. I don't want to believe there is an all-powerful God who lets people be evil. If God sent Jesus to help, it didn't work. Christians gave biblical references to justify slavery. Nations full of Christians refused Jewish refugees. My friends who call me a nigger lover go to church every Sunday.

But when I say I'm an atheist, I feel the need to apologize.

A friend gives me a book for my birthday with an inscription: *I read this book and thought of you.*

The Prophet by Kahlil Gibran. The cover is a drawing of a man I want to know. His eyes are large, round, and soft. The book is written in prose. It's beautiful, simple, and wise and makes me want to believe in the God this man knows.

I tell Freddy I might believe in God and show him *The Prophet*. He says anything written about God that isn't from the Bible is the work of Satan. And because my preacher threw sprinkles on my head and I didn't wade in the water and cleanse my whole body, the devil knows I'm easy.

Freddy talks holy, but he's done worse stuff than I ever have, and he admits it. But he says that doesn't matter since he's been saved.

That makes no sense.

But when I read *The Prophet*, it makes me feel there is something out there that will make sense. And if it is out there, I want to find it.

• Twenty-Eight •

Brother Daniel is transferring to a parish in Chicago. He hugs me goodbye, and I ask if I'll ever see him again. "God willing. Look me up if you ever visit Chicago."

Six months later, I am in Chicago with my high school band. We are at the end of our tour and staying at the Palmer House, the downtown hotel where my parents spent their honeymoon. We have free time all day until our bus leaves at 5:00 p.m. Valerie is my roommate. I tell her about Brother Daniel and make the phone call. When I hang up, she says, "Girl, you've got a crush on him . . . and he's Black. Once you go Black, you won't go back."

Her face is so serious, I don't laugh. "He's a Franciscan brother."

"He's a man. And he's probably going crazy being celibate."

I laugh. "He's not like that."

Valerie frowns. "How old is he?"

"Don't know exactly—probably twenty-five."

"He's going crazy."

I grin. "Then come with us. You can protect me from this crazed man."

Valerie shakes her head. "People will say I went out with a grown man, and my mama will have a fit."

"He wears a brown robe. Nobody will think it's a date."

Brother Daniel shows up wearing slacks and a sweater. A young

White man is with him. Brother Daniel grins. "This is Brother Glen. He's our chauffeur—and our chaperone.

I feel myself blush and ask, "Where are your robes?"

"It's our day off."

I didn't know they had days off, and Valerie gives me the look I've seen hundreds of times. It's what her face does when she thinks I'm acting like a fool.

Brother Daniel says, "We'll have lunch downtown and then go to my favorite place. I'm not telling you where because you won't want to go." He invites Valerie to come along, but she says she has other plans and gives me that look again.

I make guesses on where we're going, but every guess is wrong. It's not a museum, an art gallery, a park, or the beach. It's not Union Station, or Sears Tower, or Wrigley Field. When I guess a cathedral, he says I'm getting warm. I guess a mosque, a synagogue, and a church. He says, "You'll never guess this one because you don't know it exists. I promise you will be impressed, and if you ever get over your problem with God, you may want to check this out."

We drive along Lake Shore Drive until it turns into neighborhoods with huge houses and big churches. We turn a corner, and Brother Daniel points. "There's the top of it." Above the trees, I see an ornate dome. Soon the rest of it comes into view. It is grand, and majestic, and looks like it should be in the Middle East, not Chicago.

"This is the Bahá'í House of Worship. The Bahá'í Faith is a new religion."

Brother Daniel was right. I had never heard of it, and I am impressed. But as beautiful as this place is, I am not interested in any religion.

We walk up the steps into the massive sanctuary. Inside, there is a deep sense of calm. Hundreds of chairs are arranged in rows. A few people sit in them. Some appear to be praying, while others sit quietly. A few nod and smile. The room is circular, and I count nine doors

with large archways. Above the arches in gold lettering are quotes that
Brother Daniel is writing in a notebook. The quotes make me think of
Gibran. Brother Daniel leans back, looks up at the ceiling, and smiles.
I do the same and see that the nine sides meet at the top, and in the
center is something quite beautiful, but unrecognizable.

When we step outside, Brother Daniel tells me it was a prayer
written in Arabic.

There is a visitor center downstairs and a bookstore. A dark-
haired man greets us with what I guess to be an Arabic accent. His
smile feels like a hug. He looks from Brother Glen, to me, and then to
Brother Daniel, and his smile widens. "Welcome. Welcome. You are
welcome here."

This hadn't been our experience earlier today. When we left the
hotel, Brother Daniel made me hold onto his arm. "I'm not going to
lose you in Chicago." Everywhere we went, people looked at us, and
they weren't happy. They shook their heads and frowned. One man
stopped, crossed his arms, and glared as we passed. The waitress at the
diner wouldn't wait on us until Brother Glen called her over. She didn't
look at me or Brother Daniel as she took our order, and she slammed
the silverware onto the table so hard that other customers jumped.

Brother Daniel smiled up at her. "Oh, thank you kindly." She
sputtered and disappeared. The cook brought us the food and the
check at the same time. Brother Daniel laughed. "I guess they won't be
offering dessert."

This Bahá'í man stands looking at us with a tenderness I've never
seen from anyone. And it seems like it's because we are interracial. He
smiles at other visitors, but more at us.

Brother Daniel collects pamphlets and buys a book about the
Bahá'í Faith. He hands them to me, grins, and says, "Compliments of
the pope."

"If you like this religion so much, why aren't you a Bahá'í?"

He laughs. "Because I'd be out of a job. They don't have clergy."

We watch an introductory film, walk through the nine gardens that surround the temple, and stay too long. Brother Glen rushes us to the car and drives faster than he should. We arrive in front of the hotel where my tour bus is loading. Valerie has my luggage, and I hug Brother Daniel a quick goodbye.

On the bus, Valerie asks where we went, and I show her the pamphlets. Other kids ask what the Bahá'í Faith is, and I explain what I know. "They think all religions come from the same God, there is only one race, and women and men are equal."

One of the boys says, "Sounds like a cult."

They laugh about what I will look like bald and selling flowers in airports.

There is no point in talking. They don't want to understand.

I close my eyes and dream about tall archways, gold letters, and a man who smiles.

• Twenty-Nine •

Josephine's sister has made her a dress for our Senior Prom in case someone asks her out. Josephine says the dress is so ugly she won't go even if someone asks. But I know that isn't true. She wants a boyfriend. So do I, but neither of us have one.

White boys won't talk to me because they think I date Black boys. If that bothers them, I wouldn't want to date them anyway.

But I don't date Black boys. It would hurt Josephine and her friends, who are all dark-skinned. The boys ignore them and go after light-skinned girls.

Josephine has a crush on Franklin. He's tall, with soft eyes and a soft voice. He's as dark as Josephine. They have English class together, and a month ago, he asked her to correct his spelling for his term paper. She corrected the grammar too, and he got an A. Now she does all his assignments, and he calls her "My Queen."

We are in Josephine's room, which she shares with her sister. The prom dress is hanging on the nail where the picture of Jesus used to be. The dress was made from a cousin's bridesmaid dress. It is green satin with ruffles and puffy sleeves.

I haven't told Josephine that last week Franklin asked me to prom. I suggested he ask Josephine, and he laughed and said, "Naw... she's too Black." Instead, he asked a freshman who could pass for White.

My hippie friends from The Coffee House are doing an anti-prom dance on a bluff overlooking the Mississippi River. There's going to be a bonfire, and we'll dance to the car radio.

I invite Josephine to come with me. "Some people are dressing up. You could wear the prom dress."

Josephine says no.

She's heard Franklin's date has the flu.

• Thirty •

This is my last summer before going away to college. My oldest brother John is home and has become a Bahá'í. He read the book Brother Daniel bought me and looked up the Bahá'ís at college. He joined last spring and told my parents over the phone. Mother cried, and Dad ranted for days.

John acts the same, only nicer. He invites me to Bahá'í meetings, and I go with him. The people remind me of the smiling man at the temple. My mother is worried I'm going to become one, but I won't. I'm not so sure about God, and there's a marriage law they have that I don't like. You have to get your parents' consent to get married, regardless of how old you are. My brother says it's because the Faith is about unity, and that starts with the family.

I tell my mother, "No offense, but I would never want to have to ask for your blessing to get married."

Mother nods and says, "I wouldn't want that either."

My brother tells me about a Bahá'í meeting at the Frederick Douglass Community Center. He says, "College students from Bloomington will be there. They have a singing group." Bloomington is where I will be going to college this fall, and I know what John is trying to do.

"I have to work Sunday."

"What time?"

"I get off at 1:00."

He grins. "It starts at 2:00."

I don't want to hurt his feelings. This faith is good for him, but I don't need it.

On Sunday, the restaurant is busier than usual, and I stay longer to help. It is almost 2:00 when I get home. I look at the kitchen clock and feel sick in my gut. I run upstairs and change clothes.

My mother looks up from her recipe book as I run out the door. "I thought you weren't going to any more Bahá'í meetings."

"I won't stay long."

I don't explain why I changed my mind, because the truth will make me look as crazy as I feel. Something is pushing me there. I have a floaty feeling and see myself drive, park, and enter the building where the meeting is.

The meeting has started, and a small choir is singing on a platform in the front of the room. I see Josephine and some other friends here, but there are no empty seats by them. I stand at the back, and a man who was sitting near the door points to an empty chair in the front row. I shake my head, but he won't stop pointing. Now others turn to look. I walk around the edge, eyes down to avoid the smiling face of my brother, and sit. The choir is singing in harmony, and a deep voice rises above the others. I look up and see a young Black man.

I hear the Voice inside say, "This is the man you will marry." The voice is so loud I wonder if others heard it too, but no one else is reacting. They are all listening to the singing.

For the rest of the meeting, I watch this young man. He listens to the speaker and jots notes in a small spiral notebook. When the speaker makes a joke, his laughter is immediate. At the end of the meeting, he is asked to say a prayer and chants one. Everyone bows their heads and closes their eyes, but me. I watch as he lifts his hands up and offers his prayer.

Afterwards, I find him with Josephine, who is getting his phone number. I want to kick her, but tease instead, "Fast work, Josephine." My voice is shrill and awful.

He frowns and says, "No, she is just being friendly."

I cannot think of anything to say, so I stand and listen while Josephine talks to him. His name is George, and he is a theater major.

And he was born and raised in Chicago.

It wasn't as hard as I thought it would be to find "him."

That night, I climb out my bedroom window, sit on the roof, look up at the stars, and sing, "Goodnight, my someone."

But this time, I see a face, and I know his name.

• Thirty-One •

My college roommate has unpacked and decorated her side. Three posters cover the wall above the leopard-print bedspread. One poster is Malcolm X, another a black fist, and the last a half-naked African woman with a spear.

I regret sending the letter introducing myself and wondering if she wanted to match covers for our beds.

The university sent her name and address: Myrtle from Chicago. I laughed when I saw the name. I have a great-aunt named Myrtle who ran off with a salesman. The marriage didn't last, and she came home with a son. She wore clanky bracelets, ruby lipstick, and when she grabbed and kissed me, I held my breath. She smelled like a funeral home.

I can't imagine this being the room of a Myrtle.

My father glances at the posters and frowns. My mother chatters about the big windows and the closet's built-in dresser with a bottom drawer that won't open without lifting and pulling. She compares it to my brothers' dorm rooms. Mine is bigger, and she thinks it's because it's a girl's dorm. Dad and I don't argue her points because we don't care. I am thinking about the posters, and the books stacked on my roommate's shelf: *Soul on Ice* by Eldridge Cleaver, *The Negro Revolution* by Robert Goldston, *The Autobiography of Malcolm X*.

I hear steps outside the door pause. The door opens, and she walks in and around us to her side of the room. We are the same height, but her afro adds a foot.

I smile and speak first. She answers hello, then turns away to organize her bookshelf. My mother whispers too loud, "Ask her if she wants to come to dinner with us."

She doesn't.

My mother says goodbye, how nice it was to meet her, and hopes she will cure me of my messiness.

I flash an apologetic smile that Myrtle ignores.

At dinner, my father and I eat while Mother talks about my roommate. She is convinced the university noted my membership in the Human Relations Club and paired us up. "If I were you, I'd put up the pictures of your friends on your bulletin board. She'll see you have Black friends."

Mother doesn't understand this girl will likely consider all my Black friends as "Uncle Toms."

For three weeks, I say "Hello" when I see her and "Bye" when I leave. She nods, or sighs. I try my mother's suggestion and put up pictures. Myrtle says nothing.

One day, she is typing at her desk. I look over her head at a new picture on her bulletin board. It's a toddler, dressed in a pink, poofy dress. "Who's this cutie?"

She stands, hands on hips, eyes narrow, and says, "That's my daughter."

I think she is lying. Playing a sick game on the dumb White girl.

I point to the picture I took of my two-year-old neighbor who played in our old sandbox last summer. "This is my little girl. My parents are taking care of her."

Myrtle studies the photo. We have the same hair and skin coloring. She says, "She's cute."

"Thank you." I flop on my bed and pretend to read.

That night, Myrtle comes home drunk, stumbles into our room, and laughs. I laugh at her laughing. She tries to talk and can't. She catches her breath and spits out, "Wrong floor."

"Did you go in somebody else's room?"

She nods and giggles out, "I got in another girl's bed, and she was in it." We both catch our breath and laugh more.

When we are too exhausted to laugh, we talk.

Myrtle is a sophomore, not a freshman like I am. Last year, she had another White roommate. That one kept clothes in the closet but slept on the floor in a room down the hall. In the morning, she came to get clothes but never changed in their room. Every time she saw Myrtle in the hall or cafeteria, she waved and called out, "Hi, roommate!" One day, they were alone in the hall, and when this girl greeted her, Myrtle slammed her up against the wall and said, "If you ever talk to me again, I will fuck you up so bad you won't know who you are."

This roommate was Myrtle's first experience with a White person. She lived in a part of Chicago where there are no White people. All her teachers were Black, the store people were Black, and her family never went anywhere but to church and their relatives'. All Black.

That is almost hard to believe, but there are a lot of White girls here who have known only White people.

"I'm sorry that happened. Not all of us White people are idiots."

"No, just most of you."

That throws us into the giggles again.

Inside our room, we are friends. She teaches me how to curse like I mean it, and I write poems for her English 101 assignment. When the university clinic gives me medicine I'm allergic to, Myrtle gets me to the emergency room. When Myrtle's friends call about an apartment listed in the paper and are told it's already rented, she asks me to call. "None of us sound White enough."

I make the call, and the agent says, "Yes, it's still available." The agent makes an appointment to come to our dorm to sign the contract because he wants to make it as convenient as possible.

Some nights, Myrtle and I stay up late and tell our stories. Most are hilarious, but when we get serious, her stories are hard and sad. They make my worst days look foolish.

There are things we never talk about.

We don't talk about how she has to work to stay in school and has student loans that will take her years to repay, and my parents write a check for tuition and send money every week.

And we never talk about our daughters.

• Thirty-Two •

After a month of living in a dorm with girls I don't know and don't know if I want to know, and one-time dates with boys who won't ask me out again because I won't go to bed with them, I look up the Bahá'ís and hope to find George.

Both happen. I find the Bahá'ís and George, and it feels like I've come home. George doesn't remember me. I'm glad. This time I relax, and laugh, and talk, and listen, and when it's time to go, he finds a ride for me and climbs in the back seat next to me. His hand brushes lightly against mine. I want to tell him about the Voice and ask if he's heard it too, but I can't. This moment is perfect enough.

I go to another Bahá'í gathering a few days later, but he isn't there. A young woman hears me ask about him, and her eyebrows arch when I say his name. She looks at me with a sad smile. Later, she says, "Do you know that George has a fiancée? She's studying in France for the year. Her father won't give them consent because he's racist, but her mother has become a Bahá'í and loves George. We all hope her dad will give in when she comes back. I feel so sad for George. He misses her so much."

I wait until I'm alone in my dorm room, under covers, to cry. So now I can't trust the Voice in my head or the love I felt from George. George loves everyone. Maybe that confused the Voice.

Or maybe there is no Voice. It's just me being stupid.

• Thirty-Three •

It's Saturday night, and I am in a dorm room down the hall doing prank calls with the other girls who don't have dates. We take turns calling boys from the campus directory and score points if they ask us out.

I make the first call and talk with a southern accent. "Hello, Johnny? This is Christina, and I've been thinking it over, and yes, I'll go to the party with you."

I act embarrassed to discover it's the wrong Johnny.

"Too bad, I like your voice." When he asks for my phone number, I give a fake one and score the first point of the game.

The other girls try, but most hang up when the guy answers.

A "Donald" is picked. The girl who calls him panics and whispers, "Holy crap! He's Black."

I take the phone and say, "So, Donald, where were you? I waited for over an hour."

He's on it. "Well, baby, I've been waiting for you my whole life."

His voice is deep and rich, and I'm imagining a young Sidney Poitier. But the girls are making faces, and one pretends to gag.

I say, "Don't ever be late for another date, or it's over."

Donald laughs and says, "Get rid of your girlfriends and meet me in the student union by the Coke machine."

An hour later, I am by the Coke machine laughing so hard, people passing by stare. He's tall, skinny, and goofy-looking. I stand on a chair to look into his eyes and say, "I want to see into your soul."

Donald snaps his eyes shut and says, "You're not ready for that."

I won't go to a party with him, but I give him my number, and he calls me at 4:00 a.m. to say goodnight.

After a week of daily calls to wake me up in the morning and wish me sweet dreams at night, I agree to go out with him. I'm not going to be able to hide him from my friends, so I tell the girls what I did.

"What?"

"You met up with him?"

"Are you crazy?"

I tell them he's a good guy and invite them to meet him. I enjoy watching him with them. He's funny, and smart, and almost passes their inspection. He's nice, but . . .

"What will your parents say?"

"White men won't ask you out if they see you with a Black man."

"Okay for you, but what about the children?"

I explain my parents aren't prejudiced like theirs. If a White man has a problem with this, I wouldn't want to date him anyway, and I won't have sex with Donald, so there won't be any children.

But Donald wants sex, like every boy I've met at college. It's why I don't have a boyfriend. I dress like a hippie, and they assume I'm into free love. I just like the clothes.

Donald says I'm making too big of a deal out of sex because I'm a virgin. "It's what men and women do, baby. Grow up."

Every date, every conversation, every phone call ends in a fight. He says, "You are afraid, aren't you? It'll be okay. I'll go slow and easy."

"I'm not scared. But when I do it, I want to be in love. We're not in love."

"Do it with me, and you'll see how much I love you."

It's become a tiresome game, but we're both stubborn.

Donald tries a new strategy. "I love you enough to make you my first wife."

First wife? I think I've caught him in a Freudian slip, but I haven't. Donald doesn't know how many wives he'll have, but says I'm naïve to expect to stay married to the same man my whole life.

He looks at me with pity. "Baby, nobody does that."

"Nobody? Nobody except my parents, grandparents, aunts, uncles, and my parents' friends."

Donald thinks I'm lying. I could present proof, but there's no point.

This feels over, but we have plans to go to a party tonight. He tells me, "I'll come by at 8:00." He takes a strand of my hair, twists it, and says, "Will you wear something sexy tonight and pretend like we're fucking? The brothers tease me for putting up with your shit."

I leave without kissing him goodbye.

All I have to wear are jeans and t-shirts. The sexiest thing I can do is go without a bra, but I don't need one anyway.

I wait over an hour for him to come. Then I give up and walk to the campus quad even though it's raining. I don't have an umbrella. I'm not wearing a coat, and it's so cold the rain is turning into sleet. I imagine Donald showing up at my dorm, discovering I've left, searching for me and finding me walking alone, shivering and cold. He'll apologize and promise to give me as long as I need.

I don't love Donald, but I like having a boyfriend. I'm going to miss that.

I hear someone say, "Hey! Are you okay?"

I look up to see a beautiful man. His skin is honey-brown. He has dimples and white, straight teeth framed by pinkish-tan lips.

He doesn't want me to walk by myself. He hands me his umbrella and says he'll follow behind to protect me. That feels silly, so he walks next to me. Jonas is a business major, which is a shame. He should be in movies and on posters in the girls' dorm. I tell him my boyfriend stood me up, but don't tell him why. We come to the men's dorms.

He says, "This is where I stay." It's the same dorm Donald lives in. "Why don't we go up to my room? I'll make tea, and you can tell me about your horrible boyfriend if you like. Or just relax and listen to music."

The lobby is full of people. I look for Donald, but he isn't here. I want him to see me with this beautiful man. But that feels silly and wrong. "Maybe I should go home."

Jonas doesn't hear me. He leads me through the crowd to the elevator. The warmth of his hand makes me shiver.

He has a roommate, and I'm relieved we're not alone. The roommate is sitting at his desk studying. He stands, puts on his coat, and gathers his books. I say, "You don't have to go. I'm not staying long."

He looks past me at Jonas and nods. "Later, man," and he is gone.

Jonas goes to the door and steps out into the hall. He looks back at me and says, "I'll be back in minute."

By myself in the room, it doesn't feel right. I want to call someone. My roommate. Or Donald. I want someone to know where I am. I pick up the phone, but the rotary dial is missing. I try to open the door, but it's locked. I am about to yell but hear keys in the lock, and Jonas comes in with a tea kettle and cups.

He laughs at my questions. "For someone so suspicious, why did you come to a strange man's room?"

I am shivering, and he apologizes for the broken window. I now see the curtains blowing. Jonas laughs. "Things sometimes get a little wild in here. Drink the tea, it'll warm you up."

I sip the tea, and he asks if I want to talk, but I can see his eyes now.

I shake my head. "Thanks for being so nice and all, but I have to go. I'm meeting some friends to go to a movie."

"You're lying." He reminds me I told him about Donald. "They think you went to a party with him."

I stand to walk to the door but feel dizzy. The room feels hot now, or maybe it's me. Maybe it's the flu. Maybe I'll throw up on him.

He tells me to relax, sit back down. He takes off his clothes. I've never seen an erect penis. He comes closer, and I push him back. He laughs. "Good. You like to play games. Me too."

"I want to go home. Please, just let me go."

He lies on his bed and strokes his penis. "You can't leave now. It's after midnight, and the doors are alarmed."

"If you don't let me leave, I'll scream for help."

"Go ahead. They'll all come and fuck you like they did to a girl last week. I don't care, because I'll get you first."

A story pops in my head. "My parents are strict. They'll take me to the doctor when I come home to see if I'm still a virgin. If I'm not, they'll throw me out. Please don't do this."

"That's so sad." He makes an exaggerated frown. "That was a good performance, but not quite convincing. Try it again, and this time, cry and beg."

"You're a bastard."

He laughs. The floor tilts, and I struggle to stand still. I look at the window and try to remember what floor we're on. I could jump.

Ten.

He pushed the button for the tenth floor.

He shoves me onto the bed. "If you are quiet, I won't have to hurt you."

I feel my shoes come off, and then the rest. He evaluates my body. My breasts are too small, my thighs are too flabby, and my ankles are too thick. He tells me, "You're a C+. You should thank me for this."

He puts on a record. The music swirls around and through me. I float inside of it, and disappear.

Sunlight wakes me up. The day is too bright and beautiful. Jonas is sleeping next to me, and my clothes are folded on the chair. I slip out of bed and put them on. I feel Jonas awake and watching. He asks if I remember what happened and smiles when I don't answer.

He puts on a robe and takes me out of the room, then down the hall to the stairwell. He kisses my cheek and whispers, "I tried, but I couldn't get it in."

I go down the stairs, and he yells after me, "You were too tight. I'll get you next time."

The door alarm goes off when I open it. I make my legs run, and no one comes after me.

• Thirty-Four •

My roommate is asleep. Myrtle's bags are packed, and I remember it's Thanksgiving break. I have to catch the noon Greyhound.

No one is in the bathroom. I shower, and it stings when I wash it, but doesn't hurt inside. I don't know what it's supposed to feel like, and there's no one I can ask.

On the bus, I find a seat next to an older woman reading a book. She moves over without looking at me.

I close my eyes and see his face and remember things. The teacup was red, and chipped. It hurt my lip, and my tongue finds the wound. There were sixteen tiles on the ceiling, and two had broken pieces. His body was sweaty and smelled musky. Maybe that was the incense. He was heavy, and I pushed him away, but he came back.

My father picks me up from the bus station. He doesn't like to talk when he drives, so my silence is acceptable. My mother is in the kitchen looking at her cookbook and worrying about when my brothers will arrive. John is driving from Detroit and picking up Roger from the University of Illinois. "I thought they'd be here before you."

I say I'm tired from staying up too late and go to my room. I crawl into bed without changing clothes or brushing my teeth.

Car doors slam, and my brothers' voices mingle with my parents'. It took longer because they stopped for dinner and gas, and a deer jumped out of nowhere and was hit by another car right in front of them. They stopped to make sure everyone was okay and took the driver to the next town to get a tow. I hear my name, and my mother says, "She went up just a few minutes ago. She's probably awake."

I hear steps coming up the stairs, and my door opens. It stays open. Roger's voice whispers, "Sharon?" I hold my body still, pretending to breathe deep and slow. The door closes, and the tears that have been gathering for hours spill silently.

The next morning, I stay in my room until everyone has gotten up and used the bathroom and eaten breakfast. I am teased for being so tired, but I'm not pretending. My body wants to sleep forever.

On Thanksgiving, my brothers and dad talk about football and politics. We watch television and play card games, and I pretend to be me. No one notices anything. I'm going to get away with this.

The day after Thanksgiving, my friend Rodney calls and says, "You've got to come get me." He is visiting the White family who sponsored him in high school through a program for Black students with potential. He hated living with these people and moving away from his family in South Carolina, but his mother insisted. The program helped him win a full scholarship to the University of Illinois. He has to show he's grateful to them for all they've done, and ignore their ignorant racist comments.

I pick him up and drive to a small park on top of the river bluff. This is where we always go. He doesn't want people to see us together. "In South Carolina, I could get killed for saying hello to a White girl. It's not as different in the North as you think it is."

On the way to the park, I talk about school and the crazy girls on my floor. I push away the urge to confide.

He is silent and stares and makes me nervous. I ask, "What? What's the matter?"

"You tell me. I know bullshit when I see it. You're hiding something."

It's what I was hoping someone would say. The telling of it takes a long time. It makes it real, and it's hard to breathe while talking.

Rodney listens with eyes closed. Then he says, "You don't remember what happened?"

"Maybe there was something in the tea. Or maybe I'm crazy."

Rodney thinks Jonas lied. "He did it. He's afraid you're going to tell."

I say, "If I tell, they will make this a race thing."

"And when they find out you dated a Black man, they'll say you deserved it."

Rodney holds me and wipes my face with his sleeves. "I'm sorry this happened to you."

• Thirty-Five •

On my dorm's bulletin board is a flier:

Free Student Counseling Services
No Appointment Necessary

The flier shows a photo of three college students laughing together. Next to them is a young woman standing in a shadow.

There are forms to complete. I sign one that prohibits them from contacting my parents. Another one asks to state my reason for coming. I turn it in blank, but the woman at the front desk says, "We need to know the nature of the problem to decide who you should see."

I write, "Problem with a man."

I am surprised they assign a male counselor, but he assures me he can help. "Trust me, I've heard it all. And if you are having difficulties with men, a male perspective is useful."

I tell about Jonas and what he did. I've been practicing telling this without crying, making sure I have the facts in the right sequence. I tell him only the relevant details. He's a student and lives in the dorm. He locked me in and wouldn't let me leave. I tell about the tea, and becoming naked, and running down the stairs the next morning. I do not tell him Jonas is Black, and he doesn't ask.

He asks, "What else do you remember about that night?"

"Nothing. I want to forget it."

"Anything else you want to tell me?"

I could tell him a lot of things. Like how I don't want to sleep because I have dreams about Jonas. Not every night, but too many times. And how hard it is to walk on campus knowing he could be there. And how I won't go to the student union now because I saw him there and he saw me and waved. I could tell the counselor these things and more, but I may start crying and I don't want to cry with him.

He writes a few notes on a pad, then leans forward and says, "Let me tell you something your mother apparently never did. When a woman goes to a man's room, he thinks she wants to have sex." He flashes a sad smile and says, "This was an unfortunate miscommunication."

He talks about horse falls and getting back in the saddle and suggests I make love to someone I like as soon as possible. "I'm sure you can think of someone." He smiles and winks and says, "And if not, come back and see me."

When I get back to my dorm, I call Rodney. "You'll never believe what the idiot counselor said."

We laugh, and then Rodney says, "So when are you coming to see me?" I laugh more, but he says, "I'm serious."

Rodney is at the University of Illinois, a forty-five-minute bus ride from Illinois State. It is dark when I arrive, and I take a cab to his dorm. He sneaks me in the back stairs. His roommate is away for the weekend.

The first night, we reveal our secret crushes. I wanted him to invite me to senior prom. He wanted to ask, but was afraid of what his mama would do. He says, "She knew I liked you by the way I talked about you. When she found out you were White, she threw a fit."

We kiss and giggle. We try again and giggle more. So we listen to music, and dance, and fall asleep holding each other.

The second night, I tell Rodney this isn't going to work. "We've been friends for too long."

Rodney says, "No, this is why you came to me," and he pushes through my laughter.

It is quick and painful, and when he's done, I whisper what I've seen in movies. "It was good for me." I say that because I don't want him to do it again.

The sheet has a blood stain, and I hurt inside. Jonas didn't lie about me being too tight to get it in.

In the morning, Rodney takes me to the bus station but won't walk next to me. He walks several steps ahead because he doesn't want his Black militant friends to see us. "They think I hate White people more than they do." When we get to the station, he looks around to make sure no one is watching before hugging me goodbye.

Rodney calls that night to see if I made it home. He calls a few more times, and we search for things to say. I don't want to hear about his girlfriends, or his plans for a life without me.

What Jonas did hurt me. Losing Rodney hurts more.

• Thirty-Six •

I go out with men, and if they ask to fuck, sometimes I do, but I'm not good at it.

They say, "You just lie there."

I say, "What do you want me to do?"

"Enjoy it."

"I don't."

They don't ask me out again.

I need to talk about all of this before I explode. I think about calling Josephine or Valerie, but we haven't kept in touch. Besides, I know what they would say: "Girl, what were you thinking? You shouldn't have gone into that man's room. And then you go to that fool Rodney?"

I can't tell my brothers. I never talk to them about sex, and they will worry about my sanity and might tell Mom and Dad.

The only person I can trust with this is my Franciscan friend, Brother Daniel. He told me to come to him if I'm ever in trouble.

I call Brother Daniel and tell him about Jonas and Rodney. He listens and encourages me to tell him more. Somehow he knows there is more to tell, so I confess there are now others. "I'm not a virgin anymore, so it doesn't matter." There is silence, but I sense him there, waiting. "Nothing matters to me anymore."

"You matter to me." He suggests I come to Chicago for a visit. He will ask a female friend if I can stay with her.

"Can I come tomorrow?"

Brother Daniel and his friend, Julia, pick me up at the train station, and we go to her apartment.

Her boyfriend arrives with pizza and beer. I ask for soda, and Julia frowns. "I didn't realize how young you are. Guess we won't be going to the club tonight." She asks if I'm enjoying college, and Brother Daniel interrupts. "No talk about college allowed. For this weekend, she's a young woman enjoying the city with a friend." He smiles at me, and I smile back.

Julia and her boyfriend suggest we go for a drive.

Brother Daniel sits in the back seat with me. It's below zero, and the vinyl seats make it colder. He puts his arm around me and says, "I'll keep you warm." I still see my breath, but the shivering stops.

The city at night is beautiful. The darkness hides the trash on the sidewalk, the dried vomit, the dog shit, the cigarette butts . . . Brother Daniel points out Navy Pier and the Art Institute. He says, "I'll take you there this summer."

Brother Daniel picks up my hand, takes off the mitten, and kisses my fingers—then puts my hand on his hard penis and makes me squeeze it. I look up at his face, and he stares ahead.

I let my hand stay where he wants it and gaze out the window at the blurred skyline.

• Thirty-Seven •

A month later, I am in my dorm room alone on a Saturday night. A girl on my floor asks me to go to a party with her. I haven't gone out since coming back from Chicago. I say no, and a few minutes later, she comes back and says, "Please—I can't go by myself." There is one guy she wants to see and promises it won't take long.

The party is in an apartment off campus, and it takes half an hour to walk there. When we arrive, Ravi Shankar music is playing, and smoke swirls from incense sticks. In a corner is a lamp with an amber glow. The rest of the apartment is lit with candles. Shadows sway and vanish.

The girl whispers, "He's in the kitchen. I'll be back in a few minutes."

I find a pillow and sink into it, then hear, "I know you."

I look up to see a young man with long, blond hair and soft, blue eyes. He says, "You are an artist."

"I'm a sociology major, and we've never met."

He kneels down at my feet. "No, you are an artist. I've seen you in my dreams. I know who you are—let me show you."

He reaches into his pocket and takes out a small bag.

"I can't." The Voice has warned me about this, but I don't tell him that. I tell him another truth: My great-grandfathers on both sides were ugly alcoholics, and I see signs of addiction in myself. "I buy red licorice and want to eat the whole bag. If I force myself to stop, I get up during the night to finish it."

I tell him about my friend who tripped on LSD and thought he could fly. He survived the fall but can't talk or feed himself. "I'm afraid if I ever drop acid, I'll do that."

He writes his phone number on a pink slip of paper. "Give me a call when you're ready."

The girl I came to the party with is gone. No one knows where she is. I search all the rooms, and she isn't here. I describe her to the man who lives in the apartment. He grins. "Yeah, she left with Rick. They won't be coming back." He offers to let me stay with him tonight. "I'll serve you breakfast—in my bed."

I shake my head no, then feel my body tremble. I make it outside and begin walking as fast as I can—watching the ground in front of me, listening for sounds behind me, looking up at corners, hoping I am going the right way, and finally seeing the lights of my dorm.

I get into my room, lock the door, pull the cover off my bed, and go into my closet. When my roommate finds me under the comforter in the closet, she thinks I'm drunk.

It's better than her knowing I'm crazy.

• Thirty-Eight •

Myrtle moves into her boyfriend's apartment, so now there is no one who knows if I'm going to class or sleeping all day.

There are many things I can do now that I'm alone.

The lights can stay on all night.

I can scream into a pillow and beat on it with one fist and then the other. And then I can press my face into the pillow to see how long it takes before I struggle for air.

I can leave and walk around the town and into parks and out on country roads, and when I come back hours later, no one has missed me.

I don't want to be here anymore. But I don't want to go anywhere else. Or see anyone. I want to sleep and never wake up.

I search through my clothes for the pink slip of paper with the blue-eyed boy's number. And then my coat. And then my backpack, and textbooks, and notebooks, and desk drawer, and trash, and laundry, and every pocket of every pair of jeans, and every sock, and every book on my shelf, and the letters from my mother, and birthday cards from relatives, and shoes, and boots. And when I have looked everywhere, I start over again.

When I'm too tired to move, I give up and play *Jesus Christ Superstar*, the album my brother Roger sent me with a note: *"I love this and think you will too."*

I lie down, and I listen. Every song makes me weep. I listen again and cry more. And again . . . and again until I drift into dreams . . .

> *Try not to get worried, try not to turn on to*
> *Problems that upset you, oh*
> *Don't you know*
> *Everything's alright, yes, everything's fine*
> *And we want you to sleep well tonight.*

I wake up knowing somehow I will make it through this.
I don't know whether to thank God or Andrew Lloyd Webber.

• Thirty-Nine •

I am on my way to the dining hall and see a friend from my hometown in the lobby. The last time I saw Jeff, he was AWOL from the Army and begged to hide in my dorm closet. The time before that, he was high on LSD and invited me to ride on the back of his motorcycle and jump across the Mississippi River. He had told me, "I can do it if you come with me."

Jeff doesn't see me. I can slip past him, and when I'm finished eating, escape through the kitchen to the basement and take the elevator up to my floor. But it doesn't feel right. I tap him on the shoulder, and he turns around. His eyes are clear, and his smile is quick. He says, "I was hoping to see you."

I have questions, but before I can ask, Jeff says, "Something wonderful has happened to me." I'm guessing he has a girlfriend. Or the Army forgave him for leaving without permission and doesn't want him back—ever.

He smiles into my eyes, and his voice trembles slightly. "Sharon, I've found the most beautiful religion. Have you ever heard of the Bahá'í Faith?"

I feel my eyes roll. "Yes, I've been to their temple. Remember my oldest brother John? He's one."

Jeff's smile grows, and his stare deepens. He puts his hands on my shoulders, leans in close, and whispers, "Come to a Bahá'í meeting Saturday night."

I shake my head. "I've been to them—they're not for me."

He studies my face for a long minute, then picks me up in his arms and spins in a circle, yelling, "I won't stop until you say YES!"

I see a blur of faces and hear people laughing and say, "Okay! YES!"

The crowd claps and squeals. They think we are engaged, and Jeff makes it worse by saying, "She said YES—You are my witnesses."

He sets me down and says someone will pick me up on Saturday night at 6:00. Then he gives a quick hug and runs off. I don't know why he was here, or if he is still AWOL.

For the rest of the week, I explain to the girls in my dorm that I'm not engaged, that Jeff invited me to a Bahá'í meeting. And that leads to explaining what I know about the Bahá'í Faith: They believe in one God and we are all one race, there is a beautiful temple in Chicago, they have potluck meetings in homes.

The girls think I shouldn't go. They say it's too weird and sounds like a cult. "They'll kidnap you."

I laugh, but say, "Actually, if I was going to join a religion—it would be Bahá'í."

Saturday night, I am in the lobby before 6:00 p.m., but nobody comes. I keep waiting.

6:15, and then 6:30 p.m.

The dining room closes soon. I can grab dinner and work on my overdue term paper or go to the dorm lounge to watch *Psycho*.

But I don't move. I want to go to this meeting. I know how it will make me feel, and I want to feel that way again.

6:45 p.m.

Maybe God is finished with me. He's given me enough chances I didn't take.

6:57 p.m.

A young man rushes into the lobby, looks around, and sees me. "Are you Sharon?"

He apologizes for being late. He and his wife have one car, and their little boy is sick. He had to get medicine from the drugstore first.

He says, "I'm so glad you waited."

I smile. "So am I."

• Forty •

The Bahá'í meeting is in the house of a young couple, and it's packed with people. The man who brought me finds Jeff. "Sorry it took so long, I was late . . ." He explains why, then goes home to check on his son. Jeff takes my hand and leads me to the center of the room. He whistles, and everyone stops talking. "This is my friend. Be nice to her anyway." Everyone laughs, and Jeff leaves me alone to introduce myself. This should feel embarrassing, but it doesn't. Not with Jeff and not with these people.

The meeting begins with an older Black woman saying a prayer that sounds like a poem. "Blessed is the spot, and the house, and the place . . . where mention of God hath been made and His praise glorified." A young woman shares stories about early Bahá'ís—some who subjected themselves to horrendous torture. All they had to do was recant their belief, but they refused and were violently executed. Others walked for months over mountains and through deserts to a prison city where the prophet founder, Bahá'u'lláh, was kept in exile. They waited outside the prison until they saw His hand wave out a window. Then they turned around and headed home. The persecution of the Bahá'ís in Iran has never ended. They live under constant threat of being arrested, tortured, and executed. If they recanted the Bahá'í Faith, they would be left alone.

I say, "I don't know if I could ever be that dedicated."

The woman nods. "I don't know either, but I want to be."

George's name is mentioned, but he is in a play, and it closes tonight.

One of the men, Robby, talks to me most of the night and calls the next week to ask me out for ice cream. I say I have to study, but Robby says, "George will be disappointed."

"George is coming?"

"Yeah, I can't drive right now, and he offered. George loves ice cream."

"I guess I could go for a little while."

I get a single cone, and George and Robby order the biggest banana splits I've ever seen. It takes more than an hour to eat them.

Robby tells hilarious stories about his drinking escapades. That's why he has a car but can't drive. He's got a court date and is hoping for community service instead of jail. George laughs with him, but there is an edge of sadness in it.

I tell George I heard he is engaged. He nods, but doesn't offer details. Robby does. Her name is Pamela, they sing together, and it is so beautiful it makes the old ladies cry. They have consent from all the parents except Pamela's father, who doesn't want a Black son-in-law. She flies back from France in June, and if all the millions of prayers everyone has been saying work, her father will give consent. Robby says, "They'll get married and dance away into the sunset . . . unless George eats too many banana splits."

I attempt my own joke. "Too bad—You'll lose your transportation."

Robby says, "It's okay, I'll still have you."

He grins and George looks on, amused, or maybe curious.

I don't know what to say to that, so I ask what their zodiac signs are. George is Libra, and Robby has no idea.

I'm Aquarius. George smiles. "Libra and Aquarius get along well."

He knows this because it's Pamela's sign too.

Late that night, Robby calls me from a phone booth and recites a love poem he's written. He doesn't want anyone else to hear it. It's just for me. It's corny, and if I liked him, I'd think it was sweet.

I need to stop going out with Robby to see George. The Voice was wrong this time. George is engaged to Pamela, and they sound perfect for each other.

She's a Bahá'í, and I'm not. They harmonize, and I am tone-deaf. My singing would make the old ladies cry too.

The next time Robby asks me out for ice cream, I say, "I have to study for finals."

He insists I need a break. I tell him I can't because I've procrastinated, which is true.

Robby says, "George will be disappointed."

I hesitate—I may never see George again. "I'm sorry, Robby. I like you as a friend, but I think you want more than that."

He doesn't call again.

Two weeks later, I go home for summer break, and George's fiancée flies back from France.

• Forty-One •

I have a summer day job as a waitress at Walgreen's Grill and hang out with friends at night. We debate religion and social justice. Some are devout, and others are atheists, and I'm in between. I like the Bahá'ís, but I can't fake a belief with them. It's easier with Christians, especially Presbyterians. A one-hour church service on Sunday is enough.

A Catholic friend who wants to become a priest invites me to a conference for young Catholics committed to living a saintly life. The conference is being held at Quincy College just a few blocks from my house. I want to see how they do this.

At the opening session, one of the organizers gazes over the crowd and says he loves us all. I stifle a laugh, but others smile up at him and at each other. He asks everyone to find a partner. People get up and mingle. They find partners, and I move toward the door. My friend has already found someone, and I'll explain tomorrow that this isn't for me.

Before I get to the door, a young man taps my shoulder. He is the only Black person in the room and looks as awkward as I feel. He says, "I don't have a partner yet. Do you?"

The leader shouts the instructions. "One of you is a dog, and the other is a cat. You decide." People around us meow and bark. My partner and I both like dogs, but I say it doesn't matter, and he says it doesn't matter to him either. So I am the dog because I said it first.

The leader says, "Cats, you have two minutes to talk about yourself. Dogs, you listen and don't talk, or bark, or do anything. Just listen. Then it will be the dog's turn to bark." Laughter. "I mean talk." More laughter.

Barry talks, and he says almost what I would say. He was born two days before me. He is a sociology major and doesn't have many friends at college because he doesn't drink or do drugs. He thinks it will hurt his brain, and that scares him. He has two older sisters, and his father is an engineer, and his mother stays at home. He feels like he's supposed to do something important in the world and but doesn't know what it is.

Barry is me, except he believes in God and Jesus.

I tell him about my life, and he nods his head even though he's not supposed to do that. When we are allowed to talk to each other, we talk about all the ways we are alike and find more in common. We both love to dance and canoe, and have read the book *The Prophet* by Kahlil Gibran.

I tell him I know what the difference is between us. "I think Jesus is a good man, but the dying for my sins sounds superstitious. And I'm not sure about God. How could an all-powerful God let people be so horrible to each other?"

He says it doesn't matter. "You'll figure it out."

For the next two days, I go to the conference after work. Barry saves a seat for me. People sing songs they've just written. They share poems, and stories about rebirth. They cry, and the audience roars approval. One girl flops to the floor and wiggles around in a circle. A boy kneels down and holds her head in his hands. I see her eyes open, and she smiles, then convulses again.

Barry nudges me, and we sneak out. When we're clear of the building, I bust out laughing. "That was so fake."

He says, "I'm sorry you saw that."

"I'm not. It was funny." I laugh again, but he is serious.

"My faith isn't like that. I want you to come in here with me." We walk a block and a half to a small chapel I've passed hundreds of times but never been inside. This is a Catholic chapel, and I thought it was against the rules for a Protestant to go in.

"There is a power here. I feel it every time I pray."

He opens the door, and I follow him inside. Barry kneels at the altar. I sit in a pew in the middle, watching Barry until it seems rude.

There is a quiet so deep, I hear my breath and feel my heart beat. But that is all I can feel. I don't feel what Barry must feel here.

I look around the chapel. There are a dozen benches and kneeling pads. A plain wooden cross is suspended at the front. On either side are two stained glass windows with red, blue, and golden rectangles of varied sizes. A row of candles sits at the altar, a few of them lit.

On the ceiling is a mosaic of someone's vision of Christ. He has dark hair, and tan skin with luminous eyes.

I watch those eyes watch me, and then I feel it. A warmth that begins inside. I feel embraced, and loved.

Barry sits next to me. We sit for a long time, and then I whisper, "Thank you."

• Forty-Two •

I tell my friends I now believe. I debate with agnostics and atheists. We talk about patterns in nature, but that's the only logic I can find. This is a feeling thing I can't explain. Since this happened in a Catholic chapel, I think it's a sign I should become a nun. One of my Catholic friends suggests I talk with one, and we go to the convent. We ring the door, and the sister who answers introduces herself as Sister Sharon. We squeal and explain that Sharon is my name too, and it's another sign I should become a nun. She smiles sweetly and says, "Well, isn't that something?"

Sister Sharon takes us into a study, offers tea, and invites me to tell her more. I tell everything I can think of.

She asks, "My dear, are you Catholic?"

"No. Actually, my family hates Catholics." I smile, but she doesn't.

"Do you want this more than you want a husband and children?"

"Maybe."

"Can you obey the Pope without questioning?" I laugh, and she looks concerned. "My dear, perhaps you should think about this some more."

The next morning, I wake up remembering a promise I made to myself three years ago: "If I ever believe in God, I'll become a Bahá'í."

I go to a Bahá'í meeting at the home of a young couple from Germany who have two little girls. I step onto the porch, and the door flies open. The girls yell "Welcome!" and grab my hands and drag me into the living room. In one corner, an older White woman sits cross-legged on the floor. She is laughing and talking with a young Black woman.

On the couch is the Persian doctor and his pregnant wife whom my brother, John, introduced to me to last summer. She looks both tired and radiant. The doctor stands to greet me. His wife tries to stand, but I tell her to stay put and lean over to kiss both cheeks. A young man with flowing brown hair is playing a guitar and humming. The girls serve iced tea and cookies they made.

The young man with the guitar stops playing, everyone quiets, and the girls sing a prayer. "Oh God, guide me, protect me, illumine the lamp of my heart . . ."

I close my eyes. There is nowhere else I want to be.

The Persian doctor is the speaker. He invites us to imagine a world where it is understood we all come from the same God and we are all one race, that women and men are equal, that extremes of wealth and poverty are eliminated, that science and religion are united, that we honor all cultures and consider ourselves world citizens.

Sitting in this living room with these people . . . that feels possible.

The woman sitting next to me is visiting from my college town. She remembers me and is good friends with George and his fiancée. When the talk is over, she asks, "Did you hear what happened?" She looks ready to cry. "It's tragic." My mind races to possibilities of car crashes, murder, terminal illness.

"When Pamela came back from France, she broke up with him. I can't believe it."

"Maybe she'll change her mind."

The woman shakes her head. "No, she's engaged to someone else. They are getting married in a few weeks. He's White, so her father had no objection."

I make my face look sad, like hers, and ask, "So what is George going to do now?" George had the opportunity to study voice at a music academy out of state. His voice professor had recommended him for a scholarship.

"He decided to go to graduate school for education at Illinois State . . . so I'm sure you'll see him."

• Forty-Three •

All summer, my brother Roger has been reading the Bible, the Koran, Hindu scriptures, and Bahá'í books. He's decided to become a Bahá'í too. Our parents are still upset about our oldest brother's conversion, so Roger plans to present a convincing argument during a weekend camping trip. There won't be a television to distract Dad or a bathroom where Mother can hide. Nature soothes the soul. Perhaps they will be more mellow.

Roger waits until the last day. I hover and listen, but don't talk. He knows how to talk while he thinks. I know what I feel, but it takes time to find the words.

There is no yelling or tears, but Mother and Dad are disappointed. It doesn't feel like the right time to tell them that I am joining too.

Walking to the student union on my first day back on campus, I hear a deep, beautiful voice call out my name. George tells me he is enrolled in the Master of Education program and has a job working at a juvenile home for boys. He gets room and board, so doesn't have to sleep on his friend's couch. "Not sure why, but it felt right to stay here."

I don't tell him that I know why it feels right—that he is supposed to be here because we are supposed to get married. If I tell him that, he'd think I'm crazy.

He says, "You broke Robby's heart. He moved away."

I search for words to say, but George laughs. "Don't worry. He's with someone else now."

I wait for George to say that happened to him too. But he doesn't, and I don't know what that means. Maybe it hurts too much to talk about.

The next week, we run into each other again. My bike almost crashes into his. We talk for an hour, and I hear myself say, "There are too many children in the world. If I ever get married, I'll adopt." I feel stupid for bringing up marriage and babies. It's too obvious, and I'm acting like an idiot again.

George is quiet for a moment. "I've always thought having my own children would be something extraordinary."

I hear the Voice correct him. "Our children."

George's face doesn't change, so he didn't hear it.

In October at the weekly Bahá'í Fireside, a meeting for people who are interested in learning about the Bahá'í Faith, I announce I will officially enroll after I talk to my parents face-to-face. "Next time I see them."

It is the truth, but it also gives me more time. I'll have until Thanksgiving break.

That night, I make my weekly phone call to my parents, and they say they will come visit next Saturday. They have no reason other than it will be nice to see the fall leaves. I want to tell them not to come, that I'm not ready, that this is just a joke God is playing on me. But instead I tell them that would be great. I have one week to reread the book and pamphlets I have and rehearse what I will say.

They take me out for dinner, and I look for ways to bring it up, but Mom is talking nonstop. I go to the restroom, and Mom follows. We're at the sink, and she stares at me in the mirror. "I know you're going to tell us tonight you're joining Bahá'í."

She hands me a postcard of the Bahá'í House of Worship in Chicago.

I recognize my brother John's handwriting. It was addressed to Roger and sent to his college address, but because his mail was forwarded to our parents' home for the summer, it went to their house. The postcard said, *"Sharon's going to become a Bahá'í. 3 down and 2 to go. We just need to convince Dad because Mom will do whatever he does."*

Mom's stare hardens. She says, "We will never become Bahá'ís, so don't bother trying to convert us."

"It's a joke, Mom . . . but it isn't funny. I'm sorry."

"I didn't show it to your father. I don't want to make him madder than he already is."

Mom has one question: "I thought you said you'd never become a Bahá'í because you'd have to get consent from us to get married."

I forgot I had told her that. "I guess I have to trust you to do the right thing." I laugh, but she doesn't.

We return to the table, and over dessert, I say, "Guessing this is no big surprise, but I've decided to become a Bahá'í." My father assumes I'm doing this because of my brothers, and there is no winning that argument. To explain how I came to this would reveal things about myself I don't want them to know.

They leave town at noon, and that night, I go to the Bahá'í Fireside. George's birthday is tomorrow, so it's more of a party than a meeting. Before I leave, I ask if anyone has a pen so I can sign the enrollment card. One of the Bahá'ís does a handstand, and pens fall out of his pockets.

I walk home alone in the rain. This moment feels like it's been waiting to happen my whole life. I see a massive puddle in a parking lot. I run into the water, raise my hands to the sky, and yell, "Thank you!"

• Forty-Four •

Happiness is a magnet. I think that's why several men like me. There is the young man from my hometown who was going to be a priest but is reconsidering because of me, and my soul-brother friend Barry who wants to take me to Mardi Gras, and a man I work with at a telephone crisis center. He already hints at marriage, but I had a warning dream a month before I met him.

I was wandering through a house where people were gathering for my wedding. I felt panicked and wanted to run away. I kept asking everyone who I was marrying, and no one knew. Then I went out on a balcony and saw a Middle Eastern-looking man in a suit. He turned and smiled at me, then his face disappeared.

I woke from the dream in a sweat, heart racing. Once I finally met this man, he felt familiar, but I couldn't place him. We dated a week when I remembered the dream and told him we would never be more than friends.

I see George at Bahá'í gatherings, and he is friendly, but I watch and see that it is his nature. He's nice to everyone. I look for signs that he feels something special for me, but there aren't any. Maybe I've been fooling myself. The Voice doesn't work if I'm the only one hearing it.

A few weeks later, my brother Roger asks if I'd like to give a Bahá'í talk at the University of Illinois.

"Sure."

He asks, "What do you want to talk about?"

I say what I think will be the easiest to do. "Equality of Women and Men."

I tell people I'm doing this and get concerned looks, especially from George. He asks if I know what the Bahá'í Faith says about the equality of men and women. "It may not be what you think it is." I don't answer the question. I have read . . . a little. Not much. But enough. Maybe. Dang.

My friends Bob and Helen offer to drive, which is more dependable than my plan to hitchhike. George offers to come along.

The night before the talk, I take my Bahá'í books and my feminist books to the student union and try to make an outline. My feminist books include: *The Feminine Mystique* by Betty Friedan, *Diary of a Mad Housewife* by Sue Kaufman, and *I, B.I.T.C.H., Have Had It* by Caroline Hennessey. My Bahá'í books are *Gleanings* by Bahá'u'lláh, *Paris Talks* by 'Abdu'l-Bahá, and *Bahá'u'lláh and the New Era* by J.E. Esslemont. I go back and forth between the books and see what George meant. This isn't what I thought it was.

On the way to the Fireside, George and I sit in the back seat. Helen and Bob joke and tell crazy stories to keep my mind off being nervous, and it almost works. George joins in but is more guarded. Or maybe he's nervous for me.

We get to the Bahá'í Center. It's an old Victorian house close to the university, and the woman who owns it is a Bahá'í. She lives in a small room upstairs and has given the house over for meetings. The downstairs is filled with a couple dozen or more people sitting on couches, chairs, and the floor. The meeting begins, and my brother introduces me. I have notes, but it doesn't feel right to use them. This isn't a lecture, and I am not an expert on anything. I abandon the notes and tell my story.

I grew up with two older brothers and always felt like being a girl wasn't good enough. I thought to be equal, I had to be like them. I tried to compete physically, and that didn't work out so well. I once insisted on taking Wrestling in high school for one of the gym electives. The teacher said if I could find another female to wrestle, I could do it. The only girl willing to do it was one hundred pounds heavier than me. All she had to do was roll over on me and I was done.

Marriage looked like slavery. I didn't want a life of cooking and cleaning. Children were a different matter. My heart melted around them, and I thought that was not a good thing. It could suck me into a life I didn't want. There were enough children in the world, I didn't need to have any. I could be free to have a career doing something more important.

When I saw "Equality of Women and Men" was a principle of the Bahá'í Faith, I didn't investigate what that meant because I thought I knew. But when preparing for this talk, someone asked if I had actually read what Bahá'u'lláh had to say about it.

People laugh, and George is grinning.

Last night, I sat up all night reading. If anyone watched me, they would have thought I was crazy. I was laughing and crying. What Bahá'u'lláh taught was that women and men are equal. Period. We always have been. Any perception that we are not is an inadequate understanding of who we are. Equality is not sameness. Women have a keen intellect and strong intuitive sense. We have developed the capacity for compassion, and when women attain the full equality that has been denied in the past, they will bring about peace in the world because they will not be willing to send their sons to war.

There is no need to hide my emotions, or intuition, or degrade myself for not running as fast as my brothers. I know things with my heart, and then check it out with my head to see if it seems right. I've always done that, but I felt ashamed of that and tried to hide it.

I feel a weight lifted. I can be married and have children and still be me.

Everyone claps, my brother gives me hug, and then someone asks if George will sing. He sings a song he has composed that is beautiful and meditative. I close my eyes to listen until the last long note. I look at him, and he looks at me. No one has ever looked at me like this.

The Voice was telling the truth. *"This is the man you will marry."*

And now George knows it too.

I am staying for the weekend with my brother. When I say goodbye to George, we hug, and I tell him I'll be back by Sunday evening. It feels natural to tell him this. From now on, there is someone who wants to know when I'm coming home.

My brother and I walk to his apartment, and I tell him, "George Davis is going to ask me to marry him."

Roger asks how I know. "Are you dating?"

"No."

"What did he say that makes you think that?"

"Nothing." Roger laughs, and I say, "You'll see."

I'm not ready to tell my intelligent, logical, scientific brother about the Voice.

This freedom to be me and honor my intuitive gift will take time.

• Forty-Five •

From the time I knew what a marriage proposal was, I daydreamed about them. First it was the down-on-one-knee proposal at a candlelit dinner. During my middle school Beatles era, it was a proposal at the rock concert of my lead singer boyfriend who looked like Paul. And then in high school, it switched to the Oscar acceptance speech for Best Actor by my famous boyfriend: He would peer into the crowd to where I sat and say, "And I'd like to take this moment to ask Sharon Nesbit the question I've had since the first moment I saw her. Sharon, will you marry me?" I would say "Yes!" during my Best Actress acceptance speech.

In all scenarios, the enormous engagement ring was an exact fit, and the scene ended with me twirling in his arms as onlookers cheered.

I get back from the weekend with my brother in time to go to the Sunday night Bahá'í meeting. George offers to walk me home afterwards, and I say, "It isn't necessary," knowing he will insist. And he does.

We walk, and I talk about the visit with my brother, a paper I need to write, and how I'll be going home for Thanksgiving in another week. We walk past my old dorm, and I point out which room was mine. We are under a streetlamp, and I can see his face. He wants to say something, and I know what it is.

He stops walking and turns to face me. "Well, I've been thinking of asking you to marry me, so I guess I should go ahead and ask. Will you marry me?"

I am already in his arms before he finishes the question.

If anyone was watching us and cheered, I didn't hear it. Or need it. This is perfect. There's no ring because he doesn't have money for that, and I don't like diamonds now that I understand they are stolen from Africa.

All I want is a gold band when we get married.

Married. The Voice was right.

After I scream "YES!" George laughs and suggests I take time to think about this.

I want him to understand this is not a surprise, so I tell him about the first time I saw him and heard a Voice say, "This is the man you will marry."

I tell George it wasn't only the first time I saw him, but it happened again a month ago when we talked about children and I said I wanted to adopt and he said he hoped someday he'd have his own. The Voice agreed with him and said, "Our children."

The look on George's face makes me wish I had waited to tell him I hear a Voice. He pauses a moment, then grins. "Life with you will be interesting."

The rest of the walk home, we hold hands, and George talks. My head explodes with a thousand thoughts, but when I force myself to listen, he is talking about marriage being the foundation of human society and the part it plays in the advancement of civilization. It hits me how much like my father he is . . . turning a romantic moment into a lecture. This makes me laugh, so I explain why I am laughing, and then I get the giggles. George laughs too and apologizes for being too serious for the occasion. That is not like my father. Mother's biggest complaint is Dad never, ever apologizes.

When we get to my boardinghouse, George doesn't come in. He gives me a hug, and I ask for a kiss. He kisses my forehead.

George wants us to wait until we are married to have sex.

I think he said that when I wasn't listening.

I wake up my roommate, and other girls in the house come running. They shriek and clap. One girl grabs my hand and says, "Where's the ring?"

I shrug. "Soulmates don't need diamonds."

A few laugh, a few say congratulations, and one asks, "So which one is George?"

• Forty-Six •

George asks how I think my parents will take this, and I tell him not to worry. "Mom and I talked about what would happen if I wanted to marry a man who wasn't White. She said they'd accept it."

He flashes a sad smile, and I know he finds that hard to believe, but he'll find out soon. My parents aren't prejudiced.

I ask about his parents. George says it won't be a problem. He's been through this with them before, and they weren't the ones who withheld consent.

I could take this slow and ask Roger to invite George home for a weekend visit. Let my parents learn about his family, and how he is working his way through school, just like my father did. He'd search our record albums, play the musicals, and sing along. My mother would say he's better than people on television. He'd offer to help cook, and she'd say some girl would be lucky someday. He'd watch football with my dad, and they'd swap stories about short-lived sports careers. We'd all play Monopoly and Hearts. They'd see his graciousness, win or lose. When he leaves, they'll say, "Come back anytime."

I could have done that, but it would have felt like a lie. Besides, Mother would see the way I look at him and know.

I come home for Thanksgiving break, drop my bags on the floor, and announce, "I'm engaged!"

My parents look at each other and laugh. I laugh too and say the dumbest thing I will ever say. "I'll bet you stop laughing when you find out he's Black."

The look on their faces makes me regret those words. But it's too late, and they are true. They did stop laughing.

Mom screams and cries, "I know we told you to love everyone . . . but not this way!" She runs to the bathroom, and her wails echo.

My father says, "If I had known this would happen, they'd have been called 'nigger' from day one."

I brush past him and retreat to my room. These people are hypocrites, and I hate them. I want to leave and never come back.

But I can't. I can't marry George without their consent. This had originally made me hesitant about becoming a Bahá'í. If it didn't hurt so much, I'd laugh about it.

My brothers arrive, and I hear their voices with my father's. They will defend George and me, but my parents aren't happy with them either. My father wrote a letter to me last week: *I raised my children to become thinking human beings, not religious fanatics.* I didn't answer his letter. I thought we could talk about it when we all got together for Thanksgiving, but now I don't want to look at him.

My father said the horrible "n" word . . . the one he taught me was evil and hurtful and wrong. He wishes he didn't raise me the way he did. He doesn't want me to be who I am.

For the rest of Thanksgiving break, I pretend to study, read, and sleep. I am quiet during meals and beg off playing card games. I don't mention George to my parents again. If they ask a question I respond with a yes, a no, or a shrug. I see the looks they give each other and hear them whisper in bed at night. I hear my mother cry.

I cry too, and remember.

I remember my mother worried Valerie's parents wouldn't let her come to my birthday party because she would be the only Black girl. Mom wrote a note on her invitation saying she hoped Valerie could come, and met her father at our door. Mom said how happy she was Valerie came because I wouldn't have been happy if my best friend wasn't there. Mom embarrassed me, but Valerie's father smiled. I'd never seen him smile before.

I remember Perry, a Black boy in my father's Boy Scout troop—the scout troop my father started because no one else was willing to form the first integrated troop in our town. Dad talked about how smart Perry was, but he made poor grades. His teacher accepted the mediocre work, but Dad didn't. Perry loved to camp, so Dad made a deal with him. If Perry improved his grades, he could go on camping trips. The first time Perry made the honor roll, his mother thanked my father. "His teachers always said he was slow."

Everything I know about my parents says they can accept George and me. If I give up now, things will never be right between us. I won't ever forget this hypocrisy, and neither will they.

Somehow, someway, this will work. I don't know how, but it will.

I dread telling George and practice what to say so he understands this isn't over. I am not like Pamela. I won't give up.

• Forty-Seven •

Two weeks after Thanksgiving break, my mother writes that she and my father will come to meet George. I am ecstatic. "Once they meet you, they'll understand why I love you."

George is encouraged, but skeptical. "I guess we'll see."

My parents arrive on Saturday but say they will only see me today. Tomorrow, my father will meet with George alone.

My parents and I go out for dinner and talk about family, sports, politics, my classes, my brothers, and the pair of doves my mother still has that are breeding. She's worried she'll run out of people to give the babies to. I don't mention George, and they don't ask.

The next morning, George meets my father at a donut shop, and my mother and I have breakfast at my boardinghouse. She talks about nothing while I silently send prayers for George and Dad.

In my head, I see them talk and laugh and smile.

At noon, George and Dad appear. There's a stilted politeness between them. Neither looks at me, or each other. I introduce my mother to George, and he reaches out to shake hands. The handshake is brief. She glances at him, and then at me. Her eyes are watering.

They need to go. Dad has work tomorrow, and they are stopping to see my grandma on the way home. I wonder what they'll say when she asks about me.

We say goodbye without promises for next time. George and I stand on the porch and watch them get in the car. We wave, but they aren't looking at us. My mother is turned to my father. I think she asks Dad the same question I ask George: "So what happened?"

George says they had a civil conversation on the nature of society, the current racial climate, and the difference between the ideal and reality. Those things they agree on. They disagree on what to do about it. Dad says the world isn't ready for us. George says it will be people like us who make the world ready.

I think that sounds good, but George says, "I doubt your father would say that, and your mother could barely look at me."

That night, I say Bahá'í prayers for patience, and strength during tests and difficulties, and acquiring wisdom, and unity of humankind. And I add one of my own: "Please make this happen a little faster."

• Forty-Eight •

I hear nothing more from my parents. George writes a letter to my father, but Dad doesn't respond. I call my parents to tell them I'm going to visit George's family in Chicago before coming home for Christmas break. They say, "Let us know what day you'll get here."

Since they don't object, maybe they are warming up to the idea. Maybe we could be married this summer.

But first I have to meet George's parents. He hasn't told them yet.

I am nervous, but George says there's no need. His mother may not be happy about it, but she won't stand in our way.

There are other reasons she may not like it. I haven't graduated from college yet, and I have no career plan. I don't cook. I have not developed any talents. I'm quiet and not adept at expressing thoughts. She may think I'm not good enough for her brilliant and talented son. She may think I'm going to hurt him, like Pamela did.

George says, "I'm not worried about my mom."

"What about your father?"

George laughs like I've told a joke. "Stop worrying. They'll love you."

His family lives in Maywood, a suburb west of Chicago and the first one that allowed Blacks to live there. They moved out of public housing when George was eleven and wanted to get a knife because he was tired of being mugged. In the ten years since they moved, the neighborhood has turned almost entirely Black.

We park in the alley behind the house and smell dinner before we get to the door.

His mother accepts a sideways hug from him, smiles at me, and keeps cooking. This is the first big difference between his mom and mine. My mother sees cooking as a chore. She follows recipes, needs silence to focus, and apologizes before we eat.

In George's house, everyone gathers in the kitchen and talks while his mother cooks. Liz throws snatches of this and that into the pots and doesn't fret if it will be okay. She says, "Hope you like it. If not, there's always tomorrow."

George's father explodes into the room. He slaps George on the back and laughs while talking. "Hey! How you doing?" He doesn't wait for an answer. He grins at me and says, "Mama, lookie here who George brought home."

Liz pouts without being mad and says to me, "If you ignore him, he might go away."

This makes him laugh more, and his laughter starts me up. I don't know why I'm laughing, but it delights him. He says, "See, Mama? She thinks I'm funny. George, I like this one."

And I like this family. I want it to be mine.

• Forty-Nine •

I go home for Christmas, and Dad says nothing about George's letter, so I ask if he got it. He did, but it didn't make a good impression.

Dad grunts and looks up from his newspaper. "George doesn't love you, and you don't really love him. You two want to protest racism, and that isn't enough to make a marriage work."

The meeting between George and my father was not the magic I thought it would be. Dad shakes his head. "For as smart as he is supposed to be, the letter he wrote was illegible and had spelling errors."

I laugh at that. The look my father gives me makes me wish I hadn't, but it's too late, so I keep going. "Mom is the only one who can read your handwriting, and you ask her to check your spelling."

"Right, so I know better than to write my own letters."

"Okay, so I'll do what Mom does and write the letters for him. But I inherited your spelling gene."

My joke attempt fails. Dad sighs instead of laughs. Everything I can think to say will make it worse.

Dad goes back to his newspaper, and I pretend to watch TV.

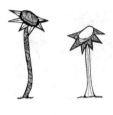

• Fifty •

The one good thing about my parents' reaction is they aren't asking questions about George. If they did, I probably couldn't answer them. I love him, but I don't know the details.

We are working on that. On weekends, we stay up talking until dawn.

I grew up in Quincy and thought I was in a big city because we had 47,000 people and my cousins lived in a town with barely 300. George thinks that's hilarious. He grew up in Chicago in the first public high-rise apartments.

In the summers, I rode my bike to the Mississippi River and played on the banks until it was almost dark.

George and his friends played on the Lake Michigan beach. When they were around eight years old, they decided to walk around the lake. They started off early in the morning and walked all day. When it started to get dark, they asked a White man who was in the public bathhouse for bus fare to get home. He gave it to them, but they were so hungry, they bought hot dogs instead. They got home after midnight, and the only thing that saved their butts from a whipping was the relief their parents felt to see them alive.

Both sets of parents are still married to each other. That's true of grandparents and great-grandparents, though there are some twists. His paternal grandmother died when his father was eleven. She made her husband promise not to marry another woman. George's grandfather kept that promise, but had a girlfriend and a child with her.

I have a great-grandfather who stayed married but had another family in another town. We think our great-grandmother was the legal one.

Both our fathers served in World War II. His father was wounded in the foot; mine never saw combat.

Dad was a flight instructor and stationed in the United States. After the war, my father finished college on the GI Bill, got his master's, and worked as a research scientist. He was shy one credit for his doctorate, but never finished. He didn't see the need because he was happy with being a researcher. He would have gotten a promotion he didn't want if he had his doctorate.

George's father didn't go to school past eighth grade. He joined the Merchant Marines when he was fourteen, and when World War II came along, he enlisted. He was assigned to an all-Negro unit and went to Africa. The GI Bill couldn't help a man with an eighth-grade education, so he did odd jobs until he married, and they moved to Chicago. He's never been without work, but he's never liked his jobs. They hurt his lungs, his feet, and his pride.

My grandfather was a farmer in Colorado and hired migrant workers. My grandmother had been a teacher before they got married. She created a school for the children on the farm.

George's grandfather was a sharecropper. He saw no point in his children going to school when they were needed in the fields. George's mother challenged him on that and was almost beaten to death, but she won her freedom to go to school. A teacher encouraged her to prepare for college even though there was little hope she could go.

My mother worked as a telephone operator in high school and put herself through business college. She was the first in her family to go beyond high school.

Our fathers are tall, and our mothers are short. Our fathers have never been without jobs, and our mothers both worked until babies were born. There are three children in both families. There would have been more in his, but his mother miscarried. I think my mother did too, but she won't talk about it.

Once all the kids were in school, George's mother worked the night shift at factories. My mother worked as a secretary until my oldest brother was born and never went back. She said other women needed the income more than she did.

George's mother helps family and friends if they need a place to stay, food to eat, or a phone call to a negligent landlord. My mother makes baby clothes for the Congo.

We have good families with a few quirks: My father thinks communists are everywhere, and George's dad thinks aliens are.

George and I laugh and cry at the same places in movies. He is considerate to waitresses and my female friends without being flirty.

His serious nature calms my impulsiveness. My spontaneity erodes his reserve.

We make each other better.

• Fifty-One •

"Why do you love me?"

We are sitting in George's car, and it is after midnight. We both have classes tomorrow and should be asleep, but I can't sleep. This question won't let me.

He laughs until he sees I'm serious. "First, because you are so innocent."

"I'm what?"

"You are innocent. There is something very pure about you."

I am shocked he thinks this, but I shouldn't be. I have spent hours telling him about my life, but I didn't tell him everything.

Being with George makes me almost forget what happened with Jonas. And the stupid counselor and Rodney and the nameless men who followed. He knows Brother Daniel took me to the temple, but he doesn't know why I no longer speak to him.

I cannot look at George's face while I tell him.

"Now that you know, I'll understand if you want to break up. I'm not who you thought I was."

There is a silence. I look up at him and see tears streaming down his face.

He reaches for my hand and places it on his chest. "Sharon, the more I know about you, the more I love you."

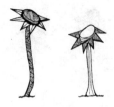

• Fifty-Two •

George and I have been engaged for three months, and he hasn't kissed me. I thought it was sweet for the first week. Now I'm worried. Maybe my father is right and George doesn't love me.

Maybe he still loves the girl who broke his heart. One day, we run into Pamela at the Bahá'í House of Worship. She comes up to him, grabs both his hands, and they stand gazing into each other's eyes for so long I have time to consider several strategies to interrupt. I choose the nice one.

I clear my throat and hold out my hand to shake hers. It makes her stop staring at George and let go of his hands. "Hello, I'm Sharon. I'm glad to finally meet you."

In the car going back to his mother's house, George says he's sorry but didn't know what to do when she came up to him like that.

I don't think it is that hard to remember you have a fiancée standing next to you. But I don't say that because there is no point in fighting over something that will go away. She gave up on them and married someone else.

I don't know why she gave up and will never ask. George's mother says she knew Pamela would not marry her son. She cared too much about disappointing her father. "And she was nervous around Black people."

I feel George's mother sizing me up, but she doesn't tell me what she thinks, besides wondering why her son has lost his mind. "Nothing personal, but I can't understand why George wants to marry a White girl. Life is hard enough for a Black man the way it is. But it's what I get for letting him make his own decisions."

George holds my hand. The warmth spreads up my arm but stops at the shoulder. I want more. I want to know if I can feel more without flashes of Jonas interrupting. George's love might make Jonas leave, maybe forever. But I don't know that. When I daydream about being with George, I hear Jonas laugh.

George wants to wait for marriage. That's admirable, and one of the reasons I can trust him. He says, "Once we are married, I'll help you through this."

I want to marry George. Soon. Now.

Someway, somehow, I have to make my parents understand that George is the one. But I can't tell them all the reasons why.

• Fifty-Three •

I am a sociology major, but it's second semester of my sophomore year before I take the introductory class, and I'm not impressed. I don't like the definition: "Sociology is the study of the development, organization, functioning, and classification of human societies."

I don't want to classify anyone.

The first topic we explore gets our attention: dating, marriage, and sex.

What gets my attention is a subtopic: Interracial Dating and Marriage. It is classified as "deviant behavior." This is a scientific term. It deviates from the norm, and I can accept that, but the professor explains that people who engage in this behavior have low self-esteem. Whites feel they can do no better, and Blacks want to improve their low status. Either way, it doesn't work and most will end badly.

I suggest another possibility. "What if the two people simply love each other and believe we are really one race?"

I hear a mean laugh behind me, and the professor looks up and shakes his head. I'm not sure if that was for me or the laugher.

He says, "In theory, that might be true, but the conditions in our society make that almost impossible."

This feels like a test I need to pass. I have to learn how to respond to this ignorance with reason and logic, and not say the first thing that comes to mind.

"Well, it's true for me and my fiancé."

I am in the front row and do not turn to see the reaction. I hear it. Whispers, feet shifting. Someone makes an odd sound, and someone else laughs.

The professor says this is interesting and asks if I mind answering a few questions.

I nod and think of the nightmare I've imagined: Waking up in an insane asylum and trying to prove to everyone that I'm sane.

The professor asks where I grew up, what my experience is with Blacks, what George's experience is with Whites. "Is he the first Black man you dated?"

I try to explain how it's been. I tell him how I was raised, that I was labeled a "nigger lover" in high school, and that I didn't date until college. I tell him I've dated both Blacks and Whites, and that some Black guys worried about what people would think and some White guys were intimidated that I had dated Black men.

I don't talk about Jonas, or the assault. I know how it looks. It looks like I have low self-esteem, and I did. I came close to losing everything. George didn't save me. But being with him feels like a reward for fighting back.

I talk about George, and what a good man he is. How comfortable he is in his own skin, and how encouraging he is of me. I can't imagine a better man.

The professor smirks, and there are grunts behind me.

When class is over, I stay until the room is empty.

• Fifty-Four •

George and I have been together for six months, and he's been angry with me twice. The first time we already laugh about.

After pictures of my boardinghouse appeared in the Illinois State University newspaper as an example of the slum conditions college students live in, I found a new place. George had a car, so he offered to help me move.

On moving day, he walked in, and I was reading. Books were still on the shelves, clothes were in the closet, pictures and posters were on the walls.

"You aren't packed?"

"I thought we could just throw this stuff in the car."

He looked at my dresser with my china dog collection and said, "These will break."

"I'll roll them in towels and clothes."

George unplugged my record player and wrapped it in a sheet from my bed. For the next seven hours, all I heard from him were sighs. My chest felt tight, my stomach hurt. I couldn't look at him. I didn't want to see the look on his face. This didn't seem like a big problem, but his silence said it was. I thought maybe he was thinking he asked me to marry him too quickly. Maybe he wished he hadn't and was now mad enough to say it.

On the third and last trip to the new place, I said I was sorry. "I didn't think I had this much stuff." I looked out the window and held back tears.

I heard another sigh, then a laugh, and felt the warmth of his hand on mine. "Next time, I'll bring you boxes."

We will never laugh about my second mistake.

A friend I worked with at the telephone crisis center was getting married and wanted me to come to her wedding. But her father was a racist, and she was afraid he would cause a scene if George were there.

The wedding was in a quaint country church, and I needed a ride to get there. I told her I couldn't go since George was the only person I knew with a car. She begged me to find a way. "Please—I need you there. If it wasn't for you, I might not be getting married."

We worked the night shift at the crisis center, and in between crisis phone calls, we shared our own. I was the first one she told about the pregnancy. I encouraged her to tell her boyfriend before getting an abortion she didn't want. I manned the phones when her boyfriend came at 2:00 a.m. to talk. I sat with her when she called her father.

I explained the father-of-the-bride situation to George, and he offered to take me if that was what I wanted. I thanked him for understanding.

The day of the wedding, George picked me up. He had the radio on and hummed along while I read him the directions. We spotted the church. He drove past and pulled over a few blocks away. I took George's hand. He let me. We listened to a couple more songs until I said, "Well, I guess I'd better go."

George nodded. I told him, "I won't be long. I'll only stay for the ceremony."

I got out of the car and turned back to wave, but he didn't look at me.

Inside the church, there were no seats left, so I found a place to stand. The smells of perfume and sweat made me lightheaded. I had already missed the bridesmaids.

My friend entered with her father, and the organ began the "Wedding March." The bouquet she held quivered, and her father whispered something that made her smile. They walked past me and down the aisle.

No real friend would have asked me to do this—but I should have refused.

I slipped out while the soloist was singing The Carpenters' "We've Only Just Begun."

George was gone. I stood where he had left me and hoped he would come back.

In a few minutes, his car came into view. As I got in, he stared ahead and wouldn't look at me.

"I'm sorry. I shouldn't have gone without you."

He sighed and closed his eyes. "You have no idea how this makes me feel. I can't explain it to you."

Saying I was sorry wasn't enough. Promising I wouldn't ever do anything like this again didn't take away the pain.

But after a long silence, he reached for my hand.

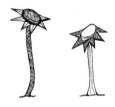

• Fifty-Five •

"Do you think I'm prejudiced?"

I ask George the question I have wanted to ask my Black friends, but never felt okay to ask.

Maybe it still isn't.

George doesn't answer. The long silence stings. If he didn't think I was prejudiced, he would have immediately said, "No, of course not. How could you ever wonder about that?"

That's what I wanted him to say, but his face is sad and thoughtful. I wish I could snatch the question back. I don't want to hear the answer.

He finally says, "I'm so tired of White people asking that question. If you weren't concerned about it, you wouldn't ask."

I try to hold back the tears, but I can't. He's right. There are words and thoughts and images in my head I don't want. I stuff them down so far I can almost forget they're there—until they escape without warning.

George wipes my tears with his sleeve. "This is what I see: You are educating yourself on racism and don't deny it exists. At our family gatherings, you are comfortable being the only White person there. Even though my mother would rather I marry a Black girl, she's come to love you. And nobody fools my mother."

He lifts my chin and says, "You love me in a way no one else ever has, and I love you more than I imagined was possible—that's what I know."

And what I know is that loving George, his family, and my Black friends doesn't erase the inherited disease of racism, but it's part of the remedy.

• Fifty-Six •

Summer break comes, and I haven't talked to my parents again about consent. They are too upset about my brother's decision to go to Lewis & Clark College's law school in Portland, Oregon. It doesn't have a national reputation, and Roger could have gone to the University of Illinois with a full scholarship. The U of I is one of the best schools in the country. Every phone call home becomes a tirade on how my brother is ruining his life. It doesn't feel like the right time to remind them I want to marry George.

I could go home for the summer to be with my parents, or do a Bahá'í service project with George in a little town in southern Illinois. I choose George.

The town was built by a mining company that no longer exists. The people who live here now never worked for the company. They didn't hire Blacks. The roads are dirt, and there's one gas station where you can buy eggs, milk, and candy.

The houses are three-room shacks, and most have outhouses. With five boys and four girls on the project, we rent two houses. The girls' house needs a new hole for the outhouse, and the boys offer to dig it. They dig the hole too wide, so rather than dig a new hole, they place boards over the hole and put the outhouse on top of them. You walk a plank to go inside, and the wind makes it sway. I do my business quick and pray to not fall in.

We walk around the town and introduce ourselves, but they know who we are. "You the ones who dug that big hole?" They don't laugh until we do.

We explain we are here for the summer to do whatever we can to help. They ask why, and we say we believe in God and want to be of service to others. "Well, all right then. But don't dig any more holes." They suggest we do something for the children. We create a day camp and teach them songs, tell stories, and take them swimming.

George and I agree to keep quiet about our engagement. We don't want to worry them. In a small southern Illinois town barely over the Mason-Dixon Line, an interracial couple could trouble people. Keeping our distance lets me watch George from across the room. I see how he smiles at children, listens respectfully to old women, and belly laughs with men.

I think we've done a good job hiding this, but one of the girls whispers in my ear, "You have a boyfriend." She points to George and giggles.

There's no point in denying it. "How did you know?"

She says, "Everybody knows, and the church ladies are praying."

I wonder what they are praying for.

• Fifty-Seven •

The summer service project has two more weeks left, but I'm going home. My parents agreed to drive my brother to Oregon and camp along the way. Roger suggests I come, in part because he doesn't want to be alone with them, but also to help me with our parents. In his annoying older-brother role, Roger reminds me the marriage consent law is to establish family unity. He says, "Maybe you should try getting along with them. Taking a family trip could help."

My parents have resigned themselves to my brother's foolish decision and are now focused on turning the move into a family vacation. Mom says, "This may be our last camping trip together."

Dad purchases a new tent that claims to be waterproof, airtight, perfect for the mountains, and sets up in five minutes. Roger and Dad plan the route to go through the Badlands, Mount Rushmore, and Yellowstone. Mom and I sort through the boxes of stored equipment, replace flashlight batteries, wash sleeping bags, and check air mattresses for leaks. We pack the car the night before and get up before dawn because Dad wants to beat the traffic. Roger and I refrain from pointing out to him there will be no traffic. The route they planned avoids cities until we get to Portland.

We ride for hours and hours. Dad drives most of the time, and Mom does a running monologue about scenery and grocery store prices. They never ask about George, so I talk to Roger and speak loud enough for them to hear. My mother tilts her head, listening. She hears how well George did in school, and the humorous things he says, and how nice his family is. She knows he is the oldest of three boys, that he can cook and clean better than I can, and that he was the first in his family to go to college. He got a theater scholarship that helped, but he has worked his way through it.

My brother says, "Yep, George is remarkable," then makes a face that signals "Enough for now." We go back to reading our books, and Mom's monologue resumes.

After four days of travel and squeezing into the four-person mountain tent that nearly suffocated us when we closed all the flaps on a cold night in Yellowstone, we arrive in Portland and meet my brother's college recruiter. That is when my father discovers the Lewis & Clark Law School has not yet received accreditation. The recruiter assures Dad they will have full accreditation by the time Roger graduates. Roger knew about this but chose not to mention it.

My father is furious that his brilliant son is now an idiot. Not only does Lewis & Clark not have accreditation, it hasn't earned the reputation needed to build a scholarship program. Roger will have to pay for this private college himself. He declined the offer of a full scholarship to the University of Illinois Law School.

The next day, Mom and I hug Roger goodbye, and Dad waves from the car. All the way through the California redwoods, my father rages. In moments of silence, my mother points out the big trees.

I make attempts to explain Roger's reasoning. He was tired of cornfields and flat land. He wanted mountains and an ocean. Portland has all that, and Lewis & Clark Law School wanted him, even though they couldn't offer a scholarship. Roger would rather pay to go to school in a place that makes him happy than go to school for free in a place that makes him miserable.

"Your brother is a damned fool. He'll be studying or working and won't have time for scenery."

I make a stab at humor. "He'll see mountains out the window."

"Portland is rainy and cloudy most of the time. Did he consider that? Idiot."

My mother sighs. "Well, you can't do anything about it now."

Dad's temper is making him drive crazy. Mom glances back at me, and I recognize the look. She needs my help, so I say, "Sorry, Dad, but I need to stop for a restroom."

We stop at a rest area. I go into the restroom and stay long enough to make it seem necessary. When I come out, they aren't in the car. They are walking down a path holding hands, which takes effort because my father is a foot and a half taller than her and they don't match up. They reach the end of the path. My mother hugs my father's waist, and he strokes her hair.

When they get back to the car, my father hands me the keys. "Your mother thinks I should let you drive." He winks, grins, and says, "So I can enjoy the scenery."

We drive through forests and along a beach, then stop at a cafe where I eat fresh clam chowder for the first time. It will take months before I'll eat the canned version to revive the memory.

We cross the desert and stop in Reno, Nevada, and Dad offers my mother and me money to gamble. We refuse. My father is a joker, and he'll tease us about this forever. "You should have seen them at the slot machines . . ."

Besides, Bahá'ís don't gamble, so if I won, I'd give it away and my father would think he had another idiot child.

I pretend to read while thinking about George and how to convince my parents he'd make a good husband. That is the reason they sent me to college. They never said it, but it was clear by what they didn't say. I said I wanted to be a social worker, and they said, "Fine." They didn't ask why I chose that career. They didn't bring up the low pay, the emotional drain, the long hours, the bureaucratic nightmare, and the challenge of statistics for someone who hates math.

They had plenty to say when my brother John switched his major from biology to education. They brought up the low pay and lack of opportunity for advancement. They didn't consider it worthy of my brother's intelligence.

For a Sociology 101 project, I debated with my father about the waste of talent when college-educated women stay home to raise babies. My father's position was that babies need smart mothers.

George is going to graduate school for education, but he's tired of school. He has an opportunity to work for General Electric, and a friend who works there got him an interview. It's a part of a new program to increase staff diversity. George took an aptitude test and is waiting for the result. If he gets the job, he will make enough money for us to live. I could finish school or have a baby. I'm thinking baby because I'm not excited about school. I don't want to be a social worker. I've always wanted to be an actress. And now, I want to be a wife and a mother.

What my parents hoped would happen, has happened: I went to college and found a husband.

Someday, after George and I are married, I'll remind them of that.

• Fifty-Eight •

When we get home, there is a letter from George. He writes about how the rest of the summer project went, sends greetings from the children, and drops the bomb: He's taking a job in Paducah, Kentucky—a seven-hour drive from me.

During the summer project, we had gone to Paducah to hold an informational meeting on the Bahá'í Faith. Three people showed up, and one of them was Margaret. She was a sassy White woman who had enough money to not care what people thought of her. She dabbled in astrology, world religions, and rebelled against her racist upbringing. Margaret thought the Bahá'í Faith was charming and that George was as impressive as a man can be. She was on the board of a county mental health organization and told the director to hire George. He starts in two weeks as a case manager.

George is back home in Chicago, and I call collect.

I ask, "What about the General Electric job?"

"Haven't heard yet, but this sounds better for me."

It does sound like a better fit. He likes people, not machines. "But your degree is in theater."

"That doesn't matter. It's an entry-level position that only requires a bachelor's degree."

George is happy about it, and I should be happy for him, but the thought of him being so far away hurts. I don't want to go back to school if he isn't going to be there.

"Then I'll move there too."

I expect George to argue, but he doesn't. He misses me too. He'll come get me in a week, and we'll go down together. I'll look for a job, and my parents will see I'm serious about George and I won't give up. If they give their consent, I'll never ask for anything else from them again. They can save the money they are spending on college for me. If they never want to see me again, that's their choice. But they will always be welcome.

For two days I rehearse what I will say, and how I will say it.

I give my speech at dinner, and my father says nothing. Nothing. He gets up from the table, walks to the living room, turns on the television, and reads his paper like he does every night.

My mother gets up and runs the water for dishes. I watch her back for signs of sobbing. It remains soft and straight. She gathers forks, plates, and bowls. She scrapes remaining crumbs off the plates and into the garbage, then opens cupboards and takes out containers for the leftovers. I walk over to the sink and pick up the dishcloth.

"What do you think you're doing?"

"I thought I'd help with the dishes tonight."

She grabs the dishcloth away and shakes her head.

After they go to bed, I call George, and he asks, "So, how did it go?"

"They didn't say anything."

"What do you mean?"

"They didn't say anything. Dad read the newspaper, and Mom washed dishes."

He says, "That doesn't sound good."

"It's better than them saying no. Saying nothing is close to 'Okay.'"

This sounds odd to him. But I tell him it will be fine because I want it to be. And I'm home in my own bedroom with my great-grandmother's antique mirror. It knows my secrets and holds my dreams and has made me feel that all things are possible. I need to believe in magic now.

I tell my parents George is coming to get me. I tell them what day he will arrive, what day we will leave, and they still say nothing.

The day George is coming, Mom cleans my brothers' room. I offer to help, and she shrugs. I dust while she vacuums and puts on fresh sheets even though no one has slept in these beds for months. I am happy but keep it to myself. She is not happy, but that's too much to expect.

It takes six hours to drive from Chicago to my parents' home. George will stop at his old apartment at the university to pick up a few things and say goodbye to friends, professors, and coworkers.

My parents and I eat dinner and watch television. I listen for a car. The street is quiet, and it is after midnight. My parents say good night and go upstairs while I wait. An hour later, a car door slams outside, and I run out barefoot and jump into his arms.

He is sorry it took so long and that it's so late. "Where am I staying?"

"Here. Mom got my brothers' room ready for you."

He smiles at this hopeful sign. I don't tell him we cleaned the room together without ever mentioning his name.

The next morning, I come down to breakfast before George does. My mother's eyes are puffy, and my father is furious. He says, "You never asked if he could stay here."

I look at my mother. "But we cleaned the boys' room yesterday. I thought that meant . . ."

My mother turns away, and Dad interrupts. "No, you weren't thinking. You haven't been thinking about anyone but yourself. Do you see what this is doing to your mother?"

"I'm sorry. I'll find another place for him to stay."

My father leaves and slams the door. Mom won't look at me.

I go upstairs to tell George. I am sad and confused but too angry to cry about this.

Mom cleaned the room and changed the sheets the way she does when company is coming. That wasn't my imagination.

George packs, and we slip out the front door to go to a restaurant for breakfast. We talk about everything except what just happened.

I want George to see my favorite places in my hometown. We go past my grade school, junior high, and high schools, parks, and the hospital where I was born.

My favorite place is down on the banks of the Mississippi River where Roger and I used to launch our canoe. There is a green pickup truck where we park, but no one is around. George and I stand, arms wrapped around each other watching the river. Out of the corner of my eye, I see two men come back to shore in their boat. I glance over at them, ready to wave, but stop. They stand staring, faces meaner than I'd ever seen in real life. I'd only seen that hatred in movies on the faces of murderers just before they killed someone.

George and I don't move. We continue to watch the river and wait for them to leave, but they don't, so we do. Before we reach the car they call out to me. "Hey, whore! You like that nigger's cock?"

George stops, and every muscle tenses. I take his hand and squeeze. "Please—don't say anything. Let's go." I didn't need to say that. He knows better than I do. We get in the car and drive away. They jump in the truck and follow. The narrow two-lane road is deserted except for us. They are at our bumper, but George doesn't speed up. I pray silently and erase horrific images that keep popping into my head.

The truck pulls around and comes even with us, but George stares ahead, so I do too. They yell more racial slurs and then speed off. The gun rack on the back of the cab is empty. They had come to fish that day, instead of hunt.

When we get back to town, we go to a park and find a quiet place to sit. George takes my hand. He squeezes and kisses it. "Sharon, you know I want you to come with me, but maybe this isn't a good idea."

"Because of those men?"

"Not them. It's your parents. They are against this."

I give the reasons I've thought about for days.

My father says he doesn't believe we love each other. This will prove we do. They think I am not serious. This will prove I am. They think I am too young. When I get a job and pay my own bills, it will prove I'm grown. And they raised me to understand we are all equal. They didn't just say those words, they acted on them. "They can accept this, I know they can."

Those are the logical reasons, but not the real reason. George is the one. He's the one I am intended to be with. Everything in my life has prepared me to be with him. I ignored my intuition once, and I won't make that mistake again. If I had followed it, I would have waited for George. I never would have gone into a strange man's room. Bad things happen when I don't follow my heart.

I can't tell my parents about the Voice. I know it sounds crazy. I can't give them evidence to justify their doubts about me. They think I am naïve. I'm not. I know that my marriage to George will mean my social status will be reduced to lower than a Black person. I learned that in Sociology 101. The professor made the point while standing in front of me and tapping his pencil on my book. It means that when we're out in public, how I dress and act will be noted and judged. There is no hiding.

We will be hated, but not by everyone. And I'll need to detect the difference between surprise at the unexpected and genuine hatred.

I will need to know how to deal friends that I love who say racist things. And I'll need to check myself for the thoughts that creep up without warning.

George considers my arguments and says he'll trust me on this. "You know your parents better than I do."

"They just need time to get used to the idea." The parents who raised me will come back.

We get George settled at my friend's house and visit with him for a while. Then I take George to meet my rebel high school teacher, Mrs.

McNeely. I expect her to be happy for me, but she pulls me aside and suggests I take more time to think about the consequences. She is more like my parents than I realized.

George and I are leaving for Kentucky tomorrow. I need to pack and spend my last night with my parents. George drops me off at my house after we had dinner at Maid-Rite, my favorite diner, the one my family went to when I was a kid. Back then, I had watched the teenagers on their dates and dreamed I would do that someday. But George and I were not laughing and teasing the way those couples did. My stomach was too jumpy for the pork tenderloin sandwich, and George was uncharacteristically silent.

On my way to the front door, I imagine what I want my parents to say tonight: "Since you are bound and determined to this, we'll give you consent."

I walk in the door to the same scene as this morning. Mom's eyes are puffy, and Dad is furious.

"Your mother cooked dinner for the two of you, and you never bothered to tell us you had other plans."

I don't know who these people are. "How am I supposed to know that? After this morning, I didn't think you wanted him here."

Dad says, "We don't want him here. But you aren't giving us much choice, are you?"

Thoughts fly and whirl. If they were willing to have him here for dinner, maybe there is still a chance. I make myself smile. "Dad, you'd like him if you got to know him. He's a good man. Talk to anyone who knows him."

Dad explodes. "Do you think I haven't checked? He's got everyone fooled . . . especially you!"

I remember George saying that a man had come to his work asking questions about him. He thought it was because his friend, Fred Hampton, was a Black Panther and had been killed by the FBI. Now I think my father hired a private investigator.

My mother sits with her head in her hands and says, "How can you do this to us?"

"How can I do this to you? How can you do this to ME? You told me all my life to think for myself, and that Black and White people are equal, and not to worry about what other people think."

Mom cries, and Dad yells, "You took it too far, and you know it!"

"I didn't try to fall in love with a Black man, but it happened. George is my best friend."

My father's eyes narrow. He leans forward and spits his words. "Your mother and I are your best friends. We are the best friends you will ever have."

Now he's said the wrong thing. "My best friends? Mom hates me."

My mother looks up and says nothing.

"You criticize everything I do. You don't like my sense of humor, or the stories I write. You don't like me. You don't want to touch me."

They are both silent, but I'm not done. I've held this in for too long. "Years ago, I hugged you, and you pushed me away and asked what was wrong with me. Why did I do that? I decided to never hug you again, but kept hoping someday you would hug me, but you never did until that day at Freddy's church—and that was because somebody told you to do it."

Mom looks at my father and shakes her head, then looks back at me and says she doesn't remember this. "You probably surprised me."

The incident that hurt more than all the spankings, yelling, and groundings, she doesn't remember.

"Hug each other now." My father demands it.

Mother throws her arms around me, buries her head in my chest, and cries. I stiffen and wait until she's done, and then I go to my room and pack.

In the morning, my father takes me to meet George. He pulls over and asks me to wait. I'm hoping he will pull a consent note out of his pocket, but he says, "I know what people say about White women who are with Black men. I hate the thought of people saying that about you." His voice is as soft as I have ever heard it.

"But, Daddy, you taught me to not be concerned with what other people think . . . especially if it isn't true."

He almost smiles. "Since when do you follow my advice?"

We get out of car, and he gets my luggage out of the trunk.

Dad leans down to hug me and says, "Honey, please don't do this."

I look at his sad eyes and almost relent. "Daddy, I have to go."

He walks away and doesn't look back.

• Fifty-Nine •

My stomach hurts. It's that deep-in-the-belly pain that will go away if you can convince yourself what you did is right. Or you know it's wrong, but you pile good thoughts on top to smother it.

I didn't do this to hurt my parents. Someday they'll understand that.

My family is stubborn. We joke that it's a family trait, but it is not a joke. It's our family creed. To give up means you don't want it. And I want to be married to George more than I've ever wanted anything.

There are rules to this creed. No begging, no crying. Make your case, present evidence, and wait for Mom and Dad's decision. If the decree is a yes, it comes with reservations and warnings. If it's a no, there is nothing else to say. Their position won't change unless a more compelling reason presents itself. That happened when my brothers and I petitioned for a canoe.

We stated facts. We had all successfully canoed at scout camps, we were all certified lifeguards, and we could take the canoe on family camping trips and save on rental fees.

They said no, but before our next family vacation, Dad bought one. He thought of a reason we had not considered: sharing a canoe would necessitate our learning to cooperate.

He was tired of our incessant fighting.

I've stated my case for marrying George, and they said no. Now

I have to wait and hope more compelling reasons emerge. Or maybe they'll give up when they see I won't.

We drive through town and pass the park where I played tennis, and the gas station where I smoked my first cigarette. I wonder if this is the last time I'll ever be here. Maybe my parents will give us consent but won't want me to embarrass them by coming home with him.

The ache in my belly won't go away. It wants me to tell George to take me back to my parents' house. But that thought brings a worse pain. I'd be miserable, and my parents will think I'm trying to manipulate them with my sadness because I've done that before.

But this is different. The thought of giving up George brings a sadness so deep it scares me.

George asks how I am, and for the first time, I lie to him. "Fine. I'm just tired."

I close my eyes and pretend to sleep. I wish we could drive to another reality, like a *Twilight Zone* episode, only this one would not be weird, or strange, or scary. It would be the world as it should be.

Hours later, we cross into Kentucky, and I notice Confederate flag decals on trucks and cars. There are Confederate t-shirts for sale in the gas station. We buy two sodas and chips, and I ask for the bathroom key. The attendant slaps it on the counter and shoves it so hard it slides off the edge and falls to the floor.

In the bathroom, I lock the door and plan what to do if people are waiting for me when I come out. I'm not a fighter. I will scream and hope that stops them. But what if everyone in the gas station wants to kill us? What if I come out and George is gone?

I say a quick prayer before opening the door. No one is waiting, but people watch me as I return the key. I walk with deliberate ease to the car where George sits waiting. He appears unconcerned.

I ask, "Did you see what that clerk did?"

"Yes."

"Do you see all these Confederate flags?"

He frowns. "Do they bother you?"

"I don't like them."

He laughs. "Sharon, this is the South. You're going to see them everywhere."

We pass by fields, and I imagine slaves working them. The road we drive on once brought slaves to the plantations.

My father was stationed in the South when he was in the Army. He once said, "They're still fighting the Civil War down there." It was why he thought Dr. King was irresponsible. "The South isn't about to change, and King's putting people in danger."

Two days ago, my father said I was naïve. "You don't know what you are walking into."

I told him, "Things are better now, and Kentucky isn't the deep South."

I dismissed his worry as overprotection, but now that I'm here, I see that Dad was right. I didn't understand how I was going to feel here.

George hums and then outright sings. He drums the beat on the steering wheel, and my body finds the rhythm. It makes the sadness softer.

Within twenty-four hours of arriving in Paducah, not only are people yelling obscenities at us from passing cars, but on his way to work, George gets into a car accident with a semi. The crash totals his car, but George is not hurt. He only has a scratch above his left eye.

Rather than seeing this as a sign to leave, I see it as proof that we can take whatever is thrown at us.

I wait for the consent letter from my parents. The one where they say they understand. They understand that a love as deep as ours is a beautiful thing.

• Sixty •

Margaret, the woman who offered George the job, lets me live with her. Her ninety-year-old mother lives with her too. Margaret doesn't tell her I am George's fiancée, but she suspects it, and it frightens her. The woman warns, "They're going to burn a cross in the yard. Or worse."

Margaret assures me I can stay as long as I need to. "It's my house, so my mother has nothing to say about it."

Her mother is polite, but nervous around me. My being here is causing friction between them. Margaret says it's normal. They always fight about something, and from our dinner conversations, that appears to be true. But I need to find an apartment soon. I search the want ads for a job. My two years of college don't qualify me for anything.

There is a job for a children's librarian. I don't have the required bachelor's degree, but I love books and I have ideas. The library is newly built, and the children's area has room to create a puppet theater. The head librarian loves my enthusiasm. She lets me fill out the application but warns me not to get my hopes up because the director is a stickler for rules. "He won't hire you without a degree."

Margaret knows someone who might help. Bill is a Black man married to a White woman. They are the only interracial couple in town. He owns a bookstore and knows everyone. Margaret grins and winks. "Bill has a way of convincing people."

She calls him and says, "Hello Bill . . . remember that couple I told you about? Well, they're here, and she's looking for a job . . ."

I clear the table while she tells the story. She laughs through the telling, listens to his response, and laughs harder.

She hangs up and says, "Bill wants you and George to come to dinner tomorrow."

I imagine a charismatic man who charms with his wit and brilliance.

George and I get to Bill's house at 6:00 p.m. The house is surrounded by an eight-foot chain-link fence and has spotlights that light up the yard like it's the middle of the day. The gate hitch is stuck. George jiggles it, and two Doberman Pinschers rush at the fence snarling and barking. The door of the house opens, and a tall man appears in the doorway with a rifle.

George yells, "Hello, Bill? It's George and Sharon!"

Bill yells, "Halt!" and the dogs back off and take positions on either side of him. He comes to the gate and opens it with a key.

Bill looks up and down the street, ushers us into the yard, and then relocks the gate. "Come on in."

We walk with him into the house, then into the living room. His chair is in the corner facing the front door. A pistol sits on a side table, and he puts the rifle in a converted magazine stand. "You two sit on the couch." The dogs follow him and sit at alert next to him. "They'll be fine as long as you don't make any quick moves."

His wife, Bonnie, comes in the room. She is petite, blond, and beautiful. Her clothes are casual chic: grey silk blouse, tailored black pants, and ballet slippers. My clothes are from the thrift store, but she doesn't seem to care. She greets me like we're already friends, leads me into the kitchen, and hands me a platter of fried chicken. "We need to get this dinner started before Bill starts talking."

I may have been right about Bill being brilliant. During dinner he presents his theories on race in America, economics, and politics. Bonnie is quiet. We smile at each other while Bill lectures.

After dinner, Bonnie and I wash dishes while Bill and George talk in the living room.

Bonnie is ten years older than me. She stays in the house and watches television and cleans. I search for something in common, but there isn't anything. She reads romance novels, has no interest in civil rights, doesn't care for children, and Bill is the first Black person in her life. Bonnie is from a small town near New Orleans and met Bill when he came for Mardi Gras. They met at a bar where they danced and drank all night. He gave her a ride home the next day, and her mother told her to pack her bags and get out. She and Bill left and got married in a week. Her people have disowned her, and no one will be friends with her here.

There is the race thing. But there is that other thing.

She laughs when I ask what it is. "Margaret didn't mention the porn shop?"

Bill's bookstore has a hidden porn shop in the back.

Decent women, Black and White, shun her. Only Margaret talks with her because she doesn't care what anyone thinks.

Bonnie loves Bill. "He's nicer than people think he is." She pauses and listens to his raging about the White man who won't let a Black man succeed in this world. "You'd think he hates White people by the way he talks, but how could he have married me if he did?"

Bonnie and I bring in coffee and dessert, and Bill changes the subject from the local KKK to the Bahá'í marriage law. "Margaret said you are in some kind of religion that won't let you marry without your parents agreeing to it?"

George explains that this law establishes family unity. In asking, adult children show honor and gratitude to their parents. By consenting, the parents promise to be supportive of the marriage, not contentious.

Bill says that is the dumbest thing he has ever heard. "What will you do if they never give you consent?"

George looks at me, and I wish he didn't. I want to be as strong and committed as George about this, but I'm not. It feels odd to me too, and if Bill pressed too hard, I might admit that. But I also see what George sees. If we married at the courthouse, it wouldn't feel right. That deep bellyache would be there forever.

I smile at George and say, "My parents will give consent. We can wait."

Bill sneers, "Wait? You best get over that and do what we did. Get married and forget about them."

He grabs Bonnie and pulls her to his lap. "I'd never let anyone stand between me and this woman. I'd have to kill them."

The dogs are on alert, watching, confused. They whine and bare their teeth.

Bonnie shakes her head. "Stop! You're scaring them."

I don't know if she means George and me, or the dogs.

Bill says he will help me find a job and help George understand the local politics. He shakes his head and leans toward me to whisper loudly, "George doesn't think it's necessary, but he's wrong. You got to know your enemy and plan your defense."

Some of the things Bill says make me feel uneasy, but I won't argue with him. He knows what he knows. I wasn't there to witness the looks, the snubs, the disregard, the patronizing, the disrespect, and the outright injustices. George experiences all this too, but he chooses another way to fight it.

George and Bill agree on the systemic problem of racism in our country but not how to address it. Bill thinks it will change only by physical force. George thinks it's through recognizing we are all God's people and putting that belief into action.

"No disrespect, George, but religion will not fix this. The racists sit in church on Sundays and preach from the pulpit."

We thank them for dinner and walk to the door as Bill keeps the dogs from attacking us.

* * *

The next day, the woman from the library calls to ask if I am still interested in the children's librarian job. She says, "The library director will interview you next Monday."

I am excited until I tell George. "I guess Bill made good on his promise."

George laughs. "There's something you don't know about this." He explains that the director of the library is a regular customer in Bill's porn shop and wants to keep that a secret. This job is payment for Bill's silence.

The same day, I get a letter from my mother. I speed-read through it, looking for magic words: *"We give our consent"*—*"You have our blessing"*—*"We give up."*

But there are no magic words. Just a note to say they received notice from the university that semester registration ends in two weeks. It's not too late if I want to return to school, and Mom says they'll still pay my tuition and living expenses.

I show George the letter. "Your parents aren't any closer to giving us consent, and nothing is working out here," he says. "Maybe if you go back to school, your parents will see that I am not ruining your life."

I don't want to admit I was wrong to come here with George, but I was.

I suck up my pride and make the call. I hear the relief in their voices. If they listen to mine, they will hear how unhappy I am. Even if they do hear it, they ignore it and say, "Good! We thought you might have changed your mind."

Within hours, arrangements are made, proof that the universe is conspiring to make this happen regardless of me. Girlfriends have rented an apartment and have room for me. George's parents are coming for a visit to his grandmother next weekend. It's less than an hour from Kentucky, so he will bring me there and his parents will drop me off at school on their way back to Chicago.

I go to the library interview because maybe my parents will give consent soon and I'll be back looking for work in a few months. The director sits at his desk and welcomes me in without a smile or a handshake. I wait for him to say something, but he doesn't, so I explain my change of plans.

The director says, "Let me make sure I understand. You came here today to say you do not want the job?"

"Yes, but I hope to return to Paducah soon and hope you might consider me for a job. I really love books." That sounds childish, but the director's stare makes me nervous.

He pauses and asks, "Will you tell Bill I offered you the job?"

"Yes, I'll tell him."

The director has one more question for me. "You seem like a nice girl. How do you know Bill?"

"A friend introduced us."

He nods, finger-drums the desk, and says, "If you change your mind, the job is yours."

I tell George about the interview, what the director said, and how he stared at me. George laughs, and I realize the director may have imagined things I wouldn't want anyone to imagine about me. I'll never walk into that library again.

Bonnie cries when I tell her I'm leaving, and Bill is angry. I know why Bill is upset. He loves Bonnie, and he can't make up for the family she has lost. Or give her girlfriends. Or make her feel less alone.

Bill glares. "Your parents will never let their daughter marry a Black man. I don't care if they let your little Black friends come home and play with you."

I can't explain it to him without sounding rude. We are not them. My parents are not hard-core racists. And George and I are not fighting alone against the world. We have friends and family who love us, and a faith community that believes there is only one race—the human race. When our marriage does happen, it will be blessed by both families.

I smile and say, "We'll invite you to our wedding."

A month later, Bonnie goes home to visit her family and does not come back.

• Sixty-One •

A Bahá'í woman named Pearl, who is old and lives half her time in a meditative trance, sends George and me a message through a friend: "Her parents will give consent, but it will be very hard and it will take a long time. There will be a lot of pain, but it will happen. They need to pray every day." She gives us a specific prayer to say and says she "sees" us married.

I am elated. George is skeptical, but I have so much belief so it doesn't matter. It will keep us going. He loves me enough to want to believe.

I sign up for my college classes and go to most of them. I laugh and talk with my roommates and my friends. I pretend to listen but mentally construct arguments and proofs to convince my parents to say yes to me and George.

The thoughts bounce around and do odd maneuvers. I wonder how long my parents will live and average the death ages of my grandparents. But one is still alive and healthy, so it throws off the calculation. It looks like my parents will be around for another thirty years. That would make me fifty-one—the same age they are now.

I worry about things. I worry that without me there with him, George's reason and logic will rule, and he'll give up. And I worry about sex. What if we wait until we get married and I still hate it?

George and I talk on the phone, and neither of us wants to hang up, even when there is nothing to say. More and more there is nothing to say. He's slipping away. I cry, and he asks what's wrong, but I won't say it aloud. If I do, he might admit it's true.

I tell him I'm coming to visit, and he asks, "What will your parents say?"

"Nothing. I'm not going to tell them."

"Okay. We need to talk."

It takes over eight hours on the Greyhound. Plenty of time to replay our last conversation and hear what George didn't say.

He's lost hope for us.

I see him through the window before he knows I'm looking. He is solemn instead of excited. He doesn't have to say the words, but I won't make this easy.

We greet and hug, and I act as if I don't know what he's thinking. We talk a little, walk a little. He asks if I want to see a movie, and I do. In the dark, we hold hands and I have an excuse to cry. We go to a diner afterwards, dissect the movie, and after choking down burgers, there is a pause that stretches so long I have to end it.

"What's wrong, George?"

He looks at me, then away, and sighs. "I don't think this is going to work."

"Why? Have you met someone?"

He shakes his head. "No, I'm not looking for anyone else, but I don't see how things will change with your parents."

"Are you forgetting that the Voice told me I'd marry you?"

"Sharon, I've never heard a Voice."

"But I did, and it was real. And what about our dream?"

One night, I had a dream that George and I were at a party with other people. It was so vivid that I could remember every detail, but it was frustrating. My roommate woke me up before it was over. I told George about my dream, and he described the house we were in, the people who were there, the conversations we had. We had the same dream the same night, but he knew the ending: We were sitting on a couch, and an older man pointed at me and told George to remove my veil. George turned and saw I had a scarf over my head. And that was the end.

We didn't know what it meant, but co-dreaming seemed like a positive thing.

Now George says he doesn't understand why that happened, but it doesn't feel like we are going anywhere.

There is a long silence that I finally break. "If you want to give up on us, I can't stop you. But don't expect me to say you're right. I love you, and I'm willing to wait for as long as it takes."

George looks down at his hands and clenches them. He shakes his head, then looks back at me. Tears roll down his face. He wipes them away and laughs. "Why did I think I could have this conversation with you?"

Maybe it's the relief from almost losing each other, or the long absence, but whatever it is after a year of holding off, that night we make love.

It isn't wonderful, but I don't hate it.

• Sixty-Two •

The nurse calls my name and takes me into a private room. She asks, "Is anyone with you?"

I tell her no, but let her know I'm not alone in this. "My fiancé is working down in Kentucky."

I sit on the loveseat, and she puts a box of tissues on the coffee table. I know what's coming.

"The test was positive. You are pregnant."

"So my breasts didn't finally decide to grow?"

She smiles and continues her prepared presentation: the importance of prenatal checkups, avoiding drugs and alcohol, eating fruits and vegetables, and sleeping.

I act interested, but want her to hurry so I can call George.

She hands me a Planned Parenthood pamphlet and says, "You seem happy about this, but I want you to know where to go if anything changes."

There is a phone booth in the lobby, and George answers on the first ring.

"I was right! We are having a baby!"

He's quiet, so I keep talking. "It's going to be okay. My parents will be mad, but they'll get over it. They'll give consent, and they'll love the baby, and when they get to know you, they'll like you."

George sighs. "I guess we'll find out if that's true."

His practicality is irritating, but it's one of the things my father will like.

We make a plan. George will talk to his mom in person because that's the way they do things in his family. She will be disappointed, but she's been through worse. This won't seem like the end of the world to her.

I will write a letter to my parents because I can't think when people yell. I don't want to hear the first things my father will say. Mom will make him calm down before he talks to me. And that is exactly what happens a week later when my father calls after they get my letter.

"Well, you've gone and done it now, haven't you?"

"I'm sorry, Dad."

"Not as sorry as we are. You know we are not happy about this. But we'll give our consent, and George had better marry you and take care of you and the baby because we won't."

I apologize again, and my father hangs up. It feels horrible, but this baby will make everything okay. My parents will see what a loving father George is. They'll see that he is good, and kind, and smart. In time, they'll know he is the perfect husband for me. It's backwards, but this will work. This baby will make it happen.

George has gone to visit his parents for the weekend. He'll come see me on his way back to Kentucky, and we'll make wedding plans. The ceremony will be simple. There's a nondenominational chapel on campus we can reserve. Our friend Helen will help organize the reception.

Just before midnight, I look out the window when George's car pulls up. He shuts off the motor, but doesn't get out. My heart tightens. I run out to him, and he says, "Let's go somewhere to talk."

There is no chatting or catching up. Inside the car, the only sound is breathing.

We go to a chapel on the Illinois Wesleyan campus and climb a spiral staircase to the bell tower room. George's voice is barely above a whisper. "My mother won't give consent while you're pregnant. If after the baby is born we still want to be married, she'll consider it."

"What? Why? I thought she liked me. You said she likes me."

George says she has made her decision, and that's it. No one will make her change her mind. No one.

We hold each other and cry. I beg him to ask her again. He says it's no use. I tell him I can't go through this alone. I wait for him to say we'll go ahead and get married, but he doesn't, so I say, "Can't we just go ahead and get married at the courthouse to please my parents? And after the baby is born and your mom gives us consent, we'll have a Bahá'í ceremony."

George says it's manipulative. We need to deal with the situation we have made for ourselves.

It's 2:00 a.m., and George has to leave to get back in time for work. He takes me back to my apartment. I'm crying too hard to say goodbye. I stand in the street, watch him drive away, and let out a scream. I fall to my knees and continue screaming, crying, and yelling for George to come back. I am on the edge of insanity. I want to let go and fall into it, but my mind makes me get up and go back inside.

I go home to talk to my parents. They already know because George's mother called them. She loves me, but she won't give consent. She won't allow her son to be forced into marriage, regardless of the baby. She tells my parents, "Women have babies without being married. It won't be easy, but she'll survive."

My father says if George loves me, he'll marry me. "What kind of a man is he to allow you to go through this alone?" He says George is using his religion as an excuse to escape responsibility. He says George broke the promise he made at their one and only meeting. "He promised I didn't have to worry about this. If he won't marry you now, don't bother asking for consent after the baby is born."

Everyone says they love me, but it feels like no one does.

I go for a prenatal checkup and have my first scare. My doctor does a pelvic exam and detects something unusual, but he can't be certain what it is. "Everyone is a little different, so it might be nothing, but it could be an ectopic pregnancy. That's when the embryo is attached to the fallopian tube instead of the uterus."

If this is an ectopic pregnancy, I'll know in a week. He places his finger on a spot on my stomach. "If you start feeling pains here, come to my office, or the hospital, whichever one is closer." He emphasizes this is serious. I could die.

For six days, I worry and wait for something to happen. On the seventh day, I wake up to a sharp, throbbing pain in the spot the doctor touched. I make it to his office, and he checks and says, "You and the baby are fine."

"What about the pain?"

He winks and points to my head.

The pain subsides, but a square inch of stomach muscles is sore for days.

I tell my brothers, my roommates, and a few good friends that I'm pregnant. They listen, empathize, and console. No one has any solutions.

I spend the most time with my friend, Helen, who has a baby. She teaches me everything she knows about pregnancy and breastfeeding. I practice changing a diaper, and it falls off within seconds. But she tells me not to worry. She doesn't even like kids, but she adores her daughter, and as long as she doesn't think too much, she knows what to do with her.

I tell Helen about Jonas and how scared I am that it ruined me and that even though George wanted us to wait until we were married to have sex, I didn't. I wanted to see if I could enjoy it.

"My father blames George, but he shouldn't."

Helen suggests I tell my parents, but I can't. They'll wonder why I didn't tell them before. And because Jonas was Black, they'll think that's what messed me up and that's why I'm with George. But if Jonas had been White, would anyone think I was messed up if I wanted to marry another White man?

Helen makes lists with me. We list pros and cons and predict the future. She and her husband struggle to pay bills, so it would help to have another income. We could share a house together until George and I get married. We talk about exchanging babysitting so we can both work.

At night in bed, my hands rest on the hard-moving lump. This is a girl. George doesn't think I can possibly know, but I do. And her name will be Elizabeth Janice after both grandmothers.

I fall asleep whispering to her. It's the only time the space between the rock and the hard place lets me breathe.

It's almost the end of the school year, and our lease is up. My roommates are all going home for the summer. Since my parents don't want me to come home, I'm going to stay here. Some friends have an apartment. There isn't a bedroom for me, but there is an extra room by the back entrance with enough space for a daybed. George pays my rent and sends money for food.

My parents help me move in. They barely speak to me, but after they leave, I find a baby care book left on my bed. It's a newer version of the one Mother had, and she wrote a note inside.

"I didn't know anything about taking care of babies. I found this helpful and think you will too. Love, Mom."

A couple days later, I receive a note from her in the mail. Besides telling me they made it home safely, she invites me home for Mother's Day. *"I was surprised with as far along as you are, nobody could tell you are pregnant. That won't be the case soon, so we thought you'd like to come home one more time."*

My roommates are all going home for Mother's Day too. They leave Friday, but I wait until Saturday. Alone in the house, I decide to decorate my walls. I have rice paper and write a Bahá'í prayer for expectant mothers: *"... I dedicate that which is in my womb to Thee ..."*

It looks unfinished. I take matches and burn the edges. A crazy thought floats up: *This celebrates death.*

I pack to go home and feel a sharp pain in my stomach that makes me feel dizzy. I make it to the bathroom and pee blood. There is no phone in the apartment. I don't know the people in the apartment downstairs. Don't know if anyone is home. But if I stay here, I'll die. No one will be back for days. My parents know I'm coming home today, but it's hours before they're expecting me. And they may think I changed my mind about coming.

I make myself walk down the stairs and bang on the door. A woman answers and calls for an ambulance. I sit on the floor in the hall, holding my stomach, trying to make this stop.

* * *

The elevator doors open, and the nurse pushes my wheelchair onto the ward. She says, "I'll be right back, hon. Just have to check something."

I hear a baby cry. My mind is messing with me, making me hear what I want to hear. But there are more baby sounds, and a bassinet by the nurse's station.

The nurse returns, and I ask, "Is this the maternity ward?" She pats my shoulder and pushes my chair down the hall. "I'm sorry, hon, it's hospital policy. But we are giving you a room by yourself and won't give you a roommate, unless we have to."

My room is the last one on the left, past the nursery, and past rooms with mothers rocking babies and fathers making phone calls.

The nurse closes the door and turns on the television. A local commercial advertises a special Mother's Day brunch.

The nurse asks, "How hot do you want your shower?"

I don't know how to answer the question, but she has already turned on the water, so it doesn't matter. She offers to help me undress, but I tell her she can go.

She asks, "Are you sure?"

I get up to show her that I can. "I'm all right now. Thank you." I keep my voice steady and smile to make her go away.

The water is not hot enough. I make it so hot I want to scream, but don't. I hit my stomach with my fist. With every punch, more blood flows. When the bleeding stops, I hit harder.

"You doing okay in there, hon?"

"Yes, I'm fine. It feels good."

"You have a visitor waiting."

My mother is sitting in the room watching television.

I had given the hospital Helen's phone number for my contact, and she had called George and my parents to let them know.

Mom gets up and stands next to me. "Helen said that George won't get here until tomorrow, so we came."

I don't want her here. If she and Dad had given permission, George and I would have been married and God would have let me keep my baby.

I thank Mom for coming, but tell her I'm tired and want to sleep.

I see her thinking about the wasted four-hour drive for a five-minute visit. "Your dad is here, but they only allow one visitor. I thought we could walk down the hall and you could see him through the window."

I don't want to see him. He will look serious and unhappy because I am. But his eyes won't lie. With no baby, he thinks George and I are done, and I think so too.

"I can't." The tears start and won't stop.

I don't know when or how I fell asleep. I wake up when her hand touches mine. "I'm going now." By the time I can say goodbye, she's gone.

• Sixty-Three •

Noises in the bathroom wake me up. A nurse's aide comes out with the dirty towels. She wears a flower corsage for Mother's Day. "Good morning! So, what did you have last night?"

I feel sorry for how stupid she's about to feel.

She asks, "Did you have a boy or a girl?"

"I had a dead baby."

I watch long enough to see her face change, then turn away.

I want it to be night again. Every time I wake up crying, someone sings me back to sleep. Is it my girl? Does she already know words? Would she have been a singer like her daddy?

A month ago, I dreamed my baby was born too soon. She was perfect, but fit in my hand. Then she began to grow, and I couldn't find clothes fast enough to keep up. At the end of the dream, she was a young woman. She climbed a ladder to a platform and gave a speech. She spoke in English, but what she said was beyond what I could understand.

I thought the dream meant she was going to be smart.

Another nurse's aide brings breakfast. On the tray is a plastic flower vase in the shape of a baby shoe. She smiles. "The vase is a gift for Mother's Day."

I tell her to get it off my tray and suggest if she knows how to read, she might want to read my damned chart.

"Or put a sign on my door: 'Mother of the Dead Baby.'"

She stands still for a moment, then grabs the vase and leaves.

I don't care that I made her feel stupid.

A doctor comes in with a nurse who seems to know me.

"Feeling better today, hon?" She reports that I took my own shower last night, ate breakfast, and my parents came to see me yesterday.

"She is waiting for her fiancé to come. Do you expect him today, hon?"

I don't like her smile, so I don't answer.

The doctor presses on my stomach. It's flat and uninteresting. He sees the bruises and asks how I got them.

"I fainted yesterday when this happened. I bruise easy." I won't tell him I did it to myself. I don't know what he would do if he knew that.

The doctor glances over my chart. "Looks like you are coming along fine. Any questions?"

"Yes, I want to know why. Was there something wrong with her?"

"There were no abnormalities. These things happen." He pauses and leans closer. "If you were my daughter, I would tell you this is for the best." He winks, pats my hand, and asks, "Any more questions?"

I shake my head. I have more questions, but not for him. I want to know if the hurt ever stops. And if my parents will forgive me and give George a chance. And if George loves me enough to wait.

I like my afternoon nurse. She's calm, not cheerful. She warms her hands before taking my pulse, and says she is sorry I lost my baby.

I ask, "Is my baby in the morgue? Who do I talk to about the funeral?"

She frowns, sits on the edge of the bed, and says, "Someone should have talked to you about this. Your baby was under two pounds. They don't have funerals for babies this small. The hospital takes care of the remains."

"I would not trust this hospital to take care of my shit."

She smiles. "I'll let the doctor know."

My baby is not "remains." Her name is Elizabeth. I was alone in the emergency room when she was born and held her before they came and took her away. She had her daddy's nose and my fingers. Everything was there and in the right places. I want to bury my daughter. It is the only thing I will ever do for her.

The doctor explains this is a legal issue. Funeral homes only take bodies with death certificates, and death certificates are not issued for babies who weigh less than four pounds.

The hospital has an incinerator in the basement. "We'll take care of this for you."

"No. I want to bury her. I'll let you know when I've made the arrangements."

Within an hour, the funeral plans are made. Elizabeth will be buried on our friend's farm. Another friend is making her casket. All I need is a date, time, and my baby.

George arrives, removes his shoes, and climbs into my bed. My body falls into his, and waves of tears release. He rocks and holds on to me with each wave. "What's going to happen to us, George?" He doesn't answer, and another wave crashes.

Every time a staff member comes into my room, I ask the same question. "When will I get my baby?" They look irritated, uncomfortable, or sad, but say they'll check.

I feel George watching me. He thinks I am going to break. I can't find the words to make him understand who I am now.

My favorite nurse delivers the doctor's message. "The lab will release her to you tomorrow as a 'specimen.' It's what the lawyers advised."

I don't know what that means, but it doesn't matter. I get to take my daughter home tomorrow.

George stays until the end of visiting hours. He is reluctant to leave, but I want to be alone in the dark and hear her songs again. I fall asleep waiting for her.

After breakfast, a nurse brings the wheelchair and release papers. Before I can ask the question, she assures me they will bring the baby soon.

George reads over the papers, and I talk about the funeral ... who is coming, who will say prayers, who will recite a poem written for her. I want him to sing, but he shakes his head. He tells me the casket is in his car. Our friend Floyd stayed up all night to finish it, and his daughter chose pink satin for the shroud.

Two nurses walk in, one of them carrying a white cardboard bucket. On top, written in black marker:

SPECIMEN

She stands for a moment, not sure what to do.

I reach out my hands. "Give her to me." She places her in my lap, and I breathe in formaldehyde.

We share the elevator with another couple and their baby. They had a girl too. She is bundled in a soft pink blanket, head covered by a pink-and-white knitted cap.

I want them to ask about what's in my bucket. I want them to stop smiling.

At my apartment, George suggests I lie down while he prepares her body.

"But I want us to do it together."

He almost yells, "How much more do you think you can take?"

I wait in my room and listen until I hear the sobs. George kneels by the casket, pink silk bundle in his arms. I kneel beside him and hear what he whispers.

"She was perfect."

• Sixty-Four •

There is no baby to bring us together. Nothing ties us together now. I don't know if George still loves me. Why would he? There is nothing about me worth loving. God knows that. That's why He took my baby. George says it wasn't a punishment. If it wasn't a punishment, what was it? Intentional? Am I so horrid that I don't deserve a child? She's better off dying than having me for a mother?

George comes to see me before he goes back to Kentucky and out of my life. He says he doesn't know where we'll go from here, but I know he's being careful with me. He is a case manager for the Paducah Mental Health Department and knows the signs of insanity.

I beg him to stay with me one more night.

Be with me, one more time.

He stays and slips away when he thinks I'm sleeping.

Two months later, I go to the doctor because I haven't started my period yet.

The doctor tells me, "You are pregnant."

That makes no sense. How could I ovulate four days after a miscarriage? Maybe these were twins, and somehow this baby was from the first pregnancy. That is what my gut tells me, but the doctor looks at me like I'm insane. I think he is. Someone is. I can't go through this again.

I call George from the pay phone on the corner. He says he loves me and we'll be okay. We'll get through this.

I do not tell him what I've decided. If God is going to make me pay for every mistake, I am done.

I walk home and make a detour to the railroad tracks behind my apartment. I walk on the tracks, then settle myself across them. I close my eyes and wait. I've never paid attention to the trains. I know they come through because I hear them, but I don't know if it's every day. There are beer cans along the side of the tracks. Teenagers probably come here at night. But this is the afternoon, so maybe no one will come by, and if they do, what would they say? If it's a kid, he might run home and tell his mom. Or maybe he'll think I'm a bum, sleeping on the tracks. I curl up to look like I'm relaxing and not trying to kill myself.

A car with a bad muffler drives by, and I jump up. If it had been a train, I would be running by now.

That makes me laugh, and then cry until I'm tired of crying.

When I get to my apartment, my roommate is gone, but on the table is a Bahá'í book. The page is open, and I find this: *"Abase not thyself, neither sigh, nor weep."*

I write it in fancy letters and tape it to my bedroom wall. I go to sleep with it in my head and wake up to it every morning.

This baby is dead. I know it, even if the doctors say it is too soon to tell. I feel nothing, but pretend in case I am wrong. But I'm not.

When I miscarry this time, the doctor says he can't tell if it was a boy or a girl. But I know. We name him Jeremy Edward Davis. This time a funeral home is willing to bury the baby. They've discovered there is a market.

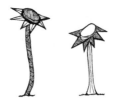

• Sixty-Five •

No one but me thinks George and I have any chance now. My brothers say it is time to give it up. Friends who love us pray and hope I'll come to my senses.

I have a dream that George and I need to separate for a year to give everyone time to heal. If we still want to be married when the year is over, my parents will see that we love each other. It will be proof to them, and proof to us.

I wake up knowing it is what we should do, but I don't want to do it. And I don't tell George about it.

Later that day, George says, "I think we should separate for a year. I've prayed, and this seems like the answer."

I accuse George of trying to get rid of me. "You are leaving me when I need you more than I have ever needed anyone." I bounce and sway and almost fall into madness, but something holds me in place.

Then I tell him about my dream.

George sighs and looks up at the ceiling, then at me. His face is sad and serious and exhausted. "Then why did you fight me on this?"

"Because you want to do it, and I don't. Which means you don't want to be with me."

His next sentence confirms my fear. "Sharon, you are driving me crazy."

• Sixty-Six •

Our one-year separation begins. We have no rules other than not seeing each other. We can talk on the phone, or not. We can write to each other, or not. We can date other people, or not. I tell him about men who ask me out so he knows I could date . . . if I wanted to.

I'm not going back to school. I apologize to my parents for wasting the tuition money they spent and resolve to never ask them for help again.

I need a job.

The nurse I liked at the hospital had encouraged me to consider nursing. "We have a paid nurse's aide training course starting soon."

I like the hospital shows on television, but I'm not sure I could poke people with needles, or tolerate pus and vomit. I sign up for nurse's aide training, take the six-week session, ace the test, and get a job working on the geriatric unit.

My first patient is an eighty-four-year-old woman with dementia. My supervisor tells me to bathe her, change her sheets, and, most importantly, encourage her to eat. She's losing weight, and if she doesn't start eating, they will force a feeding tube down her throat.

I help with her bath, and she whispers, "A man came into my room and raped me. I'm pregnant, but no one believes me." I give her the breakfast tray, but she pushes it away. "I'm not hungry."

"If you're pregnant, you need to eat."

She takes my hand and squeezes it. "Thank you. I forgot that."

She eats her breakfast, a snack, and then lunch.

My supervisor asks what happened, so I tell her.

"You did what?"

"I told her that if she's pregnant, then she needs to eat for the baby."

"This is a dementia patient. You need to get her to understand what is real, not encourage her fantasy."

"But I thought you wanted her to eat. This is what makes her want to eat."

The supervisor doesn't like my attitude. She thinks I think I'm too smart for this work. If I'm going to change the treatment plan, I should go back to school and get the credentials.

The hospital environment looks more fun on television.

My friend, Jane, comes for a visit and has a suggestion. Move into the house where she is staying until I figure out what I want to do.

Jane lives with a Bahá'í couple who have adopted two biracial children and have a house with extra rooms. They recently moved across Illinois from Bloomington to Danville. I know them, but George knows them better. He slept on their couch his last semester in college because he had run out of money.

Ann and Dick invite me to live there in exchange for helping out with the kids and occasionally teaching at the school they started, New Day Child-Parent Center. Jane works there too. It's unlike anything I've ever seen. Parents and teachers plan the curriculum together based on what is exciting to the kids. There's art and science. Kids and adults learn together. This is where I would have wanted Elizabeth and Jeremy to be.

Besides Jane and me, two young men live with Dick and Ann. We are all Bahá'ís, everyone has long hair, and the men all have beards. We all wear jeans and drive around in a VW bus. It looks like a commune, but only the married couple sleeps together.

We eat healthy meals, share household responsibilities, pray, sing, play with kids, joke, and linger over dinner talking.

I share an L-shaped bedroom with Jane and the children. When the kids wake up during the night, we help them get back to sleep. I don't mind. It's what I would have been doing if I hadn't lost my babies.

• Sixty-Seven •

I go home for Thanksgiving. The bus is full, and a young woman sits in front of me holding a baby. She tells another passenger the baby is two months old. Elizabeth was supposed to be born in September. She would have been two months too. This woman and I should have had stories to share.

Dad meets me at the bus station and smiles when he spots me. He picks up the red suitcase that was my high school graduation present, and I follow him to the car.

"Your brothers will be here tomorrow." The rest of the ride is silent. He doesn't talk unless there is something to say. There are things to say, but they will never be said. He won't ask me how I am, and I won't tell him. I won't tell him how I make myself smile during the day and pretend to have interest in what people are saying. I won't tell him how I wait until it seems reasonable to say to the people I live with, "Think I'll go to bed now." And I won't tell him that I've learned how to cry so no one hears me.

I haven't seen Mom since her hospital visit. We've spoken on the phone twice. The first time we talked, I let her know I was moving to Danville and gave her the address and phone number. The second call was two days ago when she asked me to come home for Thanksgiving.

I don't want to be here with them. They are glad my babies died. They want to pretend they never existed.

Mom is in the kitchen tearing stale bread for the dressing. This is the job she always gives me, but it's almost done. She looks up when I walk in and asks how the bus ride was and if I'm hungry. Chili is on the stove and will only take five minutes to warm up. She didn't put it away yet because she thought I would be hungry.

"The bus ride was fine. I'm not hungry, just tired. I think I'll just go to bed."

My room is the same as when I left for college except it's clean. I can smell the lemon scent from the dust spray. My mother's rocker is by the north window. She calls it her prescription rocker. When she was two weeks away from her due date with my oldest brother, he was in the wrong position. The doctor recommended buying a rocker and rocking hard and often. It worked, and John came out headfirst.

When I was still pregnant, I imagined rocking my baby in this room and in this chair.

I rock in it now, in the dark. I rock until I hear my parents' steps on the stairs. They stop at my door, then go to their room next to mine. When I hear my father's snores, I rock again until the tears stop.

The next day, my brothers are home, and they bring noise. John plays records, and Roger talks to Dad about politics and current events. Mom works in the kitchen and gives me simple chores. Set the table. Set up the relish tray.

No one else is coming for Thanksgiving, so we will not hold hands and say grace. We will not talk about what we are grateful for. We fill our plates and eat. No one talks except Mom. She wonders if the turkey is moist enough, and we say it is and prove it by taking second helpings. The television is off during dinner and turned back on when Dad is done. He's done in ten minutes.

Mom and I clear the table while Dad and my brothers watch football. I wait for Mom's instructions because she color-codes the containers and I don't know the code. I put away the leftovers as instructed, and Mom puts them in the refrigerator. She has a system for that too because it saves electricity. She can find cranberry sauce in two seconds.

I offer to wash the dishes, but she suggests I go rest. "You look tired."

I nod. I could take this moment of concern to tell her that I haven't slept through the night since my baby died. Every night, I fall asleep crying. Then I dream I'm still pregnant and wake up to feel my belly. And then I cry again.

I could tell her because she knows I wanted this baby.

I also could imagine she's sad to lose her first grandchild if it weren't for what she told Helen: "Her father and I hoped this would happen."

I go upstairs for a nap, but can't sleep. I haven't told them we are separating for a year. I thought it could be slipped into a conversation, but I can barely stand to talk to them. My fallback plan is Roger. He knows about this because he called the night George left and listened to me explain it between the sobs. Roger agrees to tell them.

After a supper of turkey sandwiches, Roger suggests we have root beer floats, knowing we don't have root beer. I offer to make a trip to the store while he talks to them.

When I come back, they are setting up Monopoly. Our tokens are at the start: Dad is the top hat, Mom is the thimble, John is the battleship, Roger is the race car, and I am the Scottish dog.

Dad turns off the TV, and Mom makes the floats.

We sit around the game board, and for first time since I arrived, we look at each other without turning away.

• Sixty-Eight •

In addition to helping Dick and Ann with the kids, I get a job in a hospital cafeteria. I am in charge of the desserts and stand on alert to replace jello and pudding. Hundreds of people walk by without saying hello. I feel invisible, which is the one good thing about the job. It gives me thinking time. I need to make plans for my life:

- Plan A: George and I get married after the year is up, and we have babies.
- Plan B: George and I get married, I go back to school to finish my degree in something, and then we have babies.
- Plan C: My parents don't give consent, but we keep trying until they give in or they die.

In all my plans, I don't have a career. I wanted to be an actress, but never took the high school theater classes or tried out for the school plays. The last place I wanted to be was on stage in front of people who hated me. The one class I took in college was a disaster. I couldn't control my voice. I didn't know what to do with my hands when I spoke. I overacted and saw eyes roll. The teacher didn't bother giving me a critique. He noted I was not a theater major and said, "Taking this class as an elective, I see. That's good."

One night, a friend of Dick and Ann's comes for dinner. His name is Robert, and he is a newspaper reporter. I've read his stories. He is insightful, funny, and intense. Tonight, he is excited about his newest project: mime. He explains this silent art form expresses the essence of the human story.

Robert is taking classes from Steve, who studied mime in college and is starting a mime troupe in town. The classes are free, but when the troupe performs, he'll get the money from ticket sales. He's trying to earn enough to move to a bigger city where he can get paying mime jobs.

Robert demonstrates the mime walk. He walks in place, and his arms move in rhythm. He changes tempos and facial expressions. He can't do walking against the wind yet, but that's his goal.

While they eat dessert, I run upstairs to try the walk. It feels awkward and wonderful.

My work hours conflict with the mime class, so I quit the cafeteria job. The other workers ask if I'm going back to college. I give them something to laugh about for the rest of the week: "No, I'm joining a mime troupe."

I don't tell my parents until I have a job as a home care nurse's aide with flexible hours. My parents are pleased because it is a better job than the cafeteria and could lead to a nursing career.

Then I tell them about mime.

"You're doing what?" Mom asks, and Dad answers before I do. "She said she's doing mime. Like Marcel Marceau, the French guy we saw on *The Tonight Show*."

"She's doing *that*?"

"Yes, Mom. That's what I'm doing."

"Why?"

I don't know how to answer the question. It sounds too strange to say I feel this was meant to be, that I was born to do this, that this is what will keep me alive.

I say, "It's fun."

It feels good to stretch and lengthen my body. I discover new muscles. My hands are sore from creating an invisible wall. The heel of the palm extends at a slight angle to give the illusion of flatness. It pulls the muscles on the top of the hand. The arches of my feet ache from walking in place. My arms hurt from pulling an imaginary rope. Body soreness demands attention. Body pain makes it clear I am still here. Creating wordless stories forces me to find their core. My characters experience fear, adoration, worry, hope, disappointment, tenderness, rage, loss, and resignation.

My characters survive, and so will I.

I invite my parents to our first mime concert, and they come. Afterwards, we go out for dinner, and they give updates on my brothers, other relatives, and people at church.

I ask, "So what did you think about the show?"

Dad clears his throat. "Looks like we should have given you those dance lessons when you asked." He smiles, but looks sad. "I'm sorry we didn't."

He looks at Mom, who is almost in tears. "I didn't know . . ." she says.

"It's okay. If I had become a dancer, I might not have found mime."

Maybe someday I'll explain my body isn't a dancer's body. I inherited legs that are too short and ankles that are too thick. But tonight, that feels like too much to say.

When I get home, I call George but hope he isn't there. I hope he did what I suggested when he said he wished he could be at my first performance. I told him he could. "Sit in the back row. You can come and go without anyone seeing you."

Before I went on stage tonight, I imagined he was there, watching. I want him to be in his car driving back to Kentucky. But he answers the phone and asks, "So, how did it go?"

"Okay. I didn't mess up."

"That's good."

And then I tell him what people said about the show, and that I was scared but excited onstage, and that this was the best night of my life.

There's a silence. "I'm sorry I wasn't there."

I make myself smile. It confuses my body and lets me talk without crying. "It's okay. There will be other performances . . . I'm going to do this forever."

George laughs. "I guess that's a good thing."

Our weekly phone conversations become harder. My mime work is all I want to talk about, but when I try to describe the stories, they sound dumb. "I know it sounds stupid, but people tell me it makes them think, and cry, and laugh."

He says, "I'll have to trust you on that."

Every phone call makes me feel farther away from him. There are long pauses, and nothing-left-to-say goodbyes. I feel strong enough to tell him that he can leave me now.

I ask, "Do you want to keep doing this?"

George pauses. "What other choice do I have?"

"You can break up with me."

He says nothing.

"If you are doing this because you're worried about me falling apart, you can stop. I'll be sad, but I'll be okay."

George still says nothing. After what feels like too long, I ask, "Are you still there?"

"I'm still here—I don't want to give up. Let's finish the year and see what happens."

• Sixty-Nine •

I like living with my friends and the kids, but I want to try living alone, and this may be my last chance. My mother went from living with her parents to living for two years with other women at a boardinghouse while she went to Brown's Business College, and then back with her parents until she married Dad. She hopes she and Dad will die together so she won't be without him. Maybe that's love, or maybe it's fear of being alone. I want to see if I can do it.

I apply for a job with the Danville School District and get one as a reading aide for an elementary school. The job pays enough to afford a modest apartment, and I find the perfect place on my first try. It's two blocks from the school, in a neighborhood with young families and quaint, old houses.

It's a studio apartment in an attic with slanted ceilings and two large windows on each side of the room. One looks down to the street, and the other view is an oak tree so close I could jump onto a limb and climb down if there was a fire. The bathroom has a huge tub with claw feet and a pedestal sink. There is a separate kitchen with a two-burner gas stove and a refrigerator like the one I had growing up. Best of all are the wood floors and the seclusion to practice mime. No mirrors, but I'll shop garage sales.

The next day, the landlady calls saying my references checked out and I can pick up the key today. I bring a sleeping bag and camp out that night. Two days later, friends help me move a mattress, bookshelves, books, pots, pans, dishes, clothes, a stereo, and records. I find sheets at the thrift store to use for curtains until a friend can help me make some.

I eat pizza for breakfast, and pancakes for dinner. I take a bath and use candles for light. I make faces in the mirror, and create a dance routine with the broom. Morning light is my alarm. I make tea, say prayers, and meditate. This place is home. My home. I am happy in a way I have never been before.

The landlady's son, daughter-in-law, and granddaughter live below. The little girl is cute and friendly. She goes to the neighborhood school where I work as a reading aide, but she won't be one of the kids I tutor. She's in first grade and already reading chapter books. We create chalk drawings on the sidewalk, and I show her how to mime a wall.

Two weeks after moving in, the landlady waits on the front porch and hands me a letter. She walks away as I open it:

NOTICE OF EVICTION

She yells back, "And it is not because you have Black friends!"

The notice states I created a disturbance for the tenants below. I had a thank-you dinner last weekend for everyone who helped me move. We talked, ate, and laughed. Everyone was gone by 8:00 p.m. Three of the friends were Black men: David, a member of the mime troupe, and his two brothers.

I call the city to file a discrimination complaint. A case manager comes to interview me and look over the apartment. He sees code violations. "You can get her on this or threaten her with it to make her drop the eviction."

Later that day, he calls me. "I went to school with your landlady's son. He saw me leaving the apartment and apologized for his mother.

He said he doesn't have a problem with you, but the problem is that his daughter likes you and told her grandmother you have a lot of Black boyfriends. That's why she wants you out. You've got a case, if you want to go through with it."

I could fight this, but the apartment has lost its good feel. It isn't home now.

As I'm moving out, the landlady comes by. "Are you leaving?"

"Yes. You evicted me."

"I didn't know if you would go." She hesitates a moment, then turns and walks back to her car.

I don't hate her like I did when I was packing last night. She looks as sad as I feel.

I move into a studio apartment that smells musty. The landlord doesn't care who lives there or who visits. He doesn't care about anything. He doesn't fix the lock that is easily tripped. I buy groceries, and most are gone by the time I come home from work. A sweater is missing too.

I tell a woman from the mime troupe about my lousy apartment, and she invites me to live with her. Melissa is divorced with a three-year-old daughter and two cats. I have my own room, and there's a living room where we can exercise and practice mime. Melissa likes to cook, and I do the dishes. Her daughter loves books and playing Candy Land. We make up stories and laugh until our sides hurt.

I lived alone for sixty-five days. Enough to know I could do it—but I'd rather not.

• Seventy •

Our year is over, and George is moving to my town. Our friend Dick is the director of a child development facility and has a job for him. George starts in two weeks.

When I tell friends, they are more worried than happy. They ask if I think this is a good idea and if my parents will ever give us consent. I tell them it would be a miracle. But I believe in miracles, and George getting this job makes our future possible.

No one asks the question that is playing on repeat in my mind: *Do we still love each other?*

George will live with Dick and Ann until he finds his own place. On the day he is to move in, I come to the house early in the morning and stay all day. He said he will be here in the afternoon, but that won't happen because George is always late.

I clean the room he'll sleep in, play with Dick and Ann's kids, make salad for dinner, and watch television while listening for a car. The kids fall asleep waiting and are carried upstairs to bed. Dick and Ann go to bed too. I read, and pace, and sit out on the front porch praying George isn't in a ditch. He's had two accidents in Kentucky and totaled his car both times.

Headlights appear down the block. I close my eyes until I hear the car stop and a door open.

I run down the steps and into his arms like all the movies I ridicule.

We hug beneath the streetlight, and I say, "Let's just stay like this forever."

George says, "Okay."

• Seventy-One •

It takes a day to get used to each other again. And another week of staying up late to talk about all the things we didn't talk about on the phone. My worries that he wouldn't like the new-and-improved me are gone. Maybe he forgot who I was. Or maybe I'm not that different. Or maybe George loves me as is . . . whatever that is.

He wants to know when I will talk to my parents about us again. I haven't told them yet that he's back. "I'd rather talk to them in person."

"And when will that be?"

I tell him, "Soon," but find excuses:

"I have to practice this weekend for a new mime piece."

"I feel like I'm getting sick."

"My car is making a funny sound . . . not sure I can trust driving that far."

A month later, when I finally go home, there is no natural way to bring it up. We talk about politics, sports, my mother's soap operas, and watch television. Without my brothers there to expand the conversation to more personal subjects, I can't find my way in. And I'm too scared to try.

I tell George I'll do it when my brothers are home for Christmas . . . another two months. It gives me more time to pray and imagine what will happen: *When I mention his name, they'll look interested rather than explode. Then I will tell them about his job. They will nod and maybe even smile.*

We are having leftover Christmas dinner, and Roger starts the dinner conversation. "I'm going to take my cornet back with me to Oregon. I want to start playing again."

We joke about the hours of suffering through listening to him practice. But it wasn't just Roger. John played the baritone, and I played flute and then bassoon. I went from enchanting melodies to squawks and bellows.

They tease I always have to do something different. Dad says, "And now your sister is doing mime. At least it's quiet."

Mom defends me and says she didn't think she'd like it, but she does. She wants me to show them something, so I trap myself in a box, push against the walls, beat on them until exhausted, then take an imaginary marker out of a nonexistent pocket and draw a door to let myself out.

My brothers are impressed, and Mom asks when my next show is.

"I guess I didn't tell you. The director of the mime troupe left town."

Mom asks, "Can anyone else do it?"

"No. We tried, but it fell apart. But we are starting a performing group. We'll have singing, mime, and theater sketches."

Roger asks, "Who's we?"

"Some of the Bahá'ís . . . I'll do mime, Helen writes plays and acts, Phil and Greg play guitar and sing, and George is back. He has a job in Danville."

My father grunts and gets up from the table. I hear the evening news come on the TV: "In today's news, President Gerald Ford announced . . ."

My mother clears the table. Her lip trembles, and she refuses help washing the dishes.

As I leave the kitchen, Roger whispers, "Break a leg."

• Seventy-Two •

It becomes easier to bring up George's name to my parents. The performing group makes it natural, but I don't tell them we still want to get married. I think they know. They have to know it's why he came back. When I say his name, I blush, and Mom sees it, even if Dad doesn't, and they tell each other everything.

George is impatient. "When will you ask them?"

It's been a year since George has come back. I pick a date to talk with my parents, but something always seems to happen. My car breaks down. Or my grandmother is in the hospital. And then my brother Roger calls to say he's met someone and they want to get married. He will ask our parents for consent when they visit him in Oregon next week.

I ask, "Is she White?"

Roger laughs. "She's not only White, she's a redhead like Dad."

"You might have a chance."

But I don't think my parents will agree. They are still sad about his last fiancée, Monica, who Mom thought was perfect for Roger. Monica broke off the engagement a few months ago. Mom and Dad will think this is too soon, and they could be right.

A few days later, Roger calls me with the news. "Mom and Dad just gave consent. Nikki and I are getting married next month."

"It isn't fair."

"Sharon, don't be like that." I hear Mom in the background ask what I said.

"It isn't fair because your wife is going to have my stage name."

Roger laughs. He remembers the notes I wrote to practice autographs for future fans. *Wishing you the best. – Nikki Nesbit.*

I wonder if Roger told them he met Nikki less than a month ago.

I tell George I'll ask later, a month or so after they get married so it doesn't look like I'm being a brat: "You gave Roger consent, so why not me?"

But before that can happen, Roger's marriage crashes. Three weeks after the wedding, they are separated, and Nikki is pregnant.

We wait through the crisis of the next several months. I listen and console my brother. I explain what I can to my parents, who are now angry Roger had held back information—like when he and Nikki met. "If we had known that, we would have never given consent." I hold back from reminding them how different it is for me and George, that while we made mistakes, we stayed together. We know each other. Our love is solid.

After months of conflict and hurtful allegations, my nephew is born, and Roger shows up at the hospital to see him. It's the end of the immediate crisis, and George asks when I'm going to talk to them.

It has been almost five years since George asked me to marry him. The wait is wearing on us. It makes us edgy, rude, disgruntled, and sarcastic. If my parents say no this time, George will give up. He hasn't said that in words, but I know.

I tell George I need just a little more time.

In a town close to us, there is a single mom who became a Bahá'í. I see how she looks at George. She seeks him out at meetings and asks questions about passages in the Bahá'í writings. They are so deep in conversation that George doesn't notice when I come and stand next to him. She does, but ignores me. George says he won't talk to her if it bothers me. I tell him to do what he thinks is right.

A week later, I go to his apartment, and on the coffee table is a letter he is writing to her. He grabs it and goes to his room. I leave, but come back later when he is gone and find the letter and poems he has written.

In the letter, he says he dropped by her house, but she wasn't there. He is sorry he missed her, but these are the poems he told her about.

They are new poems he has written, ones I've not seen. They are about stars and light and love. I rip them into pieces and leave them on his bed.

I go to the drive-in and cry through two showings of Charlton Heston running, and sweating, and screaming about people becoming secret food ingredients.

After midnight, I call George and ask, "Do you have anything you want to say?"

"You had no right..."

"I have a right to know you are seeing her. If you want to be with her instead of me, say it."

"Sharon, of course not... but we need to talk."

We talk all night. He loves me. He wants us to be married, and have children, but if that can't happen for us, we need to accept it. This waiting in limbo is hurting us. We used to be happy just being together. Now we rarely laugh.

Lately, I've been avoiding being alone with him because I know he'll ask when I am going to talk to my parents. They could be willing, but they aren't going to offer consent if I don't ask.

By morning, we have an agreement and a plan. I will ask my parents one more time for consent, and if they say no, we'll accept it. I will move away because it will be too hard to stay and see him with someone else. I will move to Denver, Colorado, to study at a mime school. The teacher is eccentric. Students begin each day by cleaning the studio floor with a bean pod for an hour. It's the kind of discipline that makes you stay upright when your spirit has collapsed.

In a month, I will go home for the July 4th holiday to ask for the last time.

One minute this feels like the right decision, and then it feels wrong. And then it feels okay again, and then it feels like someone is kicking my stomach.

My landlord comes to look at our stove and discovers my roommate's cats. He serves us an eviction notice.

The timing is elegant. My roommate finds a new place she can afford on her own. Married friends offer to let me stay with them until I know if I'm getting married or moving to Colorado. It allows me to save money for either option. I tell my parents I've moved, but don't explain why, and they don't ask.

In a brief moment of courage, I send a telegram to the International Bahá'í Center in Haifa, Israel.

ASKING MARRIAGE CONSENT LAST TIME.
PRAY GOD'S WILL.

Then I worry about how I'll be able to talk to my parents about this. I imagine it and see myself crying. That's against our family rules: *No crying when you ask for something.*

I decide to write them a letter. I want the tone to be right. State the facts, no emotion except the obvious one: We love each other. It's been almost five years of hell, and our love is strong, and so are we. We can endure anything. It will be the last time we ask, and if they say no, we'll accept it. I won't hold it against them. I write and rewrite it so many times my hand throbs.

There is one thing I don't tell them. This is the last time I'll ever ask to marry anyone because I know I'm supposed to be with George. It would be wrong to marry someone else knowing that.

I tell the friends I'm staying with that I sent the letter and it should be there by now. "If the answer is no, my parents will call and tell me not to come. Mom will worry about me driving back upset. They'll either tell me over the phone or say they want to come here to talk."

The phone rings during dinner. My friend hands me the phone and whispers, "It's your father."

I force my voice to relax. "Hello?"

"Sharon? This is Dad." Pause, pause, pause. "Your mother wants to know if you are still coming."

I hear Mom in the background complain that he always blames her. He is the one who is worried.

"You didn't get my letter?"

"Letter? Did we get a letter from Sharon?"

Mom yells, "No!"

"No letter. That's why I'm calling."

"Okay, well. I sent a letter about something." I wait for him to ask about what's in the letter, but he doesn't.

Dad asks, "So you're coming tomorrow?"

"Yes, I'll be there by noon."

"Good." I hear Mom yell something. "And your mother says to drive careful."

* * *

Mom makes my favorite meals: meatloaf, pork chops, barbecue chicken. My stomach hurts, but I make myself eat. I sit with her in the kitchen while she cooks and catches me up on *As the World Turns* and *All My Children*. We cannot understand how someone as nice as Jeff could be married to Erica Kane.

My parents golf every Saturday, and I ask if I can go with them. Dad teaches me how to swing, and Mom is delighted to have someone score worse than her.

I tell them I'm going to drive around for a little while, but don't tell them I'm going to a park by the river where I feel close to God because right now I need to pray like I never have before. I pray to find the right words and willingly accept their decision, whatever it is. I feel confident until I step back into the house and see them again. I wonder if they suspect why I came . . . if they detect anxiety underneath my pretended happiness. Mom is good at that, but if she's suspicious, she isn't showing it.

I wait for the moment that feels right, and it isn't coming.

It's Sunday night, and I leave in the morning. We are sitting in the living room. The television is on, and Dad is reading the newspaper while listening to the *60 Minutes* introduction. I feel Mom watching me. I look at her, and she smiles. I smile back, feel a throat lump, and look away. She turns off the television and asks, "What is it?"

Dad puts down the newspaper, and they are both watching and waiting. It is time.

I look down at the flower-patterned rug and hear myself say the words I wrote in the letter. "George and I want to be married, and I'm asking for your consent. It's the last time I'll ask. I love you, and I know you love me. So if you can't give it, I'll accept it and not hold it against you."

My voice trembles but doesn't break. The tears hold until I look up. Through the blur, I see Mom smile at Dad, and Dad smile back.

The conversation that follows feels like a dream.

Dad asks, "Have you found a place to live?"

"No. We haven't looked yet."

They talk about breaking it to the relatives. Mom thinks Grandma will take it hard, but Uncle Mack will be the worst. "You need to tell your brother," she says to Dad, then laughs. "Maybe this will put an end to Mack's racist jokes." My father shrugs, and Mom gives me her exasperated look.

My mother asks when the wedding will be, and I say I will talk with George and let them know.

Dad turns on the TV to catch the last half of *60 Minutes*, and Mom goes to the kitchen to make coffee.

I go to my bedroom, look in my great-grandmother's mirror, and do a silent scream. I do not understand what just happened. My parents never agree to anything without talking it over. But this seems like they had already made their decision. Did they get the letter but wanted to make me ask? They are horrible actors. My mother would have been giving hints all weekend.

When I come back downstairs, Dad turns off the TV. It's just reruns and patriotic commercials about the Bicentennial. We play a round of Hearts and hear distant fireworks. Dad is disgusted at the amount of extra taxpayer money spent this year. He wins most hands, and Mom pouts. I try to act like I'm here with them instead of in the future with George, a sweet little house with a yard, two kids, and a dog.

The next morning when I am packing to leave, Mom says she wants me to come home before I get married so she can buy me new clothes.

"It may sound old-fashioned, but you should start your marriage with new clothes." She won't look at me, and that's for the best. If she did, we'd both cry, and we've never done that together. She adds, "And if you don't mind, Dad and I won't come to the wedding. Everyone knows we are the ones who made you wait so long."

"I understand, but you don't need to worry about that."

Her lip is trembling, and Dad comes into the room, clearing his throat. He says, "You need us to write the consent?"

Mom answers him before I do. "I thought I'd type it and send it to her." She turns to look at me. "Is that okay?"

I want her to pull out the typewriter from the closet, clear off the breakfast dishes, sit down, and type out proof this is really happening. But something in her face makes me say, "I can get it when I come back in a few weeks to go shopping."

Dad winks. "What? You don't trust the mail anymore?"

Before leaving town, I stop for gas and consider calling George from the phone booth. But I want to see his face when I tell him.

On the four-hour car ride, I imagine what I'll say and how I'll say it.

I settle on the trickster. I'll slowly walk up the stairs to his apartment. The staircase echoes, and he'll be listening for me. He'll open the door, and I'll pause, shake my head, make my face look sad. When I get to him, I'll take his hands and say with a trembling voice, "I am so sorry . . . They said we can be together forever."

When I get to his apartment building, my legs race up the four flights of stairs. I burst open the door and scream, "YES . . . THEY SAID YES!!!"

George's face goes from shock to delight in seconds. After hugging me so hard I can barely breathe, he wants to see the consent.

I tell him, "I don't have it yet, but I'll get it when I go back. Mom wants to buy me new clothes . . . because every woman needs new clothes when she gets married."

George nods, then sighs.

I assure him, "It's okay. They won't go back on their word."

Three days later, I get a letter from Mom with the typewritten consent. She thought I might want it sooner than my next visit. They also finally got my letter. I used an old stamp, and she had to pay two cents postage due.

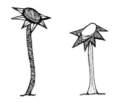

• Seventy-Three •

My father's question "Have you found a place to live yet?" is typical of him. He goes straight to practical because he knows I was evicted from my first apartment for having Black friends.

George creates our household budget. I've never done one. I just paid my rent and car note, and would stop buying gas and groceries when the money was gone. I could get most places by walking, and I made it a game to create meals from whatever I could find in the cupboard.

I'm going to search for our apartment. During summer vacation, teacher aides can get unemployment. Usually I find a summer job instead, but I didn't bother this year because I thought I was moving to Colorado.

I like streets with trees and old houses converted into apartments. I like open staircases that creak, tall windows with rectangle panes, and kitchens with hardwood cabinets.

Landlords give me tours. I see us in the rooms cooking, laughing, and making love. I tell the landlords we will be married in a few weeks, that he does social service work and I am a teacher aide, and this is in our budget. The landlords smile until I say, "My fiancé is Black. Will you have a problem with that?"

Most say that it doesn't matter—but there is another couple who wants it. If they don't take it, the landlord will call me. They never do.

One landlord is honest. "I'll rent to White, and I'll rent to Black. But I won't mix them."

The town has a Black section. It is neglected. Overgrown lots, cracked pavements. Well-cared-for homes next to abandoned ones. I'm not afraid to drive through it, but had not considered living there. Maybe I need to get over that.

I look at a three-bedroom apartment that is described as spacious. It is close to the railroad tracks, and a train comes by and shakes the walls. That could explain the loose plaster. There is an odor of stale air that hits you when you enter. The bathtub porcelain is worn, the faucet drips, and there's no shower. The kitchen floor tiles are cracked, and two are missing. There's a mousetrap set under the sink, but the bait is gone. The landlady is a White woman in her fifties. She says there's a no-smoking policy, but a full ash tray sits on the kitchen counter. The rent is the same as the last apartment I looked at—the one with hardwood floors, new kitchen flooring, and a fresh breeze flowing through screened windows. These windows have bars. She laughs when I ask if they open.

There's a slaughterhouse nearby. "Sweat or stink." She looks over my application and asks, "Why do you want to live here?"

"We're getting married, and we need to find a place. My fiancé is Black. Do you have a problem renting to us?"

She grunts. "I knew there was something. Pay the rent, and I won't bother you none."

I give her fifteen dollars to hold it. "I'll talk to my fiancé and call you tomorrow."

George asks where the apartment is and shakes his head when I tell him. "We can afford a decent place. I will not have your parents think this is where you have to live because you married me."

I hadn't thought about that. "But no one else will rent to us."

"Stop telling them we're interracial and asking if that's okay. Housing discrimination is illegal. You are giving them permission to break the law."

I hadn't thought about that either.

The next day, I go to a modern apartment complex. There is a clubhouse and an outdoor swimming pool. Young professionals live here, and it's owned by lawyers from Chicago. The apartments are expensive, but we can afford the basement level without a balcony. Here they call it the "garden level."

A young woman takes me on the tour and points out the amenities. There's a laundry room in every building, the apartments are cable ready and air-conditioned. It is close to the river, and there's a trail that leads through the woods and down to the bank. "You can even have a bonfire." She adds this after I say we are getting married next month and camping for our honeymoon.

"My fiancé's working every day up until the wedding, so it's my job to find us a place."

She gives a sympathetic smile, hands me an application, and says, "Bring it back with a check for the first and last month's rent, and we'll get you set."

"Do you need to meet my fiancé?"

"No need. Just have him sign the application."

The next day, I bring her the contract and check. "The manager is here, so let's make this official."

She leaves the room, and I push away the feeling that I'm lying. She brings back a signed copy and says, "We'll have the apartment clean and ready. Just come in and pick up your keys when you get back in town."

I consider telling her now that it's done, but don't know how to do it without sounding like an apology.

She smiles. "Good luck on your wedding!"

George is pleased, and I am worried. I imagine us walking into the office and hearing her say there's been a terrible mistake. Someone else rented it before us. Or there was a fire. Or a flood. Or it's under new management and all contracts are void. We won't have enough money to take them to court. If they don't want us here, they will find a way.

George assures me it will be okay. "We can deal with whatever happens."

He has a faith in his bones that I haven't found yet.

• Seventy-Four •

I go home for the shopping trip Mom promised. There's a name for it: *trousseau*. It sounds fancy and like something we aren't.

We spend hours in stores we've never been in before . . . the designer dress shops. I select a three-piece pantsuit, a silk blouse, and a wool coat. Mom asks if I want to look at lingerie, but that's too weird.

On our way back to the car, we run into a woman from Mom's church. The woman remarks on how long it's been since she's seen me and asks what I'm doing these days. I look at Mom, but she won't look at me.

I tell her, "I'm in town for the weekend spending all my mother's money."

The woman laughs, and I ask about her children. She tells us about their college graduations and careers and marriages. Mom looks at her watch and says we need to go home and get dinner ready.

When we get to the car, Mom says, "I don't know what to say when people ask about you."

"Really? You don't want to tell them I converted to the Bahá'í Faith and became a mime?"

She laughs. "I wouldn't know how to explain that."

"You could tell them I'm getting married."

Mom shakes her head. "I'm not ready to tell anyone."

"You don't have to say that George is Black."

She looks confused.

"If I was marrying a White man, you wouldn't say, 'Sharon is marrying a White man.' You would say I'm getting married and I'm happy. You can say that because it's true."

Mom smiles and says, "Yes, I guess I could say that."

• Seventy-Five •

The wedding will be simple because we are paying for it. I won't ask my parents. They think weddings are a waste of money. A minister married them, and their only guests were the two witnesses. Their families lived within walking distance to the church, and even they weren't invited.

I once worried how I would explain this to my future mother-in-law, who I imagined would be a sophisticated snob who wasn't pleased her son was marrying a girl with cheap parents.

George's mother has not shared what kind of wedding she imagined her son would have. She loves me, but I'm not the daughter-in-law she was hoping for. Maybe since it is me, the wedding doesn't matter to her either.

We know where we want to get married. Allerton Park is our favorite hiking spot, and every time George and I go there, someone is getting married.

Samuel Allerton owned over 80,000 acres of farmland and built a forty-room, 30,000-square-foot mansion. His son, Robert, traveled the world and collected sculptures, and transformed the estate into an art gallery. Robert willed the estate to the University of Illinois, and now it's open to the public.

Concrete pedestals holding blue porcelain Fu Dog statues line the gravel paths. Throughout the grounds are sunken gardens, raised gardens, and formal gardens. Trails through the woods lead to statues: *Gorilla Carrying Off a Stone Age Woman, Bear & Man of the Stone Age, The Death of the Last Centaur*. Beyond that is a meadow and *The Sun Singer*.

It is a fantasy land surrounded by cornfields.

We want our wedding in the massive sunken garden with concrete columns on both ends. Musician friends will play, and George and I will enter on opposite sides and dance toward the middle. As the music swells, I'll run and leap into his arms.

I dial the number for Allerton Park and talk to a woman who sounds like she just woke up from a nap. The great news is there is no cost to have a wedding there, but our sunken garden is already reserved. So are our second and third choices. The woman suggests the grove of fir trees by the pond across from the Allerton Mansion. It's close to the parking lot, and the area is shaded, which helps when you have a wedding in the middle of August.

The mansion in the background feels odd. I'd rather have it in the woods by *The Death of the Last Centaur*, but one of the guests is almost ninety years old and uses a walker.

The woman asks, "Have you thought about what you will do if it rains?"

None of my imagined scenarios had rain.

"There are no shelters at Allerton Park, and you may not put up tents or use the mansion. If you want a wedding here, you take your chances."

I book the spot before someone else does.

George has an idea for a rain site. There is a community theater in town, and it is available that day. There would be a charge, but it's reasonable. For half a second, I wonder if we should do it there instead of Allerton. It would be easier for our guests to find, and it's air-conditioned. But I let that thought go.

I create the invitations with a Sharpie, drawing two flowers—one with black petals and one with white. We copy them on mustard color construction paper and send them out.

A friend asks an interesting question. "Your rain site is in a different county. Do you have to get two marriage certificates?"

We had not considered that.

That means asking for two copies of the blood tests, and explaining to both county clerks what we are doing, and promising to send back the unused license within thirty days or be subject to a fine or jail time.

The clerks frown, sigh, and tighten their lips. I can't tell if they don't like us or the complicated situation. But I'm too happy to care.

• Seventy-Six •

When I was twelve, I promised myself that the day before I got married, I would go somewhere alone to think about whether or not I wanted to be married to this man forever. If the answer was no, I would call off the wedding. I made that vow the day my mother's cousin got married and his bride left him before the honeymoon. My mother, grandmother, and aunts talked about it for months. "That girl knew she didn't want to marry him. She made it worse by going through with it."

When I made that promise I didn't understand how hard it would be to keep. The day before our wedding, people call to clarify directions to our selected site in the middle of nowhere, and call to ask if they can bring extra guests, and since there's rain in the forecast, call to see when we will decide if we are using the alternate rain site.

My future mother-in-law calls to let us know George's aunt is not coming to the wedding but is sending her special pound cake to add to our wedding cake. "There's never enough cake for everyone."

She has that right because there is no cake. I didn't order cake because it wasn't in our budget. The reception is a bring-your-own picnic dinner. I make a run to the grocery store for cake mix.

The whole day slips away without time to be alone.

I lie in bed that night and ask myself questions:

Do I want to be with George forever?

Do I love him? Or was I just being stubborn when my parents said no? Am I strong enough to be married to a Black man?

I thought I'd answer "Yes!" without doubts—but I'm the daughter of a scientist. I question everything.

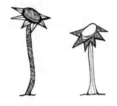

• Seventy-Seven •

I must have fallen asleep because I wake up to a cloudy day with an 85% chance of rain. The ceremony is in the late afternoon to give the Chicago relatives time to get here, and they are the first to call to ask which site we will use. They are about to leave and need the decision now. They call me because George didn't answer his phone.

I tell my almost-brother-in-law we'll have it at the park. "Bring umbrellas."

I drive to George's apartment and find him packing up boxes and labeling them. He is moving out of the apartment today and leaving his stuff on a friend's porch because our apartment won't be ours for another week.

I tell him, "You know we should be early to welcome people."

George nods and keeps packing.

There is no point in asking why he is doing this today. But I can't stop myself from saying it. I say it while I open his closet and throw his shoes in a box.

He puts his hands on my shoulders. "Sharon, I think it would be better if you go back to your place. I'll be there to pick you up at 1:00."

I leave, but not before reminding him that he has just three hours to finish packing, take all these boxes to our friend's house, unload them, go back to the apartment, shower, and get dressed.

* * *

It's 2:00, and George isn't here yet.

The people I'm staying with are ready to go and ask, "Do you want to come with us?"

"No. If George is late the way he always is, I'll be a wreck."

The cakes are done. I am dressed in the Philippine dress my friend found on a sales rack. It cost three dollars. I love the dress, but the daisy crown I ordered looks clownish. The flowers are too big for my head.

I can't sit down. I pace throughout the house, and since no one is there, I yell, "Where are you? How can you be late for our wedding? Don't you want to marry me?"

The phone rings, and it's George calling from a pay phone. "I locked myself out of the apartment and can't change my clothes."

His roommates had just left for the wedding, and George is wearing a t-shirt and cut-offs. He says, "I'm going to Sears to buy something. I'll be there as soon as I can."

I want to scream, but remember his roommates are picking up a friend of mine. "Call me back in five minutes."

I call my friend as he's about to walk out the door. I explain the situation. "Tell them to go back and let George in the apartment, and when you get to the wedding, tell everyone we'll be late."

I am so glad my parents won't be at the wedding. They might have taken away their consent: "If you can't be there on time, you have no business getting married."

When George finally comes, I can't look at him. He goes into the house to get my suitcase, and I shove the cakes and my flower bouquet onto the back seat and get in the car.

He starts the car, and we head out of town in silence. I see him out of the corner of my eye glancing over at me. "I'm sorry, honey," he says.

I nod, but don't talk. If I do, I'll cry and mess up the mascara.

We are on the highway, over an hour late, and he keeps looking at the dashboard. "George, what's the matter?"

"We're almost out of gas."

There is nothing but cornfields for miles. I wonder if anyone will pick up an interracial couple hitchhiking.

We are almost to the exit for the park. He asks, "Isn't there a gas station in that little town we go through to get there?"

Usually I can picture a place I've been to countless times. But when I try, nothing appears. "I can't remember."

If we run out of gas and can't make it to the wedding where more than one hundred friends and family are waiting for us, maybe God doesn't want us to be married. After five years of hell, it's going to end like this.

And then we go up a hill and see the Shell sign in the distance.

I sigh, "Guess God wants us married after all."

George laughs. I laugh. And everything feels right.

Aside from a kid falling into the pond, the rest of the wedding is perfect. Friends play guitars and sing "The Wedding Song" by Peter, Paul and Mary. Other friends recite poems and chant prayers. George and I read the essay "On Marriage" from Kahlil Gibran.

And stand together yet not too near together:
For the pillars of the temple stand apart,
And the oak tree and the cypress grow not in each other's shadow

The Bahá'í marriage vow is one simple sentence.
"We will all, verily, abide by the will of God."
George stumbles over it, and I giggle through it.

We kiss, people clap, and then everyone rushes to the picnic tables to eat before the park closes at sunset. Being over an hour late ruins the planned cookouts. No one seems to care except my mother-in-law, who fusses about the meat that won't keep on the long drive back to Chicago.

George and I walk around and talk to our guests. They share their food because I forgot to bring food for myself and *my husband*.

Someone puts my cakes and the fancy cake from Chicago on a picnic table, but there is no carving knife. That doesn't stop the children from grabbing handfuls.

It thunders, and the sky lights up. Everyone packs up and runs to their cars. We stand by George's orange VW bug and wave goodbye until everyone is gone.

We are almost out of the park when I remember the rings.

Our wedding bands are in the glove compartment. I wanted to exchange them with just the two of us. I imagined this on nights when I couldn't sleep: *We walk down the path past the Fu Dogs. A ray of light spotlights a patch of moss between the trees. We say the vows we wrote . . . the ones too beautiful to say aloud for anyone else to hear. We take each other's hands and place the rings on each other. George hums, and we dance . . .*

"STOP!!!"

George screeches to a halt. "What's wrong?"

"The rings! We haven't done the rings."

The rain is pounding on the car so loud I have to yell.

George suggests we wait and do it tomorrow at the campground.

"But I saw a trail back there!"

"Sharon, you're crazy." Then he backs the car to the spot.

The trail is tiny. It may have been made by rabbits.

We hack our way into the woods ten yards. We skip the private vows I can't remember, exchange rings, kiss, hug, and run back to the car.

On the way to the motel, George hums, and I watch light reflections dance on my wedding band.

• Seventy-Eight •

We camp for our honeymoon and borrow my parents' old canvas tent.

It's the tent we took on family vacations. My parents had a double air mattress and would zip two sleeping bags together. We kids slept as far away from each other, and them, as possible.

I remember waking up to birdsong and leaf shadows dancing on the ceiling.

Now I wake up to birdsong, leaf shadows, and my husband.

When I told George I worried if I would ever be able to enjoy sex, he said he thought married sex without the guilt would feel different. "It will take time, but someday you will enjoy it."

George is both right and wrong about this.

Guilt-free sex feels different.

But enjoying it took no time at all.

• Seventy-Nine •

On the drive back from the honeymoon, I read through our apartment lease. There are rules about garbage and noise, and it includes the due date for the rent. Nothing is a problem, but if they don't want us, they'll find something.

The young woman who showed me the apartment and took my application and wished me a happy wedding looks up, doesn't smile, and says, "May I help you?"

George nods. "Yes, we're here to pick up the key." His voice is firm and friendly. She looks confused.

I hold up the signed contract. "You showed me the apartment last month." I smile at her and look up at George. "We're back from our honeymoon and are moving in today."

I see the moment she understands. "Oh, yes. Of course, I'm sorry. I didn't recognize . . . um . . . Let me get the manager."

She walks out, and we wait. George takes my hand and squeezes it. "It's a nice place. I like it."

The manager is a grey-haired White man with thick glasses, stooped shoulders, and a cautious smile. He shakes George's hand and nods to me. He has our lease in his hand. There is silence, and it goes too long. He forces a smile and asks, "Do you have any questions?" George asks if they provide the garbage cans. They do not, so we'll be going to Sears today.

The young woman hands me the keys. I thank her and wonder how much trouble she is in with her boss.

George gives me a side squeeze. "I told you it would be fine."

We find our apartment, the key works, and I ask George to carry me over the threshold. My father didn't walk me down the aisle, I didn't have bridesmaids or flower girls, and none of that matters, but I want this. If someone makes a movie of our lives, I want this corny scene.

We have books, a record player, a mattress from a yard sale, and wedding gifts: bath towels, two electric skillets, three avocado-green Crock-Pots, one waffle iron, and a rocking chair.

Today when we go to Sears for the garbage cans, we'll use wedding money to buy a kitchen table and chairs. I already know the set I want. It has chrome legs, a fake butcher-block top, and four chairs with woven rattan backs. Next weekend, we'll rent a truck and go to Chicago for a bed, dresser, nightstands, and a china cabinet from George's mother.

Until then, we sleep on the floor on the floppy mattress. The mattress will become a couch bound by ribbons, decorated with pillows, and covered with a silk sheet from the Salvation Army store.

Appliances all work, the toilet flushes, and the shower is big enough for two.

• Eighty •

George's family likes the apartment.

His father walks around it, looks out windows, sits and stands for seconds at a time, and says, "George has himself a good place here."

He says this over and over until we laugh like it's a joke.

His mother opens and closes the refrigerator, stove, and cabinets. She glides her hand along the walls, takes off her shoes, and loses her feet in the carpet, then she sits at the kitchen table. George makes coffee because he knows how she likes it. We talk for hours while his father paces, goes out for walks, and finds the closest place to buy lottery tickets.

When my parents plan to come, I clean for days. My mother did this when company was expected, and I swore I never would, but I do. It gives me something to do besides worry about what we will talk about.

There was no reason to worry. Within minutes, George and Dad are discussing world issues and Bears football. I show Mom the apartment. She inspects every room except our bedroom. George and Dad keep talking while Mom and I cook.

The living room is two steps from the kitchen, so we hear everything they say. The talk sounds close to natural. What isn't natural is that my father is talking. At home, Dad watches TV and reads the paper. He isn't unfriendly, but he doesn't talk. It's my mother who talks nonstop as soon as someone is within range. But now, she is quiet too, listening.

After dinner, we go to the clubhouse, and Dad and George play pool. I didn't know either of them played. Both are rusty, but get better. They ask us to play with them. Dad shows Mom how to hold the cue, and George shows me. I mess up, George shows me again, and we tease and giggle. My parents watch us and laugh.

What I always believed could happen, has happened.

They like him.

They like us.

• Eighty-One •

I don't like to fight, and neither does George. It takes a lot to make either of us mad, but when we get mad, we are opposites. George talks and talks and talks. I go silent.

Our first married fight is about dishes. We split up household chores. Because I get home from work first, I cook dinner, and George does the dishes. But it wasn't specified how often. George waits until there are no more clean dishes, and then it takes hours to wash them. I'm in bed unable to sleep from pans clattering, glasses clinking, and George singing.

The next day, when George asks what's wrong, because it's clear something is, I say, "Nothing."

This goes on for another day. He keeps asking what's wrong, and I refuse to talk about it. George insists I tell him because it is essential we learn how to communicate, and I'm mad he's trying to force me. I go to bed and turn to the wall. George climbs in and keeps talking. I turn to yell at him to stop, but bust out laughing because he is wearing a pair of fake nose and glasses.

We laugh until we can barely breathe, and then we talk.

I tell him the stacks of dirty dishes and late-night washings bother me. George says he hates washing dishes because he had to wash too many when he was a kid. The resolution is simple. I'll cook and do the dishes. George will wash clothes and the floors.

It will take time to learn how to talk when I'm angry.
George buys me a pair of nose and glasses.

• Eighty-Two •

George and I will visit my parents for Christmas, but I don't know where we'll sleep. My old bedroom has a single bed. George could sleep on the floor, or we could sleep in my brothers' old room on their bunk beds.

We arrive, and within minutes, Mom says, "You and George will sleep on the sofa bed." She says it like she's been rehearsing it. We glance at each other, and I blush. I hadn't thought about the sofa bed. It's in the living room, and there's no privacy, but that doesn't matter. In my parents' house, we aren't going to do anything but sleep.

Grandma Sampson will come in the morning with my mother's brother, Uncle Darold, and his wife, Thelma. They live in London Mills, a small town a couple hours away. My grandmother has never come to our house for Christmas. We always go there because there are two sets of family to visit. Uncle Mack's farm is just outside of town. Now with George in the family, we won't be going there without an invitation, and that won't ever happen.

When my parents told Grandma Sampson about George, she asked how dark he was. "Some Negroes are so light you can't tell." My father pointed to the dark mahogany buffet. Grandma didn't faint away and die as predicted, but she prayed to Jesus I'd come to my senses.

Christmas morning, I wake up to the sound of my grandmother's laughter. "Well, look at the sleepyheads."

Grandma, Uncle Darold, and Aunt Thelma are at the foot of the sofa bed. I nudge George awake. I am in one of my mother's flannel nightgowns, but George is in his underwear.

I hear my mother running down the stairs. She is in her robe and hasn't taken out her hair rollers. "You must have left at the crack of dawn."

My uncle says it was before the dawn even cracked. They all laugh and follow Mom to the kitchen.

Grandma giggles about this all day. It gives her something to talk about when she can't think of anything to say. "We sure did surprise you two this morning."

• Eighty-Three •

It's the night before George and I go back home. Dad and George are watching football, and Mom and I are in the kitchen. She says, "I want you to know that all my past feelings of anger about you and George are gone."

This may be one of the most extraordinary things she has ever said.

First of all, Mom never talks about her feelings. She shows them, but won't talk about them.

Secondly, my mother is the queen of grudges. It's the main thing my parents argue about. Dad doesn't understand why she won't let go of things, and she can't understand how he can.

She has not forgiven her mother for hiring a photographer to take a family portrait just before she was born. "Grandma wanted a picture of her perfect family before I came along and ruined it."

My mother can smile and act as if everything is wonderful while raging inside. I've seen it happen with visits from friends or relatives. After everyone leaves, she rants and stomps and slams doors. She relives every infraction and insult they ever did.

My mother is pleasant with George. She notes what he likes to eat and buys Neapolitan ice cream and Dr. Pepper. But as nice as she acts, I know it could be fake.

My mother and I sit at the kitchen table peeling and cutting up apples.

"The anger has gone totally away."

This surprises her as much as it does me.

I ask the question I have had for months. "Had you and Dad already decided you'd give consent?"

Mom shakes her head. "No, your father wouldn't talk about it. I brought it up to him a while back, but he said, 'I'll cross that bridge if I come to it.' I knew what I'd say if you ever asked again, but I didn't know what he was thinking. But that night when I looked over at him—I knew he was thinking the same thing."

She still thinks it's odd that Bahá'ís have to get parental consent to marry, but it did something she didn't expect. "After I wrote it out and signed it, the anger and hurt I had felt began to go away. And now it's completely gone."

Mom is not the only one who holds a grudge.

The night I first told them I wanted to marry George has played over and over in my head, and it hurts every time. Mom was wearing a blue-striped cotton dress and a flower-print apron that she untied and threw on the floor before running upstairs and slamming the bathroom door so hard the windows rattled. My father was wearing a brown, plaid flannel shirt and tan corduroy pants. The veins in his neck threatened to explode. "If I had known this would happen, they'd have been called 'nigger' from day one."

I remember because I can't forget.

But it doesn't hurt now. That disappeared when they gave their consent.

The apples we cut up are for a pie Mom is making.

George loves apple pie.

• Eighty-Four •

George is late.

Again.

It's the one flaw I've seen in him. I shouldn't complain, but I do.

Dinner is ready, but by the time he eats, it will be worse than it was when I cooked it. It's Hamburger Helper—nothing special. I won't spend hours cooking because if I did, he'd still be late, and I would be mad. And then, if the thing I fear most happens, I would feel guilty that he died and I was too angry to feel his spirit surrounding me.

George is later than usual.

It is possible he's so late because his car is in a ditch (because that has happened to him), or he is slumped over his desk with a brain clot (because that happened to a friend), or he is lying somewhere with a gunshot wound in his chest (because that happens every day to someone, especially Black men).

I cannot read. Or watch television. I don't want to call anyone in case the hospital or police are trying to call me.

I clean. I scrub the counters. And dust bookshelves. And vacuum.

While cleaning, I imagine his funeral because if that worst possible thing happens, I need to plan it before I lose my mind. I know who I will ask to read prayers, and sing, and do the eulogy, and share stories. I will need something to wear that is in my closet because I won't be able to go shopping. But whatever I pick, I don't want it to be one of my favorites because I will never wear it again. I'll have to choose something for him to wear. His mother will want him in a suit, but I want the sweater I gave him for his birthday . . .

George yells over the vacuum, "I'm home!" He grins and says, "I see you've been cleaning again."

"Yes, and your funeral was lovely."

He laughs. "I wish you wouldn't worry so much."

"Then don't make me."

He opens his arms, and I slide into them.

• Eighty-Five •

I work at the elementary school as a Title 1 reading aide. A new reading aide looks like a younger version of my mother, but acts nothing like her. Ellen is obsessed with Elvis Presley and just returned from his funeral. Her face is puffy from nonstop crying. She slept on the street with thousands of fans. I find this fascinating.

A week later, Ellen has recovered her normal cheerfulness. She's hilarious and jokes around, but is never mean. We swap husband stories. Hers is handy around the house. Mine does laundry and cooks. They go camping, and so do we, but we are bad at it. We cut our last trip short because of raccoons. They came into our campsite at night and got into fights when they couldn't find food. One crawled into the trunk when we loaded up, and it hissed at George. He banged his new car with a huge stick to scare it away. The raccoon was more annoyed than scared and finally left, dragging our loaf of bread with him.

Ellen's husband, Danny, goes hunting but never brings home anything except store-bought steaks. He swears he has bad luck, but she doesn't believe him. He cried once when he ran over a squirrel.

Ellen loves the children. Every day at lunch, she talks about the kids she works with. She brags when they do well and worries when they don't. She doesn't talk about her faith, but I know she's a Christian. Before she eats, she closes her eyes and touches the gold cross she wears.

She asks about the Bahá'í Faith. I tell her the basics, and she says, "As long as you believe in God, it doesn't matter." I like this woman.

I'm making copies of worksheets in the lounge, and Ellen walks in. I make a disgusted face because we both hate making kids do mindless worksheets. She opens her mouth to say something, then turns around and walks out. I wonder if another celebrity has died.

Ellen doesn't come to the lounge for lunch. I see her in the hall and wave. She turns away.

I find her alone in the staff bathroom, but she doesn't speak.

"What's wrong?" I ask.

Ellen's face turns red. She looks over my head, and down at her feet, and examines her fingernails.

"I-I-I heard something about you . . ."

I know what it is but wait for her to say it.

"George is Black?" Tears roll down her cheeks. She holds her stomach, and her body trembles. "You are so nice, and smart. How could you marry a Black man? Why didn't you tell me?"

I skipped a step when I met Ellen. Whenever I meet a new person, I find a way to let them know my husband is Black. I show a wedding picture, or tell a story that needs to include that information to make sense. I can tell by their reaction if we could be friends. It often feels forced and awkward, and there are times I don't do it. I don't do it with people who I have strong positive feelings about. With those people, it wasn't necessary. I had been right—but not this time.

"I didn't think it would matter to you."

Ellen's face crumbles, like it does when she talks about Elvis dying. "I wish it didn't."

• Eighty-Six •

He is the doctor everyone says is the best, and he knows it. I don't care that he walks in and doesn't say hello to me, or warm up his instruments, and looks annoyed when I flinch. I don't mind any of that because he has discovered what's wrong with me. I have a misshapen uterus. It's bicornate, which means it has two sections. My babies didn't have enough room to grow. My miscarriages were not God's punishment. If George and I were married, it would have still happened, but I would not have been alone. George would have held me every night. My mother would have shared my sadness, and George's mother, who had lost two children, would assure me I would survive this.

My body has a defect. Maybe it can be fixed.

I am in the waiting room with a pregnant woman. She looks both uncomfortable and satisfied. Her belly is so big that the only place she can rest her hands is on top of it. I never got to that point. Elizabeth was a small bump, hardly noticeable to anyone but me. I knew she was a girl, but I am not clairvoyant or I would have known I was going to lose her. I didn't think about Jeremy. I knew he'd never make it.

The doctor is an hour late without apology. He glances through my chart and asks what I want. I'm not due for a checkup.

"I want to know if I can still have a baby. Is there anything that can be done?"

He glances at the chart again and slams it shut. "No. There is nothing I can do for you."

"Are you sure?"

He is irritated. "Obviously, you can get pregnant, so you can go ahead and keep trying. The uterus will expand with every pregnancy. Someday it could be large enough."

He can't tell me how many miscarriages it will take. It could be a couple, or a dozen. Or it might never happen.

This is my recurring nightmare. The one where I cry myself awake. *I am in a graveyard. The tombstones are small. I wander through, looking for which one is my baby's, and see they all are.*

I fight back tears and look at the doctor. He turns away and walks out of the room.

The Voice in my head screams, "Look at your chart!"

The doctor had left it on the desk.

On the second page, written in faded black marker is:

WHITE WOMAN LIVING WITH BLACK MAN

He didn't even acknowledge our marriage.

The friend who recommended him confirms the doctor is a racist. He advised she get an abortion because the father was Black. "He told me he doesn't want more mongrels in the world."

"Why did you recommend him?"

"Because he's the best doctor in town—don't doctors have to help people no matter who they are?"

I make an appointment with another doctor at the University of Illinois clinic, forty-five minutes away.

This new doctor looks through my chart, frowns, and says, "There were no X-rays taken? I may be able to reconstruct it, but I'd have to see it first."

I explain, "My doctor didn't do any. I suspect he didn't want to help me have babies because my husband is Black." I watch this doctor's face for a change of expression, a flicker of disgust in his eyes.

He looks up at the ceiling, then smiles at me and says, "You don't need to worry about that. If I can help you, I will." He explains that each bicornate uterus differs in size and shape. He has successfully reconstructed hundreds of them, but some are too small to reshape.

I go to the X-ray lab, and dye is injected into my uterus. There is a monitor, and I can see it. It is heart-shaped and tiny. I ask the technician what she thinks. She pats my hand. "Your doctor will explain everything to you."

My consultation with the doctor is in two hours, and I know he will say there is not enough tissue to work with and I'll never be able to have a baby.

I call George from the pay phone in the lobby and tell him this isn't going to work and I'm sorry he got a defective wife.

"And when did you become a doctor?" he says. "Don't jump to conclusions."

George wants to be a father so much he isn't willing to face reality. I am ready to be a grown-up about this. When it's confirmed I cannot have children, I will tell George I'll give him a divorce so he can find another wife. He will say it doesn't matter, but I know it does.

The doctor comes in, and before he sits down, I tell him I know he can't help me. "I watched the X-ray, and I saw how small it is."

He smiles, and his eyes tell me I'm wrong. I force myself to listen to every word so I can repeat it again and again and again. "You do have a bicornate uterus, but there is enough tissue for me to reconstruct it. You can have your baby."

I call George. He's too happy to remind me he told me so.

A month later, I want to back out. Maybe something will go wrong and I'll die, or worse, be in a coma and never recover, and George will stay loyal and stand by me until I finally go or finally wake up. But that could be years, and if I did wake up, I'd be too old to have a baby.

I don't tell George about these thoughts. I know he'll try to logic me out of them.

I tell him I am reconsidering the surgery and will give him a divorce so he can find someone who can have children.

George says it is my body. He will accept my decision. He doesn't want a divorce and thinks I'm ridiculous to offer it. He won't hold this against me. We'll adopt children, and he'll love them.

Knowing all this should set me at ease, but it doesn't. I can't stop thinking about it.

There's a commercial for a television special about medical breakthroughs for infertility. I don't have infertility, but the promo is intriguing. George has a meeting, so I watch it alone. The documentary depicts women with odd genetic conditions that medical science can now correct. All of them are more complex than mine, and all of them end up with babies.

George comes home from his meeting, and before he takes off his coat, I say, "I'm going to have the operation."

He doesn't ask why, or if I am sure. He opens his arms and hugs me.

My mother offers to pay our co-pay for the operation. "This is something you were born with, so it's our responsibility to correct."

She is excited about grandchildren. In public, she stares at interracial couples and their children. If they notice, I say, "Your children are adorable."

Mom smiles and adds, "She is married to a Black man too."

I've never had surgery. The doctor says it will take six to eight weeks to recover, so it's scheduled for the first week of summer break. I'll be in the hospital for a week. The doctor asks who can be with me when I go home. I tell him I'm sure I can manage on my own. He says, "No, you need someone for at least a week."

Mom offers to come and stay with us, and we exchange our mattress couch for a real one.

My surgery is scheduled for noon and will take an hour. I'll be in recovery for a couple hours and back to my room by midafternoon.

George is in the family waiting room. Nurses come and talk to other families, but no one comes to talk to him. Later, they will say they came, but he wasn't there. He left once to go to the bathroom, and once for coffee. Maybe that was when they came and they were too busy to come again. Or maybe when the nurse came, she saw a Black man and didn't think it was this White woman's husband.

When it has been over eight hours and all the families have come and gone, and no one is around except the janitor, George wanders the halls and finds the recovery rooms and sees me lying there and my toe twitching. He goes back to the waiting room.

I wake up to a nurse yelling at me. "If you ever have another operation, tell them you react bad to the anesthetic!" She gets close to my face. "Understand? You have to tell them that next time."

There is something stuck down my throat, and I can't talk. I want it out and point to it.

She shakes her head. "You're on a respirator. You aren't breathing on your own."

I'm not breathing because I have a huge tube down my throat. If she takes it out, I'll be fine.

I am a mime. I will use my mime powers to make her understand. I give commands to my face: make your eyebrows come together, turn down the corners of your mouth, tilt your head, beg with your eyes.

The nurse looks at my pitiful face. "Awww, honey. You want this out, don't you?"

I nod, and she calls for assistance. "We'll take this out, but if you don't start breathing, we're going to have to put it back in and that will hurt. Is that what you want?"

I nod and attempt a smile.

Bodies surround me as the nurse pulls out the respirator. When it comes out, I breathe, then barf. My audience claps and exits as the nurse cleans me up and says once more, but now whispering because another patient is coming into the room, "Remember this if you ever have anesthetic again." She pats my head, and I never see her again.

The breathing tube damaged my esophagus so bad I can barely talk. It hurts to swallow. The doctor says the operation was successful, and after about six months, we can get pregnant.

I ask about what happened with the anesthetic, and he says without looking at me, "Nothing was wrong. Some people take longer to wake up."

I like my doctor. I am grateful for what he has done, and I don't want to get the recovery nurse in trouble, but I don't believe him. The nurse was too insistent, and it confirms my old suspicion that LSD would have killed me.

I hope the Voice doesn't get tired of saving my life.

• Eighty-Seven •

Recovery is worse than I had imagined. Standing, sitting, lying, breathing, and laughing hurt. My mother stays for two weeks and offers to stay longer, but I know she misses Dad. In their forty-plus years of marriage, she's never been away from him for this long.

Mom has cooked meals for the next month. All I'll have to do is stand long enough to heat them up, then sit and rest before eating.

In a few weeks, I can move well enough to walk to the pool and relax on the deck chairs. The woman who lives in the apartment above ours is a teacher and has the summer off. We meet every afternoon and talk. One day, I tell her the story of how we got the apartment, and how worried I was when we came to get the key.

She says, "So that's what happened. I wondered why they didn't ask us this time."

There is one other Black man who lives in the complex. He's older, and I rarely see him. George talked with him once and said he travels most of the time for business. When this man applied to rent an apartment, the manager went to everyone in the complex and showed them his application, which stated his occupation, salary, and references. The manager asked if they had a problem with him living here. No one objected, so he was allowed.

She smiles. "I was surprised they didn't get our permission this time, but now it makes sense."

By mid-July, I am recovered from the operation in time for a project George and I had agreed to do months ago. We will tour for a month with a performance group featuring mime, music, and dance for Bahá'í communities throughout Illinois. I am still on summer break from the school district, and George is using vacation and accumulated comp time to do it.

One of the women on the tour has studied with a master mime. Her technique is better than mine, but she says I have imagination and emotion she envies. Jewel Walker, the mime master, teaches theater at the University of Wisconsin in Milwaukee, and she'll introduce me to him. She says, "I'm sure he'll let you come and study with him."

But Danville is seven hours away from Milwaukee.

Our last stop on the tour is Rockford, Illinois, a big city with a small-town feel. Rockford has incredible parks, a professional theater company, a dance company, a symphony, and is within driving distance to Milwaukee and the mime master.

Our friends Dick and Ann have moved here and offer to let us stay with them. George is building experience and credentials working in social service, and Dick can help him find a job. I want to be a professional mime, but I need a teacher.

After the tour, we wrap up our Danville lives in two months. There are yard sales, and giveaways, and goodbye parties. When George turns in our apartment key, the manager says, "I want you to know, if you decide to move back here again, I'd be pleased to rent to you."

We move on Halloween, which is perfect. I feel that mix of scary excitement. We have no jobs, no solid plans other than staying in our friends' basement bedroom. George drives a U-Haul, and I drive our VW Bug. We wind through little towns with lit porch lights and slow down for little witches, ghosts, monsters, and pirates.

I get a job as a home care nurse's aide and tell them I need flexible hours because I'm training to become a professional mime. I love telling people that because I love that it is true.

Two days a week, I sneak into mime class at the University of Wisconsin–Milwaukee. The mime master is delighted to have a dedicated student among those who think it is unrelated to their future stardom, or think it's an easy elective. The other students pay no attention to me, until we perform our solos.

"Who are you? Are you a theater major?"

I tell them bits of the truth:

"I'd like to be a theater major."

"I was in a mime troupe once."

"I'm only taking this class."

On the ninety-minute drive up Highway 43, windows down, hair flying, a silly thought pops up that makes me laugh out loud: *If everyone did what they really wanted to do, they would be mimes.*

• Eighty-Eight •

Maybe it's the influence of our friends with their adopted children, or maybe I'm afraid I won't wake up if I have a Caesarean . . . but I suggest to George we adopt. I tell him there are babies out there that need us.

He says what he always says. It's my body, so this is my decision. He's fine with whatever I decide.

Maybe he's afraid of another operation too.

I contact the same adoption agency our friends use. It specializes in biracial babies and likes to place them in Bahá'í homes because our communities are diverse and supportive. Being an interracial couple is a bonus.

I receive a phone call a week after sending the application. The woman's voice is pleasant, but I detect a note of regret. "We looked over your application, and it looks like you would be a wonderful match for our babies—but you have only been married for a year, and your income is on the low side."

It doesn't matter that we have been together for six years or that I have raging maternal hormones. We make enough for the basics, and you can get almost-new clothes, toys, and furniture at garage sales. Our families will help as needed.

The adoption agency wants us to be married for at least three years. We can do that. I ask, "How much money do we have to make?"

She won't give me a figure. She says it depends on many factors, but since we want to adopt hard-to-place children, they could be lenient, but we still need more income than we have.

That's not going to happen.

George is doing social service work with a theater degree. He's gaining experience, but to get the higher-paying jobs, he'd have to go back to school. If he goes back to school, we have to take out loans and owe more money.

I don't have a degree. I have "some college," and that means low-paying jobs. I do mime performances and rent space to teach mime classes. It isn't steady, but it's flexible, and I create my own hours. It will allow me to be a stay-at-home mom.

I could finish college in a couple years and get a job with more pay, but that means when we get the baby, I'd have to work and find day care. Someone else would raise our child.

That makes no sense.

How dare they reject us after what we saw at the adoption seminar four years ago.

A White couple who were friends of Dick and Ann organized a seminar for White families considering biracial adoptions. They had adopted and wanted to help others understand and prepare. They thought it could be beneficial for potential adoptees to meet an interracial couple. That should have warned me something was off.

The format of the seminar meant dividing people into smaller groups with a workshop leader. George and I were assigned to different groups.

In my group, the leader had everyone introduce themselves and share why they came. The first woman said she had two biological children but wanted more. Her doctor advised against it and suggested they consider adopting. She shook her head. "It's hard to get White babies, and since we already have our own children, they don't see us as a priority. The agencies said our only option is to adopt hard-to-place children, so that's what we decided to do. We thought about taking a retarded baby, but the caseworker mentioned we might want to consider a mixed-race baby. I prayed about it and feel it is my Christian duty to help these poor, innocent babies."

Then a man said his wife wanted to adopt, but he wasn't sure. They lived in an all-White small town, had no Black friends, and his parents didn't want Black grandchildren.

Others in the circle cited similar situations, and everyone said that it takes too long to get White babies.

When it was my turn, I said, "My fiancé is Black, and we were invited by the couple who organized this. They thought you might be interested in meeting us." This was before the first pregnancy, before we knew I had a problem. "We may adopt, or maybe we'll have our own."

The Christian woman gasped, then exploded. "What? We are here to help these poor babies, and you want to create more?"

The uncertain man quieted her down. He smiled at me and said, "You seem like a nice girl. Well-spoken, educated. Why would you do this?"

I looked around the circle, and they waited for my answer.

I told them about growing up with Black friends. I told them if they have White children, and most of them did, their child could fall in love with a Black person because they will know what I know: We are all human. "Unless you teach your White children their Black 'brothers and sisters' are inferior to them."

They listened and nodded and looked worried.

At the end of the conference, a Black social worker who had been checking in on the discussion groups addressed the crowd. "From what I have seen and heard today, I'd rather put our Black babies through a meat grinder than place them in your homes."

Within the year, cross-racial adoptions were no longer supported by the Black Social Workers Coalition, and a year after that, regulations were put into place that made interracial adoptions close to impossible.

White friends who longed for children, were loving and thoughtful, and were committed to eliminating prejudice were upset. I understood, but there is nothing wrong in making them prove how committed they are.

But how dare this agency reject us now. They have never seen George sing colicky babies to sleep. They have no idea how my heart hurts every time I see a baby. How do they decide we aren't ready to be parents?

I tell George what the agency said. "So forget them. Let's have our own."

The most patient man in the universe smiles.

I think we got pregnant that night. We seem to work that way.

• Eighty-Nine •

Now that we are pregnant, we need a new place to live. Dick and Ann, who now have three kids, offer to rearrange their basement to make room for a crib. Their kids are excited about another baby. Too excited. They are arguing about who will do what for the baby, and they are loud.

I want quiet.

We could rent an apartment, but I want to buy a house so we don't have to worry about anyone else. No landlords to please, no neighbors above us waking up the baby. No neighbors below to disturb when the baby walks, jumps, and bounces.

After months of looking, we find our house. It's five minutes away from Dick and Ann's. The neighbors are White, which may not have been the best choice, but this is a house we can afford, and it's unique. It's a quirky bungalow with a family room converted from an old garage. It has additional bedrooms that aren't hooked up to the furnace, but could be when we have extra money. It also has a fenced yard for kids to play in and the inevitable dog.

My parents help with a down payment. George's parents take over our co-pay for his brother's truck. The bank considers it a financial obligation and takes us over the limit of how much we can owe and still qualify.

A good realtor, equal housing laws, and a desperate seller make it happen.

On moving day, a man who lives a couple houses away comes to introduce himself. George answers, and when I get to the door, they're talking about their college careers. His name is Tim, and twenty minutes later, his wife, Janet, and their baby come.

After they leave, I tease George, "Did you say, 'Hello! My name is George, and I went to college.'"

George laughs. "No, but that's basically what he said."

Janet makes it her project to become my friend. "You two are the only ones in the neighborhood who went to college, besides us." That makes me cringe, but she's uncomfortable, and she's trying to find something in common with us.

Janet says she can see how a White person could love someone Black because she has a crush on the Black actor in *Mission Impossible*. "But your George is no Greg Morris. So, what was the attraction?" And then she laughs.

I want to end the friendship, but Janet keeps showing up at my door. "You need to get out of the house. Let's go to the park."

If she isn't going to leave me alone, she needs to understand who I am, so I tell her my stories of standing up for civil rights, losing White friends, and falling in love. And Janet tells her own. She grew up in an all-White town and only saw Black people on television. George is the one and only Black person she knows.

And then she tells me people in the neighborhood were angry we bought the house. There was talk of doing something to make it clear we weren't welcome.

Janet and her husband decided that wasn't fair and wanted to give us a chance. That's why Tim came over the day we moved in, and when he didn't return home, that was the signal for Janet to come and meet us.

She smiles. "I'm glad we did."

I refill her iced tea.

• Ninety •

Several days a week, my friend Joy, who is also pregnant, comes for coffee. We analyze her marriage and world peace possibilities. When she mentions our babies, I act happy, not worried, but she doesn't believe me. And she's right. Throughout the day, I chant a silent mantra: "Grow, baby, grow. Stay, baby, stay."

I won't talk about babies until this one has stayed longer than Elizabeth did.

At the six-month marker, Joy and I hit garage sales and hunt for baby clothes. I search through stacks for yellow and green outfits. Joy holds up a pink dress and a tiny Bears football jersey. She says, "I wish we knew the genders."

A woman overhears and whispers, "There's a way to find out." She tells us about the Drano test that worked for her and her friends.

We go back to my house, pee in glass jars, and add Drano. The concoction bubbles and stinks. Fumes rise up and choke us. I grab the jars, and the glass is so hot I almost drop them. We use dish towels to carry them outside. Mine is brownish for "boy," and hers is bluish-yellowish-greenish for "girl."

When George comes home, the house still stinks. I tell him what happened, and he asks if I've lost my mind. Didn't I realize these were chemicals? Did I consider that breathing in fumes could harm the baby?

It was a dumb thing to do because I already know this is a boy. I've held him in my dreams. He has soft brown eyes that see the insides of things.

I try to not love him until he gets here, but that's impossible.

If he doesn't make it, I won't either.

• Ninety-One •

In college, I wore blue jeans and t-shirts. Most of them were ripped. I didn't wear makeup and refused offers from girls who wanted to show me how.

Now that George and I are married, I check myself before we go out in public together. I want to break the image of what kind of White woman is with a Black man. I find clothes that are artsy, but dignified. Nothing tight. Nothing anyone would think was too sexy.

I've heard people say the only White women Black men get are the ugly ones. My looks are average, not beautiful. Makeup helps, but I keep it light, not trashy.

George and I are standing in line for ice cream. People are watching us. When I look at them, I catch the sneer before they turn away.

I ask George, "Is it my imagination, or are people looking at us more?"

He pats my pregnant bump. "They know we are more than friends."

I remember how nervous my friend Rodney was to be seen with me. I thought it was because he was raised in the South. But another Black friend, who lived his whole life in Illinois, whispered what he thought everyone was thinking when the two of us walked down the street—and what they would like to do to him.

George says he doesn't worry about what people think of us. Dwelling on it makes you bitter and angry, and that's not how he chooses to live.

I make it into a game. I pretend people look at us because we're famous. And I will be polite, regardless of how rude they are.

I won't give them more excuses to hate us.

• Ninety-Two •

When I am two months away from my due date, I let myself believe I really will be bringing home a baby. I've read all the books people loaned me and recall the birth stories women have shared. Most are about failures. I'm not worrying about a birth because I've already scheduled the C-section, but I do want to breastfeed.

My pregnant friend Joy had trouble nursing her first one. "I didn't have enough milk." From what I've read, that's rare, but Joy insists. "I hope I can do it this time." She sounds defeated already.

There is a flier on the bulletin board at my doctor's office for the local Le Leche League, a support group for women who breastfeed. I've never been to a meeting, but women I admire recommend it. The facilitators know more about breastfeeding than most doctors. They are committed and radical, and I like that. These women are potential friends for life. That's what I've been told.

I like the woman on the phone. She asks when I'm due, and if this is my first. Usually I just say yes, but this time I tell about my miscarriages, and my reconstructive surgery, and how now that it looks like this one is going to work, I need to get ready.

There's a group that meets monthly and goes through a four-part series, then repeats. We've missed the first three sessions, but we can meet the women, and they will catch me up. I've already read the recommended books.

Joy comes with me to the meeting, which is in a suburban neighborhood that goes around in circles. George says these kinds of neighborhoods give the illusion of safety because they reason criminals will get confused.

We find the house, and it's filled with pregnant women and mothers with babies. It's delightful, loud, and everyone is White. This is a situation where I usually feel uncomfortable and find a way to let people know I may look like them, but I'm not one of them—unless they too are married to a man of color.

We start with a round of introductions. We say our names and either introduce our babies or give our due dates. If we've successfully nursed children before, we tell that. And for fun, share something we notice about our changing body. Nothing else. No one mentions the work they once did, or their husbands. When it's my turn, besides name and due date, I share that I can no longer balance on one leg.

The meeting is at the home of the head facilitator, Irene. She gives a brief overview of what the newcomers need to know, like preparing our nipples with lanolin so they will be tough but supple. Then she does the monthly presentation about best foods to eat while nursing.

She invites people to share success stories and challenge stories and warning stories. There aren't many, and there is more time left, so the facilitator shares her own. She says it's funny, and she's already laughing: "The morning after I had Jeffy, the nigger nurse walked in and saw that the bassinet was empty. She ran around the room screaming, 'Where's your baby? Oh, Lordy, where's the baby?' She didn't see him sleeping in the bed with me, and I was laughing too hard to tell her!"

I thought maybe I didn't hear it right, but I look at Joy, and her face looks the way I feel. Sick.

Before I can think of what to say, someone asks a serious question. And then another one.

I retrace the incident, remembering who laughed, who smiled, who was distracted by their baby or the kicks inside their stomach, who looked surprised, and who looked upset.

There were three of us that were upset: Joy, myself, and the woman I talked with on the phone. She came today to meet me and introduce me to this woman who she said was like everyone's mother.

The leader is now talking to me. "Looks like you may have this baby before we start the next session."

I look at this woman's face and want to rip it off.

Instead, I make an offer. "May I host the next series at my house?"

She is pleased a newcomer is already that committed, but concerned it might be too much too soon.

"It won't be a problem. I have a great husband who will help me get the house ready."

She says, "How lucky you are to have a husband like that! I look forward to meeting your baby—and maybe even your husband?"

I smile. "Yes, I'm looking forward to that too."

• Ninety-Three •

I am scheduled for a Caesarian on December 15, and I want George with me for the birth. I read an article in *Parents Magazine* about fathers being allowed to be there, but my doctor says operating rooms are no place for fathers. "He could faint or get in the way. Our concern has to be you. We can't have nurses taking care of husbands." He gives me a wink. "Men aren't as strong as women when it comes to this."

The next week, I see in the newspaper a hospital thirty minutes away lets husbands in for Caesarian births. I make an appointment, and this doctor is willing to take me as a patient, but when he sees my medical history, he's worried. "We don't know how well your uterus will hold up as the baby gets bigger. If you have sudden, intense pain, get to the nearest hospital. Your uterus could rupture, and we'd lose you both."

My mother thinks it's foolish to change doctors at seven months. My father, who never saw his children until everyone was clean and settled in the nursery, asks George if this is what he wants. George laughs. "It doesn't matter what I want. I'll do what makes her happy."

George has to do an orientation before the baby comes. He is supposed to come with me for my checkup and complete the orientation then, but every time, he has to cancel. He works for an agency that deals with child abuse, and there is always an emergency

It is Thanksgiving, and because I am too close to delivery and don't want to be in a house filled with smokers, we don't go to George's family in Chicago. My parents come to our house for the weekend, and Mom insists I make a pie from scratch before the baby comes. "After that, you won't have time."

I want to remind her I don't bake and I don't like pie. Maybe it's the hormones, but I agree because this will make her happy. I search and find the unused rolling pin someone gave us for a wedding present.

Mom makes the rest of the meal, and George helps. He likes the way her turkey turns out and wants to know how she does it. She has never known a man who liked to cook.

If Mom had more of a sense of humor, I would say that's why I waited so long for consent. Instead, I say, "No man was ever going to marry me because of my cooking."

Mom nods and sighs. She whispers, "I can't get your father to make his own sandwich. You lucked out with George."

She says this like she doesn't understand how amazing it is. That she used to spend hours crying about us. That she felt she had failed as a mother.

And she hasn't even seen George with the baby yet.

• Ninety-Four •

The Monday after Thanksgiving, George comes to my doctor's appointment with me. I made him promise to not cancel this time. "We are three weeks from the due date—they won't let you be with me if you don't get the training."

On the way there, the baby is stretching, punching, tightening, rolling, and poking. Maybe he didn't like the pie.

The nurse will meet with George while I see the doctor. Afterwards, she'll talk with both of us, and we'll take a tour of the maternity ward.

My doctor reminds me of my father. He plays golf like Dad, and tells me his score as if I understand what it means. I can tell by his face if it's good or bad. Today is a good day. He checks me, and his face becomes serious. "Have you been feeling anything unusual?"

"The baby's been moving a lot. Why?"

"You're in labor. We're having this baby today."

I haven't packed the hospital suitcase. I haven't chosen the baby's coming home clothes yet. I had planned to go to the laundromat tomorrow with all the baby clothes. I was going to fold, sort, and decide.

But there is no time to go home, no time to tour the maternity ward and wonder which room we'll have.

On the way to the hospital, I ask George about the training. He can't tell me because he doesn't remember. The nurse told him I was in labor and put him in a room to watch a video. "It was on, and I sat there watching it, but I can't remember anything about it."

We don't call anyone. Our families are too far away, our friends are at work or at home with their own babies. Today is for the two of us. And our baby.

The doctor comes to check on me and says it isn't an emergency, so we'll do it in a few hours. He and George talk about Monday Night Football. The Seahawks and Jets are playing tonight. The doctor looks at the baby monitor and grins. "We can wait until after the game." George and the doctor laugh. I think the doctor is joking, but he doesn't come back until halftime, and it's a Seahawks blowout.

Attendees on both sides of the gurney wheel me into a cold room. Voices, male and female, echo. A masked and gloved nurse asks me to sit up and holds me steady. I requested a spinal to be awake. Another nurse brings a tray with a needle. She walks by quick, but not quick enough. I see the four-inch needle, and soon feel it. And soon after feel nothing.

More nurses are in the room. One puts a curve-shaped bar over my chest and drapes the sheet over it. "You'll hear us, but you won't see anything." She leaves, and I hear her voice among the others. "I'll get the husband."

George appears in a blue surgical gown and mask. The nurse positions him in a chair on my left side, and the doctor peeks over the sheet barrier. "Ready?"

I nod.

The doctor says to George, "If you want to see the birth, you can see it reflected off the light fixtures . . . it's up to you." Then his head disappears. I hear talking, but nothing distinguishable.

George's eyes are on mine. He holds my hand, which is strapped to a board and hooked up to an IV because the only veins that cooperate are on the back of my hand.

I ask, "Have they started yet?"

George looks like he doesn't understand what I'm saying. Later, he will tell me about the organs they removed and set aside to make their way to our boy. But at that moment, he stifles a laugh. "Oh, yes, they started."

I feel pulls, and tugs, and then hear a soft cry that grows loud and hovers above the laughter, claps, and shouts. "It's a boy!" "He's beautiful!"

George squeezes my fingers, then goes to him. "Welcome, son."

I hear a water splash, followed by laughter. George gave our son his first bath, and our baby was slippery.

George comes into view, holding a yellow bundle topped with a blue knit cap.

Our boy's eyes are open, soft brown, searching. He finds me. I've dreamed of this face, but this real one is more beautiful.

He made it. Our boy is here.

We name him Nathan. Hebrew origin—"Gift from God."

• Ninety-Five •

Nathan and I are in the hospital for a week for me to recover from the C-section and Nathan to lie under lights for his jaundice, which the nurses on every shift assure me is normal for babies, especially those born early.

George works as a case manager for an agency that deals with severe child abuse. He thought he had three weeks to catch up on the paperwork before temporarily assigning his cases to other managers. Now he has to do it in between hospital visits, getting baby clothes washed, and disinfecting the house because he worries the change from a sterile hospital environment to our germ-laden home will be too much of a shock for his son.

Nathan is the first newborn baby I have ever held. My friend Helen's baby had a pulsing soft spot that scared me. After several months, I held the baby twice when Helen went to the bathroom, and once I changed her diaper, but it fell off.

George is an expert. When he was in middle school, their family kept the baby of a cousin while she tried to pull her life together. When George came home from school, he went straight for the crib. He diapered, fed, burped, and played with the baby while doing his homework. When the cousin came back, George didn't want to let the baby go.

George teaches me the basics plus extras, like how to get snot out of a nose that can't blow on demand. I didn't know that was part of the deal. I cut Nathan's fingernails but snip the skin. I cry with him and cover the wound with kisses. It left a tiny scratch, and George takes over nail cutting after that. And when he sees his son's body go underwater for half a second, George adds baths to his daily chores too.

My mother gave me a subscription to *Parents Magazine* when I told her I was pregnant. I've read every article on babies. The magazines are now saved in a box for future reference on the terrible twos, and preschool options, and preparing for the first teacher conference, and helping a shy child make friends, and how to talk to your child about death, and every parenting worry I will have one day.

Nathan is a month old, and every woman who has ever had a child gives advice:

"You hold him too much. Don't spoil him."

"Use his nap time to cook and clean. You'll feel better with a clean house."

"Put him in the crib and let him cry himself to sleep. . . . Run the vacuum so you can't hear him."

"Whenever he sleeps, take a nap or read a book. Do something for yourself."

I listen and thank them.

Alone in our house, I strap him to my body in a carrier so I can make a casserole. I move his bassinet around the house as I dust. I tell him how grateful I am to be his mother and how much his daddy loves him and that I know he will become a great man, but for now he is my baby.

He naps in my arms, and I watch his breath.

His nostrils contract on the intake and flare on the release.

His lips form a circle. And then he smiles.

• Ninety-Six •

Two months after Nathan is born, I am hosting the La Leche meeting, the support group for breast-feeding women.

The leader of the group will be here early. I haven't seen Irene since the last meeting, the meeting where she told the story about shocking her nurse by having the baby in bed with her. The one where she described the nurse as a nigger.

When Irene asked who could host the next series of meetings, I volunteered. Now I regret making that offer. I should have called her out on her comment immediately instead of inviting her to my home as a way to embarrass her. I shouldn't use George and Nathan this way.

Irene arrives, and her eyes take in the tininess of our house. The part she can see could fit in her living room. There is an addition at the back of the house where we'll have the meeting. It's a converted garage. The walls and ceiling are paneled, and the carpet covering the concrete floor is a gold-speckled shag. It matches the couch left by the previous owner. The other couch is a brown plaid which doesn't match anything.

Irene smiles. "The good thing about a small house is you don't have so much to clean." She notices the table with fresh banana bread. "That's what smells so good."

"You can thank my husband for that."

"Your husband bakes? That's wonderful. I can't get my husband to lift a finger."

We hear George's voice in the bedroom. He's singing "Hush Little Baby" to Nathan.

Irene's eyes widen. "Your husband has a marvelous voice. Is he with the baby? You are fortunate . . . most men are afraid of babies. Oh my, I haven't seen you since you had your baby. Do you have a boy or a girl?"

She seems genuinely interested, and friendly, and kind. I wonder if this is misunderstanding. Maybe the nurse was from Niger and Irene didn't know how to pronounce it.

Before I can respond, George comes into the room with Nathan.

"This is my husband, George, and our son, Nathan." Irene stares with a frozen smile.

George places Nathan in my arms, kisses him and then me goodbye. He gives a quick smile to Irene. "Nice to meet you. Hope you and your friends like the bread."

George leaves, and Irene asks to use the bathroom.

Women arrive with babies and toddlers. They meet Nathan and say what most people say. "What a beautiful baby."

I lead them to the family room, and they settle in. When it's time to start the meeting, another woman announces a change of plans. She will lead the meeting today. Irene felt suddenly ill and went home.

For the next six weeks, I host the La Leche group, and Irene never returns.

I like the new leader and the group. They are smart, fun, and helpful. They give assurances I can't find in books. Like it's okay to bring Nathan into bed at night so I can sleep. After weeks of sleep deprivation, I had felt ragged and crazy. One night, I nursed him on the couch and didn't wake up until morning. With a seven-hour sleep, I became a human again. After that, I brought Nathan into bed the first time he woke up at night and kept him there. I positioned cushions so he couldn't fall out. I wasn't worried about smothering him since we don't drink alcohol or do drugs and we are light sleepers. It felt good and right to wake up to him with us.

But as right as this feels, I haven't told my doctor. He already said to not do this. All these women sleep with their babies. They say it's natural. It's the way most of the world does it. Secure babies become confident adults. But there is something else I notice. They nurse for a long time. The three-year-old toddlers, running and playing, take nursing breaks.

I ask, "How do you know when it's time to wean?" They smile and say it's nothing to worry about. My son will let me know when it's time.

My son is brilliant, and I have proof. When Nathan is six months old, he says "Na" when he wants to nurse. At ten months, he clearly says, "Nurse." When he's a year and a half, he says, "I want to nurse."

When Nathan is nearly two, we are at George's parents' house. I am upstairs reading. Nathan is downstairs with George. They are watching football with George's father, brothers, and a few male friends. Above the noise of the TV and men's voices, I hear Nathan loud and clear. "I want Mommy's breasts." There is a pause followed by explosions of laughter.

George appears with Nathan. "He wants you."

"Yes, I heard."

George grins. "Like father, like son."

Nathan is weaned in a week.

• Ninety-Seven •

Now that Nathan is walking, talking, and eating solid food, my worries shift from keeping him alive to raising a Black boy in a racist society.

Nathan is adored by friends, our Faith community, and most of our family, but I worry about the rest of the world. Is there some trick to this I don't know? I ask George, and he says the worst thing possible. "Ask my mother."

I do not want to ask his mother. I am still trying to convince Liz I'm worthy of her son. She doesn't know why Black men make their lives harder by marrying White women.

On our next visit, I sit in the kitchen peeling potatoes and ask, "So, what did you do to make George turn out so good?"

Liz teases that he still has me fooled, and then tells one story after another. Some are about her mistakes. Because she worked and George was the oldest, she put too much responsibility on him. She had no daughters, so he did domestic chores.

I thank her for that. "He's teaching me how to clean, and I don't cook!" She shakes her head, and I wish I hadn't said it, but I think she knew.

"Things will happen that you can't control, and you have to make the best of it."

She tells a story George has told me, but this time it's from her side:

George was three, and he hurt his leg playing outside. His friend came to tell Liz, but she was busy and told him to tell George to get himself up the stairs. She was tired and didn't want to leave his baby brother alone. She doesn't know how he did it, but he got himself up the stairs and was crying too much to eat his supper, so she sent him to bed. The next morning, he screamed when she touched his sheets. It was a compound fracture, and he was in Cook County Hospital for six months. Visiting day was once a week, but sometimes there was no one she trusted to watch his baby brother. Sometimes she didn't have bus fare and was too tired to walk the five miles to get to the hospital and back. When she would come the following week, George wouldn't look at her. She sat next to him talking and asking questions until he answered one. He grabbed her hand and didn't let go until she kissed him goodbye.

She never explained to him why she hadn't come. "He might have resented his little brother, and George was too young to understand about money. When I left, I said, 'I am happy you are getting better, because when you are all better, you will come home.'" She learned to only make promises she could keep.

She did things other family members criticized. It was common for Black families to send their children down South to visit the relatives who didn't migrate North. She refused to send George and his brothers because they would have had to learn how to act around White people: Don't look them in the eyes, don't speak unless they speak to you, say "Yes, ma'am" and "Yes, sir" and say it like you're happy. When a White person walks toward you, get off the sidewalk, and if they ask you to run an errand for them, don't act as if they have lost their minds. And most important, never look at or say anything to a White woman. "If I taught George and his brothers that, no matter what I said about them being as good as White people, it would feel like a lie." She's seen what that did to her daddy and husband. "It broke their spirit—I couldn't let that happen to my boys."

In her house, nobody used the "n" word, and she didn't allow negative talk about White people. "There are good White people, and if you distrust all of them, you miss opportunities."

She did not tell her children they had to work harder than Whites because her expectation was already high. She would not let them attribute any failure to racial prejudice, even if it could be true. Believing that could make them feel hopeless.

She let them deal with the system on their own, but intervened once. George's high school put him in the vocation education track instead of college-bound. If the counselor had ever had a conversation with him, he would have realized the mistake. Liz insisted George be placed in the college track even though she had no idea how they could send him to college.

George won a theater scholarship, went to college, and that's how we met.

She laughs. "Be careful what you pray for."

• Ninety-Eight •

"I think I'm getting my period." George makes tea. I gather a heating pad, books, and the remote. The bonus of pregnancy and breastfeeding is no periods. It's been more than two years, and I don't remember it hurting this bad.

I fall into a nightmare. I can't breathe. I think I might die, but the pain dies instead. A minute later, it is back. It feels like labor and reminds me of the miscarriage. I dream I am dead, greeting people at my funeral. I hear my son ask for me, "Where's Mommy?" I try to answer, but my mouth disappears. I hear screams. They get louder, and then George's voice calls out, "Sharon, what's the matter?"

"Get me to the hospital."

He drives too fast with Nathan in the car. I close my eyes and clutch the seat. No crying. It will scare them.

I walk into the emergency room while George parks. They put me on a gurney. Faces ask questions. I tell them what I know. It's my stomach. It hurts. Like labor. They ask the date of my last period, and I laugh. They think I'm delirious.

George finds me. Nathan sleeps on his shoulder. An intern comes in, looks at the chart, and says he'll be back, but he does not come back. Orderlies come and take me to X-ray.

Once in the room, a lady with ice fingers asks, "Is there any chance you are pregnant?"

"Maybe."

The X-ray lady frowns. "I have to check something."

It's cold in here. I have shivers under the cramps.

The X-ray lady is back. "This won't take long." She straightens my legs and disappears. "Hold still." The machine groans. She turns me and shoots again. And again. And again. And one last time.

I pee in a cup. A thin, pale woman takes my blood. I want to ask if this is her bedtime snack, but don't.

Someone takes me back to George. He sits with eyes closed, holding Nathan. George isn't asleep. I hear him chanting a Bahá'í prayer.

"Is there any Remover of difficulties save God? Say: Praised be God! He is God! All are His servants, and all abide by His bidding!"

The nurse and intern come. The intern says, "We need to do a pelvic exam." I make George stay. The intern does it, and the pain stops. I tell them it's gone now and we want to go home, but they tell us to wait.

George and Nathan sleep in the chair. I am too cold and happy to sleep. I am okay. Whatever it was has stopped.

My own doctor walks in. He looks irritated. Why is he here in the middle of the night?

"I'm sorry they woke you up. I'm fine now."

He nods. "You are pregnant."

I look over at George. He is awake and hears. The questions are coming too fast to say them. My doctor answers the first one.

"Your uterus was tipping, and that can cause cramps. The pelvic exam most likely repositioned it."

"But they X-rayed me."

"I know."

"What did that do to the baby?"

His mouth tightens. "I'll let the intern who ordered it explain." He abruptly leaves the room.

George lays Nathan on the chair and covers him with his jacket. He takes my hand in both of his and kisses it.

My doctor returns and stands with crossed arms behind the intern. For one second, I feel sorry for the intern. He glances around the room, clears his throat, and says, "There's a chance the baby may be affected by the X-ray." He stammers the possibilities: retardation, cancer, miscarriage, stillbirth. "Of course, there's no way we can tell now. There's just as much chance the baby is fine." He looks at me, then at the ceiling. "I can't give you any advice here. But if you want an abortion, I'll make the arrangements."

I want to yell. Make him understand what he did. I won't end the pregnancy on chance. But I will wake up every morning and pretend there is no baby, so if this baby dies, I won't care. And when my body reminds me there is someone else in it, I will imagine a little girl because we already have her name. And then remember my first girl and why I don't count on miracles.

I stare at him and pour my thoughts into that glare until he cannot take it. He mumbles "Sorry . . ." and leaves.

I go home with instructions to rest. George cooks and does the laundry. I heat leftovers and fold clothes. Nathan plays on the floor next to the couch. We watch Big Bird, Grover, and Cookie Monster. He naps with me, and we ignore my belly.

Six months later, I am in the hospital hooked up to intravenous medication that makes my heart race and my body sweat. The doctor says it will keep me from going into labor. I ask, "What is it doing to the baby?"

He tells me not to worry. This is keeping the baby safe.

I want to see my boy. They say he can't visit, and I say I will check myself out unless he can. George brings him one afternoon. George holds him, but Nathan won't talk to me. He looks at the beeping machine attached to my belly and the tubes hooked up to my arms and says, "I wanna go home."

George calls me that night to tell me what Nathan said in the car on the way home. "Mommy came back."

The contractions stop, and they send me home with medication and stronger warnings to rest. "Your only activity is going to the bathroom." My mother comes for a week to cook meals. She doubles recipes and freezes them. My father comes to get her because he's run out of the meals she cooked for him.

Nathan still plays on the floor next to me and asks me to read him books. But when George comes home, he runs to him and stays by his side until bedtime.

Friends tell me they are praying for me. I try, but I don't know what to pray for. Maybe this baby isn't supposed to be here. The early exit attempts were thwarted. Maybe the prayers are prolonging the stay.

I have a doctor's appointment, and George comes with me. We bring along a friend to stay with Nathan in the waiting room.

On the way, I feel extra kicks and stretches. I can't get comfortable, and George asks what's wrong. I hold back tears, but my voice trembles. "You don't want to know."

The doctor confirms my suspicion. "You're in labor again . . . but you're further along, and the baby is viable."

When this happened with Nathan, I was a little worried and mostly excited. Now I feel nothing.

We get to the hospital. I hug Nathan goodbye before sitting in the wheelchair, wait for George to sign admittance papers, and shrug when the nurse asks how I am. We get to pre-op, and I point out the veins that work best.

The ceiling of the operating room looks familiar. Last time, I didn't count the tiles. I can see ten. The sheet suspended above my chest hides the rest. George is in position, holding my fingers. His eyes smile like they did last time. My doctor's head peeks around the sheet. "You doing okay? I'm ready to start."

I am ready to get this over with. I nod and close my eyes. I can't look at George this time. I feel the tugs and the pulls. Hear the splashes and then the cry. It's loud, and my heart jumps. "It's a girl!" George kisses my fingertips and disappears.

My girl is four pounds, thirteen ounces. She is here six weeks too soon, but she cries, poops, pees, and breathes. George holds her in one hand.

We give her the Arabic name "Bahiyyih." She's named after the daughter of Bahá'u'lláh, the founder of our Faith. I am reading a biography about her, and she is described as being small but powerful. That is what the nurse says when she wheels in her bassinet to my hospital room. She will be able to stay with me because as tiny as she is, she is strong.

Her lungs are fully developed. She nurses on the first try and sucks so hard it hurts.

A Persian friend says her name means "Light upon Light." Her middle name is Dawn, and that is the name we call her because it's easier for people to pronounce, especially the grandparents.

In a family of late sleepers, this girl wakes and giggles with the sunrise. George says we should have named her "Noon."

• Ninety-Nine •

When George comes home, Nathan comes running and jumps into his arms. George's worried face relaxes enough to play with Nathan and snuggle Dawn. But after dinner, and one more hour of play, and kid baths, and bedtime stories, and chanting prayers, his worry-face returns.

George rarely talks about his job and the child abuse cases, but what he does share is heartbreaking. The levels of perversity are unimaginable. I wonder how this affects him. He assures me he's fine and does his John Wayne impression: "Don't you fret, little missy. You must have forgotten I'm a cowboy."

The hours have been longer than usual. George says it's the paperwork. The agency gets money from the state, and there's a multitude of forms and reports required for documentation. His supervisor wants him to be more efficient and spend less time with the clients.

That isn't his style.

George spent all weekend at the office doing reports he turned in this morning. They were a week late.

He calls after meeting with his supervisor. He received an official warning about the paperwork and will be fired if it is ever late again.

I tell him, "Quit."

"I can't. It's irresponsible."

"If they can't appreciate a case worker who cares as much as you do about people, they don't deserve to have you. You'll be working even longer hours to get it done on time and spend even more time away from your kids. We miss you. Quit. You'll find something else."

"I need to find another job first."

"You won't have time to look for one. Quit. It will work out."

For a long moment, George is silent, then he says, "Thank you, Sharon. I love you," and gets off the phone to turn in his resignation.

I didn't plan to say that. It rushed out before I could think, and now I'm scared. I'm still recuperating from the Caesarian, and I can't touch my toes. It's going to be another month or two before I'll be back performing mime. At best, I get a couple gigs a week. It won't support us all.

George searches the want ads every day, talks to colleagues, and becomes a regular at the unemployment office. He signs up to work for a temp agency and gets short-term manual labor jobs.

I dread telling my parents, but since they visit every three weeks, there is no hiding it. I explain and pretend I am not worried. They pretend too.

After a few months, my father asks, "If George could do what he really wanted, what would it be?"

"We've talked about it . . . he'd love to do theater . . . but it's unrealistic."

George has been in a few productions at a regional theater. The director wants him to join the company, but the hours are long and irregular. He can't work another job to make up for the low pay. I have a few mime shows, but nothing steady. And we don't want to put the kids in day care.

Dad has a proposal. If George can get a job with the theater, he will supplement our income. "Do you think George will accept my offer?"

My father is smiling and serious. Mother is quiet but smiling too. They must have had this conversation in the car on the way up.

"I have no idea what he would say."

Dad goes to talk with him.

George later tells me my father countered his initial refusal with, "At least once in your life, you should work at something you really want to do. I've had that privilege. So should you."

George becomes a company actor with New American Theater, and the man I fell in love with is back. For the next two years, Mom writes a newsy letter every month and sends it with a check taped to the back.

I keep the running total in a notebook, and when George decides to leave the theater for a full-time social service job, I hand my father our first repayment check. He hands it back. "It was a gift, not a loan." I tell him we want to pay them back. "Mom and I wanted to do this . . . one day you may do the same thing for your children."

• One Hundred •

My mother brags about the grandkids to my uncle and aunt. She plays the recordings of the kids telling stories. They are stories with beginnings, middles, and ends. For a four- and two-year-old, they are good. Aunt Catherine was a teacher and is impressed, but Uncle Mack says nothing.

The kids and I had gone down on the train to visit my parents for a week, and they are driving us home. Mom wants to stop in to visit my uncle and aunt. She thinks they will melt once they see how smart and cute the kids are.

I walk into the house, and my uncle stares with his one good eye. He doesn't get up to hug me, but that was never his way. He always grinned and teased me about something, but this time, he ignores me and the kids. I take them into the living room while my parents visit.

My cousin, Dorothy, is there, visiting with her three girls, and her kids think my kids are adorable. One of the girls asks how they got tans. My cousin blushes, and I laugh, remembering when I asked that question about my neighbor's baby. "They were born this way. Their daddy has dark skin."

When it is time to go, my uncle doesn't say goodbye or promise a next time.

There will never be a next time.

My parents visit us every three weeks and stop at the farm on their way back. My mother reports the latest developmental milestone, plays the recordings, and shows the pictures.

She says, "They talk about their grandkids, so I'm talking about mine."

I can say it's their loss. But it's mine too. I love my uncle and aunt and cousins. The farm was a magical place to me. I want my children to know that magic.

But I won't let them be around people who wish they had never been born.

• One Hundred & One •

It's dinnertime, and I can't find George. He was working on the lawn, but the car is gone. He never leaves without saying goodbye.

I work through possible explanations . . . he ran out of gas for the lawn mower, he has temporary amnesia, alien abduction.

I do not imagine what really happened.

George was outside in the front yard. A White boy, around ten years old, rode by on his bicycle and yelled, "Hey, nigger!!!"

George got in the car to chase him down. When he caught up to him, the boy jumped off his bike and ran up to a house, screaming to be let in. George got up to the door just as woman opened it. The boy begged the woman to let him in, but George said, "I need to speak with this boy."

The woman nodded and stayed by the door.

George told the boy he was lucky. "I am a nice man, but you didn't know that when you called me a nigger. Say that to someone else, and you may not be so lucky."

The woman told the boy this man was right, he was lucky, and he best not bother this nice man again.

As George tells the story, I think he is lucky too.

Someone could have seen a Black man chasing a White boy and decided George was dangerous. It could have been the police coming to my door and taking me to the station for questions. Or to the morgue to identify his body.

Unless the boy confessed to what he did, I'd never know what had happened.

A few months later, I do a mime performance at the neighborhood school, and after the show, a boy comes up to me and says, "I seen you in the neighborhood." He shifts his weight from side to side. "You were doing something weird in your living room. I guess you were doing this mime thing."

"Did you think I was crazy?"

He shrugs. "A little."

"Do you ride a blue bike?"

He looks down at his feet. Before he can answer, his friends come up and one of them says, "Danny says he knows you."

Danny's face turns bright red.

I nod. "We live on the same block."

His friends think that's cool. They ask how to do the wall, and I give a mini-lesson until the teacher says they need to get back to class.

Danny offers to carry my boom box to my car, and the teacher gives permission. We walk without talking. He can't say the words I know he wants to say.

I could help him. I could tell him I know what he called my husband. And can see he's sorry now.

But I'm not as nice as George.

• One Hundred & Two •

George comes into the house and doesn't greet me or call out to the kids. I ask what's wrong, and he shakes his head. He doesn't want me to hug him. He doesn't want to talk.

"Honey, please tell me what happened."

George was doing errands. The car has been making an odd noise, so he stopped at a garage. The mechanic had other customers, all White. George waited and heard him speak with them. When it was George's turn, the mechanic spoke slower, using simpler words. This is not the first time a White person has assumed him ignorant.

George spoke to him as he always speaks, in a voice that has been favorably compared to James Earl Jones in theatrical reviews.

The mechanic looked at George for a long minute, then spoke even slower, as if he were a child.

"What did you do?"

"I left."

Tears stream down his face, and I don't know what to say. This is bad, but not as bad as I expected. The mechanic didn't use the "n" word or refuse him service. George didn't get into an altercation that could have landed him in jail. The mechanic's prejudice lost him a customer and money.

I wipe George's tears, hold his hand, and wait. There is something about this I don't understand.

George says he is tired of it. "You never know what you are going to get with a White person."

He usually has his guard up, especially around strangers. "Today, I forgot."

I didn't know he did that. I wonder if being married to me has made him more trusting.

He shakes his head and laughs. "Don't look so sad. I'll be all right."

I pull back tears. If I break down over this, he'll never tell me anything again. I smile. "Of course. I forgot you're a cowboy."

• One Hundred & Three •

I'm sick of being a White person.

Between what Whites did to Blacks and Native Americans, I want to apologize every day to somebody.

I don't blame Blacks for mistrusting me. I'm grateful when I'm accepted, but I'm mindful. I monitor what I say and how I say it. I don't use the "n" word ever, even if they do. I am a mimic. I easily pick up people's dialect, mannerisms, and common-use words. But I've made myself not do that with Black people. I've seen the looks when White people try to sound Black. And I've heard the behind-the-back comments. No matter how "cool" a White person thinks she is by doing that, it isn't appreciated.

After reading *Bury My Heart at Wounded Knee* by Dee Brown and *The Autobiography of Frederick Douglass*, I tell George I hate White people and give a multitude of reasons.

He acknowledges all that is true and asks one question. "Why do you only focus on the negative? White people also abolished slavery and passed civil rights laws. If there weren't any good White people, we couldn't be together."

He has a point, but so do I. "I don't like being the symbol of oppression."

George kisses my forehead and smirks. "It's a tough job, but you can do it."

• One Hundred & Four •

One morning, Nathan is still in bed, but awake, looking up at the ceiling and smiling. He doesn't hear me come into his room. He doesn't see me kneel next to him. I hesitate, but have to ask. "Nathan, what are you thinking about?"

"Mommy, isn't it wonderful that numbers never end?"

When George was putting him to bed last night, Nathan asked him what the biggest number was and George told him about infinity.

Nathan's been making up math problems ever since he knew there were numbers. "There's three people in the house. When Daddy comes home, there'll be four." For his fifth birthday, we give him an educational video game with math equations in addition, subtraction, multiplication, and division. I show him how to do the addition and subtraction. An equation appears on the screen, and you type in the answer. If it's right, the numbers flash and bells ring. If it's wrong, a buzzer sounds and the equation appears again. You get three chances to get it right, then it shows the correct answer.

This becomes Nathan's favorite game. Bells are ringing every few seconds. There is a two-person mode to race for the answer. He challenges me and wins most rounds.

"Mommy, what's multiplication and division?"

"Honey, that's something for when you're older."

A few days later, I hear a shout and Nathan runs into the kitchen.

"I know what multiplication is!!!" He dances in a circle around me. "It's fast addition!"

I have to pause and think about that before I realize he is right and join his celebration dance.

Nathan figured it out by playing with the multiplication equations, putting in a number three times until it gave the answer. When he saw the answers, somehow he understood. I don't know how his mind made that leap. My mind doesn't do that.

Nathan goes to kindergarten this year, and I'm afraid it will squash his creative, curious mind. I'm afraid White teachers will make racist assumptions and not recognize his brilliance. I'm not being paranoid, I've witnessed this. When I do mime performances for schools, I eat in the teachers' lounge. I overhear them complain about how dumb their students are. If the student is Black, the comments are more vicious. I did a performance at our neighborhood school in the spring, but it's only two blocks from my house, so I went home for lunch. I wish I had eaten in the teachers' lounge.

A month before school starts, I receive an invitation from the kindergarten teacher to come to an orientation meeting for parents. They underline PARENTS ONLY to make it clear. George stays home with the kids while I go.

I walk into the school and feel my chest tighten so hard it's difficult to breathe. I tell myself to calm down. Don't overreact. Nathan may love it here.

The kindergarten room is the first one on the left. A woman with dark blond hair, who looks to be about the same age as me, stands at the door. She glances at her clipboard and back at me. "Mrs. Davis? You are the last to arrive." She looks at her watch and frowns.

I see by the wall clock I'm two minutes late.

Some parents stand together talking in hushed whispers. A few sit in the miniature seats— most are standing and waiting. Everyone is White, but I am too. It doesn't mean Nathan will be the only Black child, but it's likely.

The room has that fresh-paint smell. The walls are all white and blank with the exception of an alphabet poster. There are four rectangular work tables, an oval rug, and a child-height coat rack with names taped above. I find Nathan's. It's written on blue paper for the afternoon class. Around the room's perimeter are learning centers: "Construction" is equipped with a bin of wood blocks; "Art" has paper and crayons, "Reading" has a display of books, including one (only one) with a Black child on the cover, *The Snowy Day* by Ezra Keats; "Games" has checkers, Go Fish, and Candy Land; and "Drama" has a fireman's helmet, police hat, nurse cap, and a play kitchen.

We had learning centers at New Day, the school Dick and Ann ran in Danville. Kids were free to choose. The only restriction was the number of children each accommodated. I was in charge of the drama and movement center. I observed what sparked the kid's interest and added supplies as needed: masks, fairy wings, drums to accompany dances.

It's good they have centers, but they need more supplies. I'll offer to donate multicultural books and costumes, make play dough with the kids for the art area, and give one of our sets of Mancala, an African stone game for the Game center. Maybe, if I sense the teacher is open to it, I'll suggest adding a "Science" center. It was the most popular one at New Day.

The teacher raises her voice to get our attention. It is loud and shrill. "Find a seat so we can get started. . . . We're running a bit later than I planned." I feel her eyes on me, but I don't look at her. I find an unclaimed seat in the back of the room.

The teacher prints her name on the board: Mrs. Moloughney. "Your child's first lesson will be how to say my name." A few laugh, but she teaches us and then calls on us randomly to say it. Most oblige, but one woman says, "I'm bad at names. I'll pass." The teacher pauses for a moment, then says, "When your child comes home and talks about the teacher, I want you to be able to say my name." She pronounces it again slowly. "Mo-lock-ney." The woman's face is bright red, but she repeats the name and the teacher smiles. My stomach turns, and my head feels dizzy.

For the next hour, Mrs. Moloughney gives a presentation on the kindergarten experience our children will have. They will learn how to follow directions, and obey the rules, and do their work without wasting time. By the end of the year, they will count objects up to ten. "You may think your child knows numbers, but let me assure you they have only copied you. They don't understand what numbers represent." Our child will able to write the letters of the alphabet, upper and lowercase. Every day begins with a pencil and paper worksheet to practice letters, which must be completed before they go to an assigned center.

She asks if we have questions. I have one. "What happens if they can't finish the worksheet?"

She frowns. "Even the laziest children will get finished because they want to get to the centers."

I imagine my boy, sitting at this little table, trying to form the letters with tears rolling down his cheeks.

I'm not being paranoid about this either. I'm the one who made him cry.

I wanted Nathan to be able to print his name before he went to school. I thought if he could already do that, his teacher would know this was a smart boy. I bought primary lined paper and wrote his name at the top. Then I wrote it below using dots for him to connect them. Nathan was excited to do it, but soon got frustrated. His lines were shaky. They were too large and went beyond the dots. After more than an hour of trying, he tore up the paper and cried. I held him and told him not to worry about it, but I worried. A few days later, I heard a report on NPR. A recent study found that many children, especially boys, do not develop the muscles in their hands needed for small motor activity until around age seven. Expecting them to write before they are developmentally ready sets them up for failure. I told Nathan what I had learned and apologized for asking him to do something his hands weren't ready for. He said, "That's okay, Mommy. You didn't know."

Mrs. Moloughney is going to insist he complete his worksheet. When it takes him too long, she will think he's lazy. If she gets angry, Nathan will not talk with her. That's how he deals with angry people. And maybe, because I've seen it happen, especially with Black boys, she will label him slow, uncooperative, lazy and write it on his school record.

Even worse than that is Nathan may think he isn't smart.

"We can't send him to that school—it's going to crush his spirit." I tell George I will homeschool Nathan until we can figure something out. He agrees to trust me on this.

Our friend Ann has another suggestion. She stops by after going to an open house at Spectrum Progressive School. "It's a lot like New Day. They may still have openings."

I know about this school. When Nathan was a baby, there was a brochure advertising it at the end of the grocery store checkout line. On the front was a photograph of a girl, arms outstretched making a shadow, and a quote from child development guru Jean Piaget: "The principal goal of education in the schools should be creating men and women who are capable of doing new things, not simply repeating what other generations have done." Inside the pamphlet were pictures of children painting and a quote from Albert Einstein: "Imagination is more important than knowledge. Knowledge is limited. Imagination encircles the world." I was disappointed it was private, which meant there was tuition we couldn't pay. A thought had floated through my head: *You can work there as an artist, and bring Nathan.*

I search through my desk, find the brochure, and call. The next day, Nathan, Dawn, and I sit in the kindergarten room watching children construct towers with blocks, boxes, and recycled cardboard tubes;

paint pictures on easels with acrylic paints; curl up in an old footed bathtub and read books; dress up in what looks to be old bridesmaid dresses and dance to Bob Marley's *Lively Up Yourself.* Older children arrive to take them to rehearse for a play their classes are doing together. The teacher welcomes us to watch the rehearsal—or—she kneels down to be eye-level with the kids: "Or if you like, you stay here and play." They grin and run to the construction area. She laughs and says, "Your kids are beautiful. Stay as long as you like." They build a tower of boxes and blocks as tall as themselves, knock it down, and then build it even taller using wood crates to stand on. I look through books. *The Snowy Day* is here, but there are more books by Ezra Keats: *Peter's Chair, Whistle for Wille, Pet Show!*—all with brown children on the cover.

This is a predominantly White school, like our neighborhood school, but this one feels right.

George and I look over our budget. His salary covers our expenses. My mime work allows extras. If we give up cable TV, the once-a-month movie outing, and our occasional date nights, we can afford the afternoon kindergarten. Maybe I can increase my mime work enough to pay for next year's full tuition. The year after that, Dawn turns five. I may need to find another job.

Nathan loves this school. He watches the clock all morning and announces when I should be making lunch so we can go. One of his favorite activities is Alphabet Show and Tell. Each week, they focus on a different letter and you can sign up to share something that starts with that letter. "A" is the first week, and several kids bring apples, a few bring McDonald's apple pies, and one kid brings homemade apple muffins for everyone. Nathan brings the apple cores he's been saving from lunch all week. For "E" week, he brings a paper bag with nothing in it. He makes the kids and teacher guess what is in the bag until they give up. He opens up the bag to show them. "It's EMPTY."

For "M" week, Nathan wants to share me: Mommy is a MIME. He wants me to do a show. I ask his teacher if it's okay, and she's delighted.

"We've all hoped you'd do a show for us, but didn't want to impose."
She asks if it's okay to invite more classes.

That day, the other kindergarten class and preschool classes crowd
into the room. Children from the morning kindergarten class and their
parents come too. "Hope you don't mind—" Nathan's teacher smiles.
"We sent a note home."

I begin with my makeup case in the middle of the "stage" and
pretend it isn't mine, but I'm curious. I open it, shut it, open it again,
and finally take out the makeup and put it on. I do that for kid shows
to ease the terror small children often have for clowns. Mimes are not
clowns, but traumatized children do not know that or care. For this
show, I do a piece about a smile that runs away, a piece with Nathan,
who mirrors my movements to Barry Manilow's "I Am Your Child"
(which makes adults cry), and finish with "The Kite," in which I
attempt to fly an imaginary kite but there isn't enough wind. I get a few
kids to help by huffing and puffing—but in the end, I need everyone.

Kids crowd around me afterwards to ask questions, teachers
and parents thank me, and the school director calls me that night. "I
heard from teachers and parents how wonderful the performance was
and how good you were with the kids. Could you come in to see me
tomorrow?"

They cannot pay me what they know I am worth, but they offer
a part-time position as an artist-in-residence in exchange for full-time
tuition for both Nathan and Dawn and an additional stipend. My work
is to engage children in learning through mime and drama. The stipend
is enough for cable TV, a monthly movie, and date night.

My bonus is lunchtime in the teachers' lounge, protecting children's
spirits as needed.

• One Hundred & Five •

Every religion has its own calendar. The Bahá'í calendar has nineteen months with nineteen days in each month. That leaves four extra days in the year, which are devoted to charity, hospitality, and gift-giving, and they fall at the end of the Gregorian calendar's February. It's perfect timing. There are after-Christmas sales, parking is easy, and out-of-stock toys are back on the shelves.

Dawn is three when the Cabbage Patch doll mania hits. There are news accounts of Christmas shopping mamas pulling hair, ripping pantyhose, and bribing stock boys to buy a doll that resembles a hairless gopher.

Our children's only Christmas presents come from my parents, and they will never buy a Cabbage Patch doll. They say it builds character to not get what everyone else has, and it's why I never had a Barbie. I had Jan & Jill dolls with bendable joints, hips, and modest busts. They were dressed in leotards and came with an exercise manual.

George and I toss around ideas for the kids and set the budget. I do the shopping while he stays with them. With our income, it's rare to buy anything besides food and cleaning supplies. I stroll through toy aisles and estimate survival rates.

I come across three shelves of Cabbage Patch dolls. There is a bizarre cuteness embedded in their scrunched-up faces. They have names and adoption papers. I hear myself say, "Awwww," and check the price tag. At $31.99, this doll would be my daughter's only present, besides the underwear I already bought. And there is no reasonable explanation to give George. The orphan appeal wouldn't sway him.

A store clerk comes up and frowns. "I'm sorry. All we have are these Black ones. Do you want to go on our wait-list?"

I make my face smile, turn to the clerk, and say, "Thank you, but I am just trying to decide which one. *These are all so cute.*"

I tell George that I adopted "Cecelia Petunia" into our family as a stand against racism, not as a submission to subliminal advertising or because I have succumbed to herd mentality.

He laughs. "Whatever you want to tell yourself, dear."

• One Hundred & Six •

I have five students in my mime class. They are all boys, ages six to eight, and they prove my theory that young children are not mature enough to learn mime.

One of the mothers is a friend, and she made the suggestion to teach the boys, but mime technique requires repetitive practice to train the muscles to move with precision to create recognizable illusions. These kids want to skip the practice and act out skits. They move in distorted exaggeration and make indistinguishable gestures I cannot interpret. They tell me to guess what they are doing and are delighted when I can't.

The class is held at the Rockford Public Library. I rent the auditorium, a big room with a small stage. It's on the lower level, and there is a street entrance and restrooms. When the rooms are rented, the entrance door is unlocked. Homeless people watch for these opportunities to take a shower in the sink.

We finish the warm-ups and are playing Position Zero. "Stand straight and tall, stare at a spot on the wall, and do not move for one full minute. Ignore me." I weave in and out, make faces, walk like a robot, and mime-laugh at them. It's my passive-aggressive game, and how I release my irritation at teaching this class.

Two young men wander in from the street. I catch a glimpse of them as I stick out my tongue at the boy frozen in front. I feel the men watching me. One of them is tall, and he walks away when I look at them. The shorter one stands in the doorway and says something I don't understand.

I smile. I want him to know that I am not like most White people who are afraid of Black men, even though my stomach is tightening up. "I'm sorry, I didn't hear you. Is there something I can help you with?"

He mumbles, then glances around the room and back into the hallway before looking at me again.

I turn away from my students and come closer. "I'm sorry. I still didn't hear what you said."

"Can I use the bathroom?"

"Yes, go ahead."

He stares and doesn't move.

I walk up to him, step into the doorway, and point. "It's there—behind you . . ." He grabs my neck and forces me to the floor. I scream. "Please don't!"

He hits the back of my head, but not hard. Enough to keep me down. I see the feet of the tall man run into the room and out again. The man hits me once more and takes off. I get up and look at the table where my purse was. It's gone.

I look at the boys. They are where I left them, in Position Zero, but they are all shaking and one is crying.

There are many things I hate about this. I hate that the boys saw. I tell them I was surprised and scared, not hurt. They nod, but stare at my throbbing neck. I hate that I was so dumb to leave my purse by the door. I hate that I ignored my instinct and walked up to a stranger, trying to prove to myself that I am not prejudiced. I hate that the librarian who called the police and listened as I gave descriptions of the young men is startled when George comes to pick me up—and grabs my arm to pull me away from him. It takes her a few seconds to understand my words. "This is my husband."

The policeman takes my statement and says he'll be in touch. Parents give hugs. There is one more class in the session, but they all say to forget it.

When we get to the car, George asks me what happened. I tell him without describing the men. There is a space of silence before he asks what they looked like.

"One was very tall, the other was almost as short as me—They were both Black." I don't look at him when I say this, and he doesn't respond.

We pick up our kids from a friend's house, and I wait in the car. I'm not ready to talk to anyone. I just want to be home.

We pull up to the house, and I panic. My purse had thirty cents, car keys, and my driver's license with this address. George says they won't come here, but he goes into the house first, and after a few seconds, signals it's okay. But he was too quick. He didn't check the back part of the house we don't use except for storage because it has no heat. They could be there waiting behind the unpacked boxes. So I ask him to check again.

I don't sleep that night. When I close my eyes, I feel hands squeeze my neck.

The next morning, I tell George we need to change the locks. This is an expense not in the budget, and it means the mime class cost us money. George says he doesn't think it's necessary, but he does it.

The next day, there is another downtown mugging. The suspect descriptions sound like the same men. The victim is an old White man, and they beat him. He is alive, but in critical condition.

Two detectives come to see me with news about my purse. It was found in a church dumpster a few blocks from the library. Everything is in it except the thirty cents. Fingerprints on the purse match a man who is in custody for the beating of the old man. They ask if I will look at a few photos.

There are pages and pages of young African American men, and I find two who might be the ones. They nod, and one says, "You did good." They have enough evidence for the short one, but they need more for the tall one. More than the fingerprints on my purse. They want me to testify at the trial.

I agree and explain why I am a good witness. "My husband is Black, so I'm not like some Whites who think all Black people look alike. And I am a mime, so I observe body language. The tall man walks with his neck hunched forward. Probably because he's around short people like his partner."

I hear the detectives laugh as they walk to the car.

Months later, the detective calls. A court date is scheduled for the tall one. He wants me to go to the courtroom and look at the suspect. If I can identify him, I'll be called as a witness. But if I have any doubts, I am to get up and leave. "If you do testify, only answer the questions asked." He clears his throat and adds, "So unless his attorney asks, don't talk about your husband. It isn't relevant to the case."

I am alone in the courtroom until people arrive who I assume are the suspect's grandmother, mother, sister, and younger brother. The women pray and wipe their eyes. The sister holds the grandmother's hand, and the brother sits stone-faced and quiet.

The suspect walks in, neck forward, back hunched over, appearing shorter than he is. He searches the room, sees his family, and nods. I see his lower lip tremble. He doesn't look at me.

My first thought is "It's him." But he looks different in an orange jumpsuit and chains. He is younger and softer than I remember. I start playing "What If."

What if he found the purse in the dumpster and threw it back? I never saw his hands. Maybe the tall one wore gloves. Maybe he set this kid up because this kid is tall and has the same skin color. Or does he? Maybe it's the fluorescent lights, but he's darker than I remember.

I cannot look at this child-man and say, "Yes, without any doubt, he is the one." If the lawyer is good, he'll sense my conflict. If the lawyer doesn't catch it, I will want to make sure he does.

I do what the detective told me to do if I had any doubts. I slip away.

The detective calls a week later. "I have good news for you."

The young man was convicted and got seventy-five years, just like his partner. "They were lucky the old man survived, or it would have been life without parole."

With good behavior, sincere regrets, and a compassionate parole board, they could be released when they are fifty years old.

The detective is happy that I can sleep easy now that they are gone.

That night in a dream, I see thousands of soulless eyes stare at me. Hands reach for my neck, then melt. The tall one breaks through the floor. His mouth opens, and keys, coins, and teeth fall out. Bloody lips smile. The sound of women crying floats up and surrounds me.

I wake up crying too.

• One Hundred & Seven •

"Why do all the Black people live in Chicago and all the White people live in Rockford?"

Nathan corrects himself before I do. "Everyone is White here except Daddy and me and Dawn."

It isn't true. But it's what he knows.

I could explain that his relatives don't live in Chicago. They moved from Chicago to Maywood, the first suburb that allowed Blacks. Now almost all the residents are Black, but there's an older White Baháʼí who lives a few blocks away from his grandparent's. We've visited her, but Nathan was a baby and doesn't remember.

And I could tell him there are Black people in Rockford, but we don't live in Rockford. We live in a suburb too.

We bought this house because it was close to our friends and cheap enough that we could qualify for the loan. I saw tricycles, flower beds, and clotheslines in the yards. That's what made it feel okay . . . not that the people were White. That's what I told myself. I hope it's true.

I could tell him that, but it's too much for a seven-year-old, and none of that matters. What matters is Nathan is aware of the imbalance.

I tell George we need to move.

He sighs and asks why, and I tell him what Nathan said. And other reasons. This house was perfect when we got it, but now it suffocates. We have two kids, two cats, and a dog. The ceilings are so low I can touch them, and I'm only five feet, two inches tall. The family room where I exercise and practice mime has a concrete floor. That's not good for my body. My knees hurt.

"I can't breathe here anymore."

George says fine, but this will be my project. "You find the house you want and let me know."

After school, I bring snacks for the kids and drive with them around Rockford. I go to the one neighborhood I've heard is diverse. Ann and Dick moved there last year, but the houses cost too much.

They know a White couple with adopted biracial children whose house is for sale. They are moving to the country because the wife wants horses and the husband teaches at a rural community college. They love the house and want it to go to a family who will love it too.

The house is located in a predominately Black neighborhood. It's three stories tall, white with red trim. It reminds me of the house I grew up in. The fenced-in backyard has a wooden playset and enough running room for the dog. The front porch has a swing. My kids climb on it before I can tell them no, but the woman says it's fine. We watch them swing and talk about how cute they are. Hers are teenagers now. She sighs. "I miss this age."

Nathan and Dawn beg to stay outside on the swing. I am about to say yes, but the woman says, "It's best you come inside."

The wood floors are polished, and the ceilings are high with ornate trim. The fireplace in the living room has bookcases on either side. My kids want a house with stairs, and this one has one hundred and fifty-five. Nathan counted. The top floor is the attic room of their teen son. There is a poster of Gandalf, my son's favorite character in *The Hobbit* by J.R.R. Tolkien. Nathan maintains his natural quiet, but smiles. If we buy this house, I'll ask if the poster can stay. Or where I can buy a replacement.

The woman offers a cup of tea, and her daughter offers to take my kids outside to play. I nod, and the woman says to stay in the backyard. I see the stern look she gives her daughter, and the annoyed look the daughter gives back. She exits with the kids and lets the back door slam.

"She's grounded, and I don't want her to use this as an excuse to sneak off."

I laugh and say, "So that's why you want to move."

She doesn't laugh. "Our kids were the only Black children in our old neighborhood, so we decided to move here for them. We fell in love with this house, and our neighbors are good people. They have lived here for years, but . . ."

I like this woman. I like the way she looks at my children, and the pictures on the walls, and the handmade ceramic coffee cups. She is a children's book author and has a study with stacks of papers, a typewriter, and a cat climber. She's heard about me from our friend and is intrigued that I'm a mime.

She's watched me love her house.

And now she's going to tell me why we shouldn't move here.

Most of the people who cared about the neighborhood are gone. They gave up when drug dealers moved in and the police did nothing. Children can't play at the park down the street because of the needles and broken glass. Clean it up one day, and the next day there's more. A turf war seems to be going on. You often wake up to gunshots in the middle of the night. Sometimes you hear what happened, but most times you don't.

Her son reads books and stays inside. But her thirteen-year-old daughter likes to be outside. She likes the way the boys look at her and call out to her. She has started sneaking out at night and won't tell them where she's been. Her daughter is angry they are moving into the country and ruining her life.

"I don't want to scare you—most of the people who live around here are fine. But I wouldn't feel right encouraging you to buy our house without telling you why we are moving."

On the ride home, the kids pick their rooms. Nathan wants the attic, and Dawn wants the daughter's purple room.

I say we aren't ready to buy that house. "I want to look at more houses."

I see the disappointed faces in the rear view mirror and resolve to go house shopping alone until I find the right one.

• One Hundred & Eight •

A river divides our city. West of the Rock River is the older section where Italians settled. Swedes lived on the east side. I don't know when it happened, but the Italian section became a mostly Black section. There are still a few Italians in the southwest quadrant, and there is Maria's—a restaurant cherished enough that White people risk going. President George H.W. Bush ate there. It's the only good thing White people say about the west side.

I look for houses on the west side. Houses in predominately Black neighborhoods are cheaper. The neighborhoods are disjointed. There are homes with fresh paint and flower beds next to houses with boarded windows and knee-high weeds.

I go to open houses in neighborhoods on the west side that are still White but border predominately Black ones. When I find a house I like, I tell the realtors I want my husband to see it. I go home to get George and the kids, but as soon as they see George the realtors say they forgot to tell me that someone already made a bid and are waiting for final approval, or the sellers might not be selling after all. The realtors take our phone number, but never call. A month later, the house is still on the market.

On the very far southwest side of the city, I find the house I want. It has hardwood floors, a formal living room, a dining room, and an upstairs with four bedrooms. There's a fireplace in the living room and another one in the master bedroom, and the attic is a large, open space that could be my studio.

The neighborhood is zoned for horses. People living three houses down have a stable. Across the street is a school, and beyond it, a forest preserve. The neighborhood is White, but it's close to a Black and Hispanic section. It will be integrated soon, and we could be the first. I call my realtor, and he sets up an appointment.

George likes it, but is concerned. The floors need to be stripped, the windows need caulking, the wallpaper is faded and torn, and the backyard has no fence for the kids and dog.

We would have to do the work ourselves because we don't have the money to hire it out. Neither of us is experienced or has time to do remodeling. That will be a nightmare. But I'm in love with this house and don't care about any of that.

Our realtor suggests we make the offer contingent upon an inspection. The sellers accept our offer, but the inspection uncovers an electrical problem that will cost $2,000. We ask for a price reduction, and the owners refuse and set aside our offer.

That night, George and I talk. He says there are other houses. That's logical, but I can't be logical. I know what color the walls should be. It's big enough to have both our families come for Thanksgiving, and we'll make a haunted house in the attic for Halloween. There will be sunset hikes at the forest preserve and marshmallow roasts in the fireplace. The kids will take apples to the neighbor's horses.

I see us happy here.

George gives in, and we tell our realtor we'll buy it as is. But the people won't sell it to us. Another couple made the same offer we did, and the sellers have accepted it. They will fix the electrical problem for them.

Our realtor says things like this happen without saying exactly what happened. "We'll find you something else."

I don't want another house. I stop house hunting and wait for my realtor to call and say the deal fell through and they will now sell it to us. But when he does call, it's about other listings. I ask if he's heard anything about the house I want, and he says he hasn't seen a closing notice yet.

One Sunday when George is playing with the kids, I drive by the house and see a family moving in. An all-White family.

I go to the end of the block, make a right and another right, then drive down a street I've never seen before. The yards are big, and the houses are old and beautiful. On the corner is a tall, brick house with a fenced-in backyard and a "For Sale" sign.

The next day, we walk through the front door into a foyer with arched doorways and polished woodwork. It was built by the father of the man who lives here. I grab George's arm and squeeze.

This is it. It's been waiting for us.

Other people have made offers but couldn't get the financing.

The yard has a section for the dog and another section for the children. It has the staircase the kids want and the fireplace I need. The doors are custom-made to fit curved archways. Beams in the kitchen ceiling hold hanging wicker baskets. The master bedroom on the second floor spans the width of the house and has a walk-in closet and a small sunroom.

George is happy because there is nothing we need to fix. I even like the color of the walls.

We make the offer, get the loan, sell our house, and move. It's all done within two months. And that Thanksgiving, both families come for dinner.

Our realtor says if this house were across the river, it would be more than twice the price.

This time racism works in our favor.

• One Hundred & Nine •

This is the first time I've lived in a Black neighborhood. I wish I was comfortable, but I'm not, and I don't tell George. I'm ashamed of feeling this way.

To be exact, the neighborhood is not all Black. An old Italian man and his wife and her twin sister live next door. After we move in, one of the women asks if our dog bites. I say no and walk closer to talk. She grunts, "Good," and turns away.

A Hispanic family lives a half block away. They ignore us when we pass by.

The rest of the neighbors are Black. They ignore us too.

I don't assume Black people accept interracial couples. My mother-in-law makes that clear. She tells me it makes her mad that people think it's just the White family and friends who disapprove. She gets grief from relatives and friends about George. "Our men go to college and think they're too good for a Black girl."

My college roommate and her friends complained about the lack of eligible Black men. Too many in prison. Too many going to White women.

When I'm out with George, I see Black women give the cold stare. Now I have Black women for neighbors, and none of them speak to me. If I were braver, I'd go to them and say hello.

I didn't do it in the White neighborhood either. Janet, the one and only friend I had there, made the first move.

I remember when I was brave like that. When I believed everyone would like me if they knew me.

I miss being that girl. I don't know where she went.

I invite Janet to come visit. She cancels twice and then calls one morning. "I will come today."

Janet doesn't like to drive in unfamiliar places, and she has never been on this side of town. She asks for directions and more details. How long should it take? What are the landmarks? Where are the gas stations? What will she see if she misses a turn?

"I'm leaving now, so if I'm not there in thirty minutes, come look for me." I laugh, and she says, "I'm serious."

Janet arrives flushed and sweaty. "Wow, that was some drive over here."

I don't want to hear what she's going to say, but I can't stop her.

"I've never seen such odd neighborhoods. There's broken-down houses next to nice ones. And so many men just standing around. Doesn't anyone work around here?" Her laugh is loud and shrill. I make my face neutral instead of irritated.

We've had these conversations before. If I pick at every unintentional insult, it won't be a pleasant visit.

I shrug. "People work all kinds of jobs . . . not just 9-5."

We have lunch, and then I give her a tour of the house.

"It is beautiful. Too bad it's in this neighborhood. Aren't you scared to live here?"

I admit what I've never told anyone.

A week after we moved in, George's mother called and asked him to take her on an emergency trip to see his grandmother in southern Illinois. No one else in the family could take her. When he told me, I felt a fear that made it hard to be rational. I didn't want to be here without him. I asked him not to go.

"My mother needs my help."

"So do I." But I couldn't explain why, so I told him to go ahead and hoped he wouldn't.

I watched him pack. He said goodbye to the kids, hugged me, and said he'd call. The kids stood at the window and waved, but I couldn't watch him leave.

That night, I put the kids to bed, took a bath, and cried while the water ran. I couldn't sleep. I sat up all night, watching movies and listening for sounds. All I heard was a cat fight, and a few cars drive by. The next night, I was so tired I fell asleep on the living room floor, and the kids pounced on me the next morning.

They wanted to go to the park down the street. Along the way, neighbors were out in their yards working in their gardens, painting fences, playing with kids. We smiled at each other and said good morning. One asked how I liked living here and remarked on how beautiful the kids are. Another offered help if I needed anything.

"After that, the fear left. I never told George about this. I'm ashamed of how crazy I acted."

Janet frowns. "If I were you, I'd get extra locks and a security system."

She never comes to my house again.

• One Hundred & Ten •

The Spectrum School staff Christmas party is always held at someone's house. The last few years it's been cozy—a little too cozy. The people hosting it had small, one-bedroom homes.

Planning for this year's party comes up during lunch. The chair of the committee asks, "Does anyone have a big house? One with at least two bathrooms?"

"I do!"

They turn to look at me, and the room quiets.

"Our house is plenty big."

I've shown pictures of the house with its large living and dining rooms, Italian plaster walls, and arched doorways. They've remarked on how lovely and spacious it is.

They all know where I live. Some grew up in that neighborhood when it was inhabited by Italians. I didn't ask if their families moved away when Black and Hispanic families moved in.

No one says anything. They know I don't celebrate Christmas, so I assure them the house will be decorated. "I can borrow some decorations from my mother. She has boxes of them she doesn't use."

One of the teachers says, "Maybe this year we should do something different . . . have it at a restaurant."

Others chime in that it sounds like a great idea. They start brainstorming possible restaurants.

The committee chair says, "Thank you for offering to host, Sharon. But this will make it easy for everyone."

And they all follow her lead and thank me for my willingness to hold the party. But really, this year a restaurant is a better choice.

On the drive home, I turn up the music and look at my neighborhood like it's a movie . . . I see a father walk his little boy from the bus. An old man sitting on his front porch grins and waves at them. A woman sweeps her sidewalk. The neighbor weeds her flower bed. They smile and talk. Two girls skip down the sidewalk, arm in arm, pigtails bouncing.

I see kids jump rope, play tag and baseball at the park. Young men hunch over the engine of a car. Men barbecue and laugh.

I love my neighborhood.

• One Hundred & Eleven •

My friend Lily wants a baby so bad it hurts. She and her husband can't afford any more fertility treatments.

An opportunity has presented itself. A friend-of-a-friend's niece, who lives across the country, is pregnant. She wants to find a family who will adopt the baby, and she has specific criteria. They have to live far away, be college-educated, love children, and if they are White, they cannot be prejudiced. The girl is White, and the father is Black.

I am excited for Lily. "I'll write a recommendation."

She closes her eyes and sighs. "Our parents don't want us to do it."

I think she must mean her husband's parents. Her parents adore my kids, especially her mother. She says they are brilliant and beautiful.

"Not your mom."

"Yes, my mother too."

I want to believe it is something other than race. Maybe it's concern about the private adoption. Or worry that the girl was drinking before she knew she was pregnant.

"They don't want a Black child in the family."

My friend is miserable. She wants to be a mother, and her husband wants to be a dad. This baby could be in their home in two months.

"What will happen if you go ahead and adopt? Don't you think they'll come around?"

She dismisses my questions and asks her own. "When you are out in public, how do people treat your kids?"

"They say they are cute, or they ignore us. No one has been mean to them, but sometimes they give me a disgusted look."

Lily is surprised. "Why would they do that?"

"Because it's obvious their father is Black."

She is quiet. "Lily, when you're out alone with the baby, people who don't know you may assume that your husband is Black."

She shakes her head. "I hadn't thought about that."

"And there will be Black people who think you shouldn't be raising a Black child." I attempt a joke. "My mother-in-law says my daughter's hair is proof I shouldn't be."

Lily doesn't laugh.

The conversation drifts from babies to work, books, and anything else.

The next week, I see Lily's mother in the grocery store. She is surprised at how much the kids have grown. She says she is dying to be a grandma.

She grins down at them. "Can you be my grandchildren? Would you like that?"

Nathan stares at her. Dawn grabs my leg and hides behind me. I say, "Their grandmothers will never give them up."

She laughs and calls over her shoulder, "Let me know if they ever change their minds."

I make myself smile instead of saying what I am screaming at her in my head.

Dawn loosens her grip on my leg and points to the ice cream. "Can we get some for Daddy?"

They both look adorably hopeful, and I break the budget and get Neapolitan, Rocky Road, and Mint Chocolate Chip.

• One Hundred & Twelve •

Last night, I didn't pack lunches, or get clothes in the dryer, or plan breakfast, so we are late for school again. The kids won't be in trouble because it's my fault and their teachers know it. They give me slack because I'm never late for my drama classes and they like what I do with their kids. We've dramatized a solar eclipse, created scenes from moments in history, and explored what happened after the spider frightened Miss Muffet away.

Nathan and Dawn sit in the back seat and tell knock-knock jokes. I listen to *Morning Edition* on National Public Radio. I haven't planned a lesson for the older kids, so I hope something may spark an idea.

There's a book review for a novel loosely based on Joseph Paul Franklin, a serial killer who was on a mission to preserve the White race. He targeted interracial couples to keep them from having babies. One was pregnant. This man killed eighteen people, and he was on his rampage soon after George and I were married. It could have been us he spotted at a carnival and followed home.

I remember the kids are in the car and snap off the radio.

Nathan asks, "What was that story about?" I glance at him in the rearview mirror and see his "worry look."

I wish we had that family meeting about race I suggested to George a few months ago. He said, "And why would we do that?"

I had said, "To prepare them."

I wanted a scheduled presentation with an outline of the points to cover. And I wanted George to do it. I had already failed at a "life-lesson talk."

When Nathan was six and Dawn was four, I read them *Where Did I Come From?* by Peter Mayle because I didn't want them to hear it on the playground from other kids and get grossed out. They laughed for five minutes, and then Nathan screamed, "Daddy pees in you!" Every time they see a pregnant woman, they giggle.

I want the race talk to go better. And I want George to do it.

He says to wait until they ask. "We don't know what they need to hear until we know their questions."

That made sense, but now I wish I had pushed harder for the presentation.

"So what did you hear, Nathan?"

Maybe he's asking about the story before this one. The story I can't remember right now.

"The one about some man killing interracial couples. Isn't that what you and Daddy are?"

Nathan is only eight years old. I didn't know he knew that term.

Dawn had not been paying attention, but now she is. She wants to know everything her brother knows. "What's interracial?"

Nathan tells her it's when Black and White people get married.

I add that it is not just Black and White. It can be Asian and White, Asian and Black, Indian and White . . . I list as many combinations I can think of to make a game of this. Maybe this game can last until we get to school, which is now minutes away.

But Nathan doesn't let things go. "What about the man who hates interracial couples so much he kills them."

Dawn doesn't believe him. "That's stupid. Why would anyone do that?"

I look in the mirror and see their eyes on me, waiting.

"The man who did this thought it was wrong for Black and White people to love each other. He has a sickness in his head."

I park the car, but they don't move. "What else do you want to know?"

Nathan asks, "Where is that man?"

"He's in prison. They caught him, and he can't hurt us or anyone else."

They nod, but stay in their seats. I smile at them through the rearview mirror and tell them to go on inside.

"I'll be coming soon."

Seat belts unbuckle and car doors open.

They do what they always do—race each other to the entrance, and Nathan wins. I hear his victory shout and Dawn's "No fair" response. They open both doors and disappear.

It looks as if nothing has changed. But I know it has.

• One Hundred & Thirteen •

On the drive home from school, Nathan reminds me the neighborhood ice cream stand closes tomorrow for the winter and won't reopen until May 1. "That's 181 days, or 4,344 hours, or 430 thousand . . ."

Dawn interrupts his minute calculations with, "Can we get ice cream tonight? Pretty please, Mommy?" She catches me in a smile and stops the begging. I see them in the rearview mirror make a silent cheer.

We sit on the front steps and watch cars drive by with radios blaring rap beats mostly, but every now and then a Latin tune. We eat the ice cream to the rhythms.

A boy rides by on his bike. He comes back around and says, "Hey, Mrs. Davis!"

I call back, "Hi, Demetrius!" He flashes a grin and speeds away.

My children are used to kids calling out my name and sometimes asking for an autograph. Nathan says I'm famous, but only in Rockford. I've performed my mime show in all of the public elementary schools and most of the private ones. But when these kid-fans recognize me, I don't know their names. Dawn asks how I know this boy.

"I've started to teach drama at his school . . . like I do at your school."

Nathan asks if it's the school up the street.

I answer, "Yes."

I expect him to ask why they don't go to that school, but he doesn't. He nods and licks the last drips off the cone.

Nathan may already know. Local news carries stories about the discrimination lawsuit against Rockford Public Schools (RPS 205), and George and I talk about it. The district settled to prevent the most damaging evidence from becoming public, but Dick and Ann are one of the plaintiffs, so we know what evidence was coming. Evidence that in order to make it look like schools were integrated, they placed the "Gifted" program (all White) in a predominately Black school, but kept the students separated. Each program had different start and end times, and different lunch hours, and recess. School assemblies were never whole school events. "Gifted" students had after-school music classes. Neighborhood students had sports. Parents of kids in the "Gifted" program were assured their children would never mix with the neighborhood.

The judge said RPS 205 turned discrimination into an art form. Now there is "remedy" money for predominantly Black schools to address the disparity. The principal of our neighborhood school heard about the work I am doing for the private school—creating lessons to enhance reading, science, and math through theater. I now work part-time at both schools, and it's easy because I use the same lesson plans. Teachers at both schools are surprised I don't have to make them easier for the public school kids.

My students at the public school have questions for me. "I saw you at the Dairyette. . . . Who were those kids?" And when I say they are my children, they have follow-ups. "What are their names? How old are they? Is their daddy Black?" And then the final question, the one I struggle to answer. "Why don't they come to our school?"

"Maybe someday I'll bring them to visit."

What I don't tell them is I need to keep my children safe. Safe from teachers who love them but don't expect them to be smart. And from other students who will taunt my son when he gets an A+ on his math test and tease my daughter because she loves to read chapter books. *"You acting White."*

Teachers know this happens. The ones who care lecture, take away recess, call parents, but they can't make it stop.

It happened to Demetrius. He loved drama and learned lines quick. Other kids teased him, "Oh, you're a White boy now."

I called them out on it. Told them when they hold each other back, they are letting the racists win. I thought maybe they understood. But after that, Demetrius stopped volunteering in class, stopped being curious, mouthed off to me, and laughed at my disappointment.

Today he spoke to me after he made sure no one else was around to see it.

• One Hundred & Fourteen •

It's getting late, but I don't tell the kids it's past bedtime. Not tonight.

I wish George could be here, but he's out of town. When I told him what I was going to do, he laughed—the laugh that makes him take off his glasses, wipe his eyes, and then bust out laughing again.

I wash dishes, read the paper, and keep an eye on the clock. At 9:45 p.m., I yell, "Nathan, Dawn! Time for bed!"

I hear them planning their plea.

Nathan states his case: "We are playing, not fighting. We aren't tired, and when Daddy is gone, you let us stay up late."

I frown. "It's already over an hour past bedtime."

Nathan nods to Dawn. She steps forward, looks up at me, and grins. "Pullleeaasssee, Mommy?" She scrunches her face and flutters her eyelashes.

I keep my face solemn, then yell, "MYSTERY TRIP!"

They squeal, attack me with hugs, and run to the drawer to get the blindfolds.

We form a three-person chain, and I lead them out the door, down the steps, and into the car.

There are giggles and whispers. I watch them through the rearview mirror trying to peek.

Nathan guesses it's the drive-in; Dawn guesses Disneyland. They both hope it is not the graveyard again.

Sharon Nesbit-Davis

We drive through town and onto the highway. I slow down for a county road, and then a gravel one. There is nothing but cornfields, stars, and a full moon. I stop the car, and they take off the blindfolds.

"The moon wants to leave. It's our mission to make her stay."

Nathan is skeptical. Dawn is excited and scared.

We get out, and I yell to the moon, "Please don't go!" Dawn joins in the yelling.

Nathan stands looking at the moon and is the first to see it. "Mom! It's going away."

The moon is disappearing, and we all shout and scream until it vanishes. Dawn cries. Nathan is concerned.

I open the trunk. There are capes, wands, and drums.

We drum and dance. Wands float magic into the sky.

And this time we all see it. A growing sliver of light.

The moon is coming back.

The kids tell George about the mystery trip. Nathan looked it up and explains the lunar eclipse. But Dawn sides with me and says, "We danced the moon back." And then they laugh about other mystery trips, and Halloween pranks, and the day I pretended to be an alien.

I have never told anyone why I create mystery trips because no one ever asks. Not even George. Everyone assumes it is for fun, and it is. But it is more than that.

Before we were married, even good friends worried. "What about the children? It's fine for you and George, but your children will suffer. Neither race will accept them."

My mother-in-law says, "Protect their spirits."

I'm doing my best. They have us, our families and friends, and the Bahá'í community who love them, but I can't keep them safe forever.

And I can't make the hatred go away.

So I give them this: Memories that make them laugh so hard they cry, and then laugh again.

• One Hundred & Fifteen •

"I want to be White like you." My daughter climbs onto my lap and takes my hand to examine it. She moves all my fingers and places her hand up against mine. Her fingers are long and slender like mine, like my mother's.

I say, "Let's trade. You take my white skin, and I'll take your brown."

She sighs. "I want us to match."

Dawn loves me more than I expected. I thought we'd be like my mother and me.

On my first day of kindergarten, my mother gave me a choice. "Do you want me to take you? Or do you want to go with your broth—"

"I'll go with them!" I yelled as I ran out of the house before she finished her sentence. It was a three-block walk, and I knew the way. They rode their bikes and waited at every corner for me to catch up.

My oldest brother took me to the kindergarten room and left me amongst a throng of classmates clinging to their mothers.

At dinner that night, I told how all the kids had their mother there except me. "The kids were all crying."

We laughed at how silly those children were. My mother said, "I'm glad you don't need me like that."

My daughter doesn't just love me, she likes me. She is eight, and she still feels that way. When I was eight, I had already attempted to run away three times. The last time, my mother helped me pack and suggested I take my winter coat. It was summer.

Dawn wants to live with us forever. She draws pictures of houses with us living together on a farm with horses. Every night, she comes into our bed in the space I leave for her. I feel her warmth before my eyes open. I wake to her grins and giggles.

And now she wants to be White like me.

Her skin is beautiful. She's the color White people spend hours in the sun to get. I point that out, but she isn't impressed. She says, "I want to be like you."

I tell George, and he isn't surprised or concerned. "Of course she wants to be like you. You're her mother." He grins at my worried face. "Enjoy the adoration while it lasts."

It lasted another month.

"I don't want to be White anymore. I like being mixed."

Dawn's best friend Nikki is biracial. They had a sleepover and decided they are lucky to be both Black and White.

Dawn doesn't understand why something I think is wonderful makes me cry. "You are weird." She rolls her eyes and runs out to play.

This is the daughter I expected.

• One Hundred & Sixteen •

Nathan has a family tree project due tomorrow. He's sprawled on the family room floor with the poster board and markers I bought two weeks ago. I could nag about his procrastination, but that is pointless and hypocritical. It's in his DNA from both sides.

He got Dawn to draw the tree, and I read and spell the names from family Bibles. I give the names of my great-great-great-grandparents. My paternal grandmother gathered proof we are descended from a Revolutionary War general. She hoped one of her granddaughters would join the elitist DAR, the Daughters of the American Revolution. None of us cared.

Nathan says it's far enough. I don't know if that's the assignment, or if that's how many branches his sister drew and he's tired of writing.

"What about Dad's side?"

If there are Bibles with recorded names, marriages, births, and deaths, I've not seen them. Nathan knows his grandparents and one great-grandmother. Great-Grandma doesn't know her birthday, so she guessed on the date. She was born in planting season and thinks she was thirteen when she got married.

I remember the name of a great-grandfather. George may know more names, but he isn't home yet.

I wish I told Nathan to call his father instead of what I say. "Of course we don't know the original family name. The African names were lost."

Nathan stops writing. "So Davis is not our real name?"

I tell him what I recently read in a book. People were given their owner's last name when they were bought. When they were free, some renamed themselves. By then, they didn't know their African name. "An older cousin of yours, Sally, says she's traced the family back to Confederate President Jefferson Davis' plantation. But Dad isn't so sure about that."

Nathan puts the markers back in the box. "I don't want a slave name." He goes up the stairs to his room, and the door slams.

George comes home, and I tell him what happened. "Have you ever felt that way?"

He sighs and looks at the ceiling. "I had not allowed myself to think about it."

I put the unfinished family tree on the kitchen island. Maybe Nathan will get up early in the morning to finish it. He may procrastinate, but he is conscientious. He always turns in assignments.

Nathan is still sleeping when I get up. I knock on his door and announce the time.

Dawn and I are finishing our breakfast when he comes downstairs. He grabs a bagel and an apple, picks up his backpack, and heads out the back door. Dawn and I follow, leaving the discarded family tree behind us.

• One Hundred & Seventeen •

One morning at breakfast, Dawn announces she wants to be called by her real name, Bahiyyih, from now on. She says, "Will you tell everyone?" By everyone, she means the teachers at school, all the relatives, all of our adult friends, the parents of her friends, and everyone else who will be confused.

Dawn is friendly, but shy. When strangers talk to her, she won't look at them or speak until they are gone. I ask, "Are you sure? It will be hard for people to switch. And because it's unusual, you'll have to teach people how to say and spell it."

She gives me the you-are-not-talking-me-out-of-this look.

This doesn't surprise me. We moved into this neighborhood, where the little Black girls all have interesting names: Tomika, Shaquita, LaToya. I overheard Dawn tell them she has another name. And then we had a visit from a college girl who told her how lucky she was to have such a beautiful name.

I write the name and pronunciation on a notecard for her teacher:

Bahiyyih
Pronounced: Buh HE ah

Friends and family think this won't last. "What seven-year-old decides to change her name?" They say this is a phase, but they don't know the girl I do. Once she makes up her mind, she doesn't give up.

Bahiyyih helps people make the shift by reminding them when they forget. She is patient for a month, and then won't respond when they call her Dawn.

Seven years later, Bahiyyih is a freshman in high school. The boys in her elementary school didn't appreciate how beautiful she is. The high school boys notice.

We are having dinner when the phone rings. George answers and, after a long pause, says, "When you learn how to pronounce my daughter's name, maybe I'll let you talk to her."

He sits back down and grins. I try to hold back my laughter but can't.

Bahiyyih gives us the why-are-my-parents-idiots look.

But she doesn't change her name back to Dawn.

• One Hundred & Eighteen •

It's late, I'm alone, and I need cash for an early morning breakfast. The ATM machine isn't well lit, but it's around the corner from the police station.

I find a place to park and walk the half block to the machine. My card is buried in my purse somewhere. I should be looking for it in the safety of a parked car with the motor running. I find it just as a man walks up and stops several feet away. I glance over. He is a tall man wearing a trench coat, and he is Black.

We are the only two people on the street. My heartbeats are so loud I wonder if he hears them.

I could get the money fast and run to the police station to request an escort to my car—explain a man was watching me at the ATM. But I don't want the police to overreact.

Or I could pretend the machine isn't working, walk to the corner, cross the street, and go the long way back to my car and skip breakfast with my friends.

Or I could imagine that this man is like George, who is tired of White women crossing the street when they see him coming.

The man stands quiet, his hands clasped in front of him.

I withdraw my twenty dollars and put it in my purse. The purse is on my right shoulder, and I keep it there. It is the shoulder that passes him as I walk by and say, "Hello." He nods with a quick glance and stands still until I pass.

I get into my car, breathe, and feel my heart slow down.

I wish my body was a better liar.

• One Hundred & Nineteen •

Friends tell me about a woman they know I will like. Carmen is White, her husband is Black, and they have twin girls the same age as Bahiyyih. They've recently moved to town, and she is already working with neighbors to organize a community garden. My friends met her when she came to an open house event at a resource center in her neighborhood that is sponsored by the Baháʼí community.

I call Carmen, and she knows who I am. "I've heard all about you."

We get together the next day and talk about the kids, schools, and family reactions to our marriages. It's the beginning conversation I've had with all my friends who have married interracially.

Carmen is impressed George and I waited five years for our parents to approve, and even more impressed that they did. She was fifteen when her mother died. "So she never knew. My father said it would have killed her." He will talk on the phone, but refuses to see her or the girls. He's rich and knows they are struggling, but he won't help. She has several brothers and sisters, but doesn't see them much. Sometimes they call on her birthday.

Carmen shows me a picture of her twin daughters. They are identical with golden-brown skin, black curly hair, and infectious smiles. "Your girls are gorgeous. Here's mine." I hand her pictures of Nathan and Bahiyyih. "I'm biased, but our kids are beautiful."

Carmen shrugs. "But with them being mixed, they don't look like us. I wanted my daughters to look like me."

Our children become friends, and Carmen and I try, but it doesn't feel like I expected. There's an unease between us.

We invite the family over for a barbecue. Our husbands are outside cooking, the kids are upstairs in Bahiyyih's room playing music, and Carmen and I sit in the kitchen. Our husbands' laughter jolts our silence, and I joke about them bonding over charcoal and sharing the same first name. Her George is from Haiti. "I love your husband's accent."

Carmen sneers and says, "That's the only reason I married him. If he sounded like the rest of these niggers, I wouldn't have bothered with him."

"What?"

She leans forward and whispers, "Your George doesn't talk like a nigger either, and if he did, you wouldn't have married him. You know it's true."

Our husbands walk into the kitchen, and our conversation stops. They speculate on what we were talking about, and I'm afraid Carmen may tell them. But she doesn't. She winks at me, grins at them, and says, "You don't want to know."

• One Hundred & Twenty •

Nathan and his friend, Rick, are shopping with me for a weekend camping trip. We need flashlight batteries, mosquito repellant, and a sleeping bag for Rick, who has never camped. He's acting cool but keeps asking about bears.

The boys are wearing do-rags on their heads. It's the popular look of urban Black kids, and Rick always wears one, but Nathan doesn't. He's wearing it because he's embarrassed about his hair.

He called one morning after a sleepover at a friend's house. "Hey, Mom, can I dye my hair?" Before I could answer, he said, "Too late, it's done."

Nathan should have said half done. His crazy friend dyed half of it . . . an even split down the middle. One half blond and the other half his natural black.

I slumped to the floor laughing when I saw him. George told everyone his mother's side just came out.

Nathan doesn't find any of this amusing. He does not like attention, so Rick brought the do-rag for him. He can't wear it to school because they decided it was gang clothing, but he can wear it to the store.

Nathan and Rick walk in front of me. I like watching my son when he doesn't know I am. He is a handsome young man, even with his crazy hair. I can't hear what they are saying, but whatever it is, it must be hilarious.

An older White woman walks toward them. I hope they notice and move over. And then I see her face. Her eyes fix on them. Her mouth tightens. She clutches her purse and swings it across her body away from them, then hurries past them.

Now a foot away from me, she slows down and releases the grip on her purse. She glances at me and flashes a smile.

I want to snatch her purse away, show her that danger can come from anywhere and anyone. I want to tell her about those two Black boys she is afraid to go near. I want to tell her that Rick makes breakfast and lunch for his grandmother every morning before he heads off to school. I want to tell her about the times I came to this store with my little boy and old White women, like her, stopped to say how beautiful he was. I want her to look and see the beautiful boy is still there.

Nathan waves for me to come to the sleeping bag section. He says, "Uhhh . . . isn't this where you bought my bear-proof sleeping bag?" Nathan's poker face is perfect, and I follow his lead.

I find a sleeping bag with bear-print lining, and Rick hugs me.

They play catch with it on our way to check out. I should tell them to stop and behave themselves, but I don't. They're just kids being kids.

• One Hundred & Twenty-One •

After a semester of driver's ed, and months and months of practice, Nathan has his driver's license.

He wants to go to a movie with Rick tonight. And he wants to drive. I cannot think of a good reason to say no.

Nathan is an easy kid. He does well in school, is never in trouble, and picks good friends. People compliment us on how polite and respectful he is. He only gets mad at his sister, and rarely asks for anything.

I tell George I think it's time to let Nathan take the car on his own.

I see George's worry face, and I'm worried too, but Nathan is a careful driver. He'll be fine.

We join Nathan in the kitchen where he is waiting for our answer.

"Your mother thinks you are ready."

They stand facing each other, the breakfast counter between them. George looks at Nathan a long time, so long it becomes uncomfortable. Nathan looks at me, wondering . . . but I don't know.

George clears his throat. "I want to make sure you know what to do when the police pull you over."

This topic has never come up because I'm the one who taught Nathan how to drive. I thought about it but dismissed it. How could they ever see my sweet boy as a threat?

Nathan laughs. "The police won't stop me. I obey all the rules, and I don't speed."

I back him up on this. "He's memorized the Rules of the Road and follows them better than I do."

George's mouth tightens. "You will be two young Black men. That's all the excuse they need."

"I know my rights." Nathan's smile has faded. "If they pull me over for no reason, I'll tell them that."

"No. You. Won't. You say nothing. And tell Rick to keep his mouth shut."

Nathan glares.

George glares back and raises his voice. "You will put your hands high on the wheel and answer their questions. When they ask for the registration, tell them you are going to open up the glove compartment. Do it slowly."

I've seen George do this. When police pull him over, his emotions vanish. He is neither friendly, nor rude. He keeps his voice quiet and steady and becomes someone I don't know.

Nathan's jaw tenses. His voice raises to match his father's. "If I did nothing wrong, I will defend myself. I won't just accept it—like you do."

George slams his fist on the counter. The dishes clatter, then silence. His voice is almost a whisper, but it is strong and clear. "I have worked too hard to let you get yourself killed because you think you have rights they don't know about."

The two stare at each other. I have never seen them like this.

Nathan backs away from the counter, brushes past me, climbs the stairs to his room, and slams the door.

George closes his eyes, and I approach, putting my hand on his shoulder. Several minutes later, he opens his eyes and sighs. "Tell him he can go."

George goes outside to mow the lawn, and prune trees, and yank weeds.

I give Nathan the message, and he attempts to subdue his elation, but he can't. He grabs the keys, bounces to the door, and says, "Thanks, Mom."

"Promise me you'll be careful."

He nods and grins. "Tell Dad not to worry."

I wave to Nathan from the window, watch him back out of the driveway and disappear.

George and I take the dog for a walk, eat leftovers for dinner, and surf through channels. We keep the volume down, listening for the sound we finally hear.

Nathan and Rick are back. The movie was good, they brought popcorn home for us, and they want to play football video games.

George and I lie in bed, too exhausted for sleep, but too tired to do anything else.

I whisper, "I think we should tell him he has to stay in the house forever because this is too hard on us. It's going to ruin our love life."

George laughs and kisses my forehead.

We hold hands under the sheets and fall asleep to the sound of muffled laughter and the electronic roar of the crowd.

• One Hundred & Twenty-Two •

My mother-in-law is the last of her generation in George's family, but she doesn't remember that. Some days she wonders when her husband is coming home and makes my brother-in-law go look for him. When he can't find him, she insists on calling the police. The police have been kind and pretend to take a missing person's report so she and my brother-in-law can get some sleep.

She still knows me and asks about me when George calls.

A few years ago at a family gathering, she announced I was her favorite daughter-in-law. I was embarrassed for my sister-in-law. I said, "It's for longevity." And everyone laughed. George's brothers have been married multiple times. Between the two of them, there have been six daughters-in-law.

Later in the kitchen, she says, "You are my favorite. And not just because you lasted the longest."

Some days she remembers that. But not today.

We are spending Thanksgiving with her, and she doesn't want George and I to get married. "I'm tired of my friends asking why my son has to go off and marry up with a White girl when there are plenty of smart and pretty Black girls around with no husbands."

She looks at me and asks why he would do that to her. "People think it's just the White parents that get upset."

She pats my hand and asks me to help in the kitchen. By the time we're peeling potatoes, she remembers my name and asks how the kids are. She is surprised to hear they are watching TV with their cousins in the living room.

I hug and kiss her goodbye, and she smiles and whispers, "Don't let my son marry a White woman."

I don't think dementia runs in my family, but my parents worry about getting it. Dad keeps up with scientific studies and has added some vitamins to his regimen. They play card games. He does puzzles to keep his brain cells active. If something happens to them and they forget they love George, I'll forgive them.

My bigger fear is me. I worry about the racism that seeped into me without permission. I've done my best to eradicate it, but if I lose control of my mind, lingering thoughts could release themselves.

If that happens, I hope my family will forgive me too.

• One Hundred & Twenty-Three •

George meets me at the restaurant. He's late, but doesn't apologize. We've stopped arguing about this. I bring my laptop and write until he comes.

We say hello, look at the menu, and place the order. We check phones for messages and wait for the food.

We look like the old boring couples I used to feel sorry for. I would make up stories to fit the faces. *He wants a divorce but is having second thoughts. What he doesn't know is she already knows. He's a sleep-talker. And his clothes are in the dumpster. She will tell him after dessert, and he'll beg for her to stay, and she'll say she wants to be with someone who appreciates who she is and that is not him. The whole restaurant will break out in applause as he storms out. The handsome chef will take her hand and say, "You deserve to be loved."*

This never happens. They finish the meal and skip dessert.

I wonder if anyone makes up stories about us. Do they see an older Black man and an older White woman and think we aren't a couple because we are too old for that trend? I heard on the radio that interracial couples are considered cool by high schoolers.

If they think we are married and tired of each other, they are mistaken.

We know before we say hello if anything is wrong.

If something extraordinary happened, we know that too.

If it's a regular day, and most are, it's enough to be together. We don't have to be entertaining.

But if anyone is watching, they will catch the moment when I look up and see him looking at me.

I try to hold his gaze, but can't.

George thinks it's hilarious that after all this time he still makes me blush.

I think I make him blush too. He laughs at my accusation and makes his one and only "racial" joke: "You'll never know."

• One Hundred & Twenty-Four •

I am working at my desk when my boss comes with my coat. "Come with me."

"Where are we going?"

She grins and hands me a button. "I know you aren't political, but wear it."

It has waves of red, white, and blue and three words:

WOMEN FOR OBAMA

"Who is Obama?"

She laughs at my ignorance. "Trust me. You want to know about him."

We walk to the building next door where the state congressional office is. There are two rows of chairs, three news crews set up behind them, and a table with coffee and cookies. A poster board sign rests on an easel:

OBAMA FOR US SENATOR

A tall Black man with a big smile walks in and is introduced as "Barack Obama, the next Senator of Illinois."

He thanks the people who put this together and glides into the importance of education and support for struggling families. He gives credit and thanks to his wife for her enlightenment on this and all subjects. What else he says, I don't hear. The thoughts in my head are too loud: *I am two feet away from a future president.*

I look up Barack Obama on the internet and discover his mother was White and his father African. He is mixed, biracial. His mother was only a few years older than me. She must have heard the same objections I did: "Fine for you to make this decision, but what about the children?"

I tell George about Barack Obama at dinner. "He's going to be president."

George shrugs. "We'll see."

Four years later, throughout the presidential election, I give George updates on the poll predictions. I tell him, "He's going to win."

George says the same thing every time. "We'll see."

On election night, Bahiyyih and I camp out in the living room watching the returns. I'm ready for an all-nighter, but it only takes a few hours. I yell down to George in his basement office, "Obama won! He did it!"

George comes upstairs to watch the Grant Park speech. Bahiyyih and I cheer, laugh, and scream. George is quiet.

The next morning, I am still excited, and George is still quiet.

"Doesn't it make you feel hopeful?"

George sighs. "Do you have any idea how much they will hate him?"

• One Hundred & Twenty-Five •

Our friend Leslie invites us to a lecture at Northwestern University in Chicago, sponsored by the university's Bahá'í Club. The lecture is on Post Traumatic Slave Syndrome, given by Joy DeGruy. This is her doctoral thesis.

The lecture is on Tuesday evening. We'd hit rush hour on the way in and wouldn't be home until after midnight. Leslie says, "It's worth it. I heard her speak a few weeks ago. She's amazing. The whole audience was in tears by the end."

Joy DeGruy lives in Portland, Oregon, and is in the same Bahá'í community as my brother Roger. He concurs with Leslie's assessment. "She's doing incredible work. You should definitely go—bring Kleenex and introduce yourself. I told her about you."

George doesn't want to go. "I know the history of slavery. I don't like talking about it."

"Okay, but I need to go. I can't explain why. It's one of those gut feelings I get."

I don't insist that George come with us, but he does. He is polite but not talkative on the drive.

The large lecture hall is close to full. The room has tiers, and we find seats close to the top. I have a clear view of Joy. She has the build of a gymnast, moves easily on stilettos, and wears a black-and-white pantsuit. Her laughter floats over the din, and she greets people with hugs. She doesn't look like someone who is about to rip out our hearts.

She begins with a warning: "This isn't the History of Racism 101. There isn't time for that." She looks over the audience. Most are Black. A few are White. "What I'm going to say tonight could upset you. If you are White, you may feel uncomfortable. If you're Black, you may feel angry, sad, frustrated. To understand the impact of chattel slavery, you have to know what it was, not the sanitized version studied in school or shown on television." She seems to look at me when she says, "If *Roots* made you cry, you may not want to stay."

For the next two hours, she tells story after story of American chattel slavery. Some stories are familiar. Others are new.

I did not know about the experiments done on women and girls whose masters said they were no longer fit for duty. The walls of their vaginas had broken down, causing urine and fecal leakage. One cause was childbirth, another was having sex too young. Dr. J. Marion Sims used these girls and women to develop the first vaginal speculum. He did not anesthetize them because he reasoned their race made them durable to great pain.

Sims treated infants of slaves who were born with neonatal tetanus. Tetanus is found in horse manure. The likely cause was the slaves' living quarters being too close to the stables, but Sims believed it was an inherent flaw of the race. He attempted to treat it through prying the bones of the skulls of infants into alignment with a shoemaker's awl. He did not anesthetize the babies either. Most died, and Sims used their bodies for further experiments.

I have never heard of the "Casual Killing Act," which excused the murder of a slave while being corrected by his or her master. For purely economic reasons, it makes no sense to murder your property. The master and overseers were skilled in punishing slaves without killing them. This law protected the White mistress when she beat a child slave to death for looking like her husband.

Joy asks us to close our eyes. "Imagine you are one of the slaves, and answer these questions:

Have you ever felt your life seriously threatened?

Have you ever seen your child or spouse threatened?

Have you ever seen someone injured or killed?

Have you heard about a serious threat to a relative or close friend?

Has a close relative or friend been kidnapped, tortured, or killed?

Have you experienced intense fear, terror, and helplessness?"

The lecture hall is silent until someone behind me sobs.

Joy says, "These are the questions you ask a patient to determine if he or she has post-traumatic stress disorder. If they answer yes to even one question, there's a possibility. If they answer yes to more than that, it's considered a solid diagnosis."

Joy pauses, then asks, "So how did you do? And remember, the trauma didn't happen just once. It was every day. It was lifetimes of trauma. Generations of trauma."

Slavery ended, but trauma continued. There's the KKK, lynchings, Jim Crow, four little girls in Birmingham, Emmet Till, mass incarceration . . .

Joy paces and throws up her hands. "And where was the therapy?"

She lists common PTSD symptoms: intense psychological distress, irritability, sleeplessness, sudden bursts of anger, difficulty concentrating, lack of expectations for the future. She says, "These behaviors are attributed to Black culture instead of what they are: human response to trauma."

Joy stops pacing and looks over the crowd. "I can tell there's a lot of educated and respectable Black folks here—but no matter how many diplomas you've got in your family, I'll bet you also have family members with felonies, addictions, and insanity." Laughter breaks out, and Joy joins in. "Mine too. That's true for every African American family I know."

I think about the story George's mother tells about her father. He was brilliant and built a radio out of scraps. In the middle of the night, he woke everyone up. They gathered around his contraption and heard music. He laughed and danced with them.

As smart as he was, he couldn't get a good job. He was a sharecropper and pulled his children out of school to work in the fields when he needed them. By the time they were in high school, they were so far behind they dropped out.

Liz knew school was the only way she would ever do anything besides have babies and pick cotton. She had an important test on a day her father wanted her to work in the fields. She told him she'd work the fields the next day. But today, she had to go to school. He grabbed her and threw her in the back of the truck. She jumped down and said, "I'll stay home tomorrow." He whipped her and threw her back on the truck. She got down again. He beat her harder and tossed her back. Again, she got off. And again, he beat her. She wouldn't give up, and he finally left her in the dirt. She made it to school, crawling most of the way, slipping in and out of consciousness. Her teacher tended to her wounds and said that it was against the law for him to beat her like that. Liz didn't take the test that day. She was too weak to hold the pencil. That night, she told her father if he ever beat her again, he would go to jail.

Her father never touched her again. Or talked to her. A few weeks later, police found him in the street pounding a hole with his fist into the pavement. They locked him up, and the next morning, he was dead. The police said he drowned himself in the toilet.

Every time Liz tells the story, she remembers more details. Recently she remembered the headlines that everyone whispered about at school: "Insane Negro Kills Self in Jail." She wondered why her mother heard the beating and did nothing to help her. Then she answered her own question: survival.

The story nobody knows is her father's pain and suffering. He didn't talk about it.

Joy says that's another PTSD symptom. "People don't talk about it.

We self-medicate with alcohol and drugs, or do something crazy to get ourselves killed."

Joy ends the lecture with assurance healing can happen. "We are an incredible people with an amazing history of survival. We need to remember who we are, build on our strengths, heal ourselves and our communities."

There is a space of silence before the standing ovation. People cry and hold each other.

There is a look on George's face I haven't seen before—a mixture of sorrow and relief. He closes his eyes and whispers something. I lean closer to hear. "It makes sense. It all makes sense."

We sit and watch as people line up to talk with Dr. Joy. Some are crying. She listens and smiles, offers hugs or touches a shoulder.

I wish I had the power to disappear. I'm holding in tears because this isn't the right place to release them. I don't want George to comfort me. I want to comfort him, but I don't know how.

George asks if I'm ready to go.

"Yes, but I told Roger I would introduce myself. I don't know if I should." I don't want to impose myself on her, create a situation where she has to be nice to a White stranger. If I were her, I wouldn't want to talk to a White person right now. Or ever.

George stands. "It's up to you."

We walk down the stairs, and as we reach the bottom, the people who had been talking with her move away. She glances over at me, and our eyes meet. She smiles. She smiles bigger when I tell her I am Roger's sister. She looks over at George and laughs. "Oh . . . I've heard all about you two." She gives us both a hug.

On the way home, George thanks Leslie for inviting us. "I'm glad I came, but I'm not ready to talk about it." He squeezes my hand, then turns on the radio to a jazz station.

That night, lying in bed, unable to sleep, I think about Joy's description of the Middle Passage.

Africans stacked in the belly of the ship.
Eighteen inches of space.
It's where they ate, relieved themselves, puked, birthed babies.

George's Ancestors survived those ships.

Their descendants survived all that came after.

I see them in the faces of our children.

And I see my people too.

Forces beyond all of us shaped our lives.

If just one of them had given up, we would not be here.

I close my eyes and imagine a gathering of the Ancestors—enlightened and reconciled.

They sing, dance, share their stories, circle around us, and say to each other,

"Look what we made. Look at what we made together."

• Acknowledgements •

I wrote my first letters in crayon on the wood stairs of our house when I was four. I almost got away with it because my mother didn't know I could write. My accused brothers presented evidence to prove their innocence: "Look at the E. It has too many lines. Look at the S. It's perfect. 'S' for Sharon." I spent hours scrubbing the steps, but some of the crayon wax seeped into the grain. A faint trace of the letters could be seen if you knew they were there. For years, I'd hear my mother's grumbling as she climbed the stairs. "I'll never understand her. What possessed her to do this?" Finally my father installed a Rubbermaid step covering to conceal them. Mom showed me the bill. It was more than a lifetime of my allowance.

When I was twelve, Mom cleaned my room and found a story I was writing. She wrote a note at the top. "Sharon! Get out of your dream world!!!" After that, I stopped writing my stories on paper. I kept them in my head.

Forty-five years later, on the first anniversary of my mother's death, her voice woke me up: "Sharon! It's time to write your stories."

That night, I wrote a story, but it wasn't about heroic girls riding wild horses in magical kingdoms. The story was about my mother's death, which was followed three weeks later by my father's. And writing about it lifted me out of a sadness I didn't know was there.

I began writing stories about my life and soon felt the need for a teacher. Through a series of events I will not call magical, though it feels like they were, I met Judy Bridges. She lived in Milwaukee—

like my mime teacher. And once again I was on the highway between Rockford and Milwaukee to study my art with a master.

Judy Redbird Bridges, author of *Shut Up & Write!*, is the founder of a writing studio called Redbird Studio, where she's taught more than six thousand kids and adults to write better than they did before they met her. She is a gifted teacher who intuits what you need as a writer. It was Judy who created the Women's Writing Retreat at The Clearing in Door County, Wisconsin, a space created for artists to renew themselves through nature. Every year, for one glorious week, I had hours of uninterrupted writing time, ate scrumptious meals, honed my writing skills, presented my work to fellow writers, and had one-on-one conferences with Judy. It was Judy who led a writing exercise to walk into a scene of our lives, remember it through our senses, and write it down in first-person present tense. I loved how it felt to write this way, but assumed a memoir had to be written in past tense. Judy laughed. "It's your story. Your decision how to tell it. But if you put it in present tense, you'll take us along with you." It was Judy who looked at my collection of stories, identified themes, and suggested I select a theme and create a memoir of those stories. She asked, "Which one scratches at you?" I knew which one it was. My interracial marriage.

Judy has remained my constant mentor in this project for over ten years. The Redbird writers have been there as well, laughing, crying, and ever so gently critiquing.

The Redbird writers experience was so valuable that I joined more writer groups: Shabamoco, comprised of Molly Chestnut Sides, Connie Kuntz (who did a line edit of this book before submitting it to a publisher), and my daughter, Bahiyyih El-Shabbaz; Time to Write, led by Debby Gaines; and Write on Time, a group started by Heidi Baker, the daughter of my friend Helen, who would have been so delighted with our collaboration. Each group was unique, but they had one common thread. We all love writing, give constructive feedback, and applaud each other's success. Their positive response to the work coupled with Judy's gentle nudges sustained me when my resolve weakened.

In addition to Judy and my writing groups, the staff of Ten16 Press, their enthusiasm for the book, and their professional expertise made this publication process joyful. They all made this a better book.

While most people's names in the book were changed, the stories are as I remember them. Regardless of whether it was an uplifting encounter or a challenging one, I'm grateful for the part they played.

The first story in this book was prompted by my friend Jane Treat, who is a storyteller and a collector of stories. One night after dinner, she posed a question: "Is there a story from your childhood that would have predicted your life now?" I immediately thought of the Black doll I loved. And thinking about that story led to more stories that revealed a clear path, an intentional one to the life I have.

The last story of attending Dr. Joy DeGruy's lecture on "Post Traumatic Slave Syndrome" was the beginning of a friendship that has become family. Her thesis became a book, and she has become an internationally recognized expert in the field. The book and additional resources can be found on her website, "Be the Healing": https://www.joydegruy.com

And speaking of family, mine is remarkable. Nathan and Bahiyyih are both writers, exceptional ones. I hadn't predicted that, but now it makes sense. I think the reason George and I were meant to be was to bring them into the world. The world needs their stories.

I am always thankful for George. Without him, this book could not have been written, and that is true in every way. When I told George I was writing a memoir about our marriage, he sighed, but gave his blessing.

In our over four decades of marriage, George and I have one ongoing disagreement:

I say, "I love you."

He says, "I love you more."

Now I smile. "But I wrote the book."

CPSIA information can be obtained
at www.ICGtesting.com
Printed in the USA
LVHW082144050223
738732LV00034B/1163

9 781645 382065